Acclaim for Debra J. Dickerson

THE END OF BLACKNESS

"Stimulating. . . . Provocative. . . . Loaded with wish-I'd-said-that one-liners. . . . Dickerson has a way with words and a timely message. . . . When she says it's time for black America to get off its duff, she's not asking anyone to do something she wouldn't do—and hasn't done—herself."　　　　　—*Chicago Tribune*

"Blunt and bracing. . . . *The End of Blackness* is a solidly researched account of the evolution of black identity in America (her 'prologue' is about as concise and direct an account of slavery and its long-standing effects as you are likely to find). . . . Dickerson's is a message for all Americans, not only those who are confused about how to think about race."　　　　　—*Mother Jones*

"Fascinating. . . . A call to arms. . . . Dickerson knows how to throw a literary punch."　　　　　—*Pittsburgh Post-Gazette*

"[Dickerson is] a thinker who suffers no fools of either the liberal or the conservative stripe. . . . Revive[s] a tradition of clear-eyed, accessible writing about black political destiny in the vein of W.E.B. Du Bois, Carter G. Woodson, and Frederick Douglass."　　　　　—*The Atlantic Monthly*

"A brave, original, and angry book. . . . I find much to agree with. . . . We Americans need to get out of the 'race' routine, and black folk must lead the way. . . . The end of blackness . . . is worth striving for."　　　　　—Glenn C. Loury, *The Boston Herald*

"Compelling. . . . Exhibits a praiseworthy independence of mind, questioning everyone from the 'Black Politboro'—the civil rights establishment, which sets the tone of black politics—to white apologists who still downplay the ravages of slavery. . . . A stirring endorsement of a new marriage of responsible civic individualism and dedication to the collective good."　　　—*The Washington Post*

DEBRA J. DICKERSON

THE END OF BLACKNESS

Debra J. Dickerson was educated at the University of
Maryland, St. Mary's University, and Harvard Law
School. She has been both a senior editor and a
contributing editor at *U.S. News & World Report*, and
her work has also appeared in *The New York Times
Magazine*, *The Washington Post*, *The New Republic*,
Slate, *The Village Voice*, and *Essence*. She lives in
Albany, New York.

THE END OF BLACKNESS

ALSO BY DEBRA J. DICKERSON

An American Story

THE END

OF

BLACKNESS

Returning the Souls of Black Folk
to Their Rightful Owners

DEBRA J. DICKERSON

Anchor Books
A Division of Random House, Inc.
New York

FIRST ANCHOR BOOKS EDITION, JANUARY 2005

The Library of Congress has cataloged the Pantheon edition as follows:
Dickerson, Debra J., 1959–
The end of Blackness : returning the souls of Black folk to their rightful owners
/ Debra J. Dickerson.
p. cm.
Includes bibliographical references and index.
1. African Americans—Race identity.
2. African Americans—Social conditions—1975–
3. Self-reliance—United States. 4. African Americans—Psychology.
5. Race awareness—United States. 6. United States—Race relations. I. Title.

E185.625.D53 2004 305.896'073—dc21 2003056346

Anchor ISBN: 0-375-71319-0

Book design by M. Kristen Bearse

www.anchorbooks.com

Printed in the United States of America
10 9 8 7 6 5 4 3 2 1

To James Baldwin, Amiri Baraka, W.E.B. DuBois, Ralph Ellison, E. Franklin Frazier, Dr. Martin Luther King Jr., Albert Murray, Thomas Sowell, Malcolm X, and especially Frederick Douglass and Carter G. Woodson. Finally, worthy leaders and thinkers. Now I know how to be both black and human. Now I know how to *think* because now, having sought out the un–Black History Month, Chicken McNuggetized, contextless quote, I know how thoroughly I've been bamboozled as to my true intellectual and moral heritage and I know who did the bamboozling. Now I know that it's *black people* they strove to challenge and perfect, not the rest of the world. They loved us more than they hated anyone else. That's a gift beyond measure for an orphan race.

CONTENTS

THE END OF BLACKNESS

INTRODUCTION

This book will both prove and promote the idea that the concept of "blackness," as it has come to be understood, is rapidly losing its ability to describe, let alone predict or manipulate, the political and social behavior of African Americans. Given its strictures and the limitations it places upon the growth and free will of those to whom it refers, it diminishes their sovereignty as rational and moral actors. Nearly 150 years after the end of slavery, a generation past the end of Jim Crow, the time is overdue for blacks to reforge their identity to reflect the progress already made and to prepare for that still to come. "Blackness" must be updated so that blacks can free themselves from the past and lead America into the future.

Race-obsessed for centuries, America has sacrificed forests to create books proving that blacks[1] collectively are either inferior or equal, are either progressing or falling behind, are assimilating or balkanizing—but what about the individual black? Intracommunally as well, blacks are equally quick to assign "symbol of the race" status to anyone who draws attention to himself in any way, good or bad. But are Ward, Condoleezza, Tiger, O.J., and Latrell never allowed to simply *be*? To be a wife, a student, a sovereign human being outside the sudden spotlight of a statistician's calipers or a politician's sound bite? Isn't one real measure of oppression overcome the moment an individual loses the power to represent anyone but herself, when a neglectful welfare mom's actions taint no one but her?

As convulsed as America has been over race, little of the discussion has focused on charting societal progress at the individual level. But how does any one individual make real in her own life the sacrifices of blood, sweat, and tears that made the progress possible? *Brown v. Board,* the Civil Rights Act, the Voting Rights Act, the myriad desegregation cases, the marches, the sit-ins, the midnight bombings, the dorm room bull sessions, the interracial marriages, the "what am I?" biracial children, the assassinations, the hate-filled faces of nameless Little Rock housewives—all are macro-level upheavals of the American polity. But a generation later, what is their connection to any individual black person?

Every January 15 and every February, blacks sonorously invoke Martin Luther King Jr. and Malcolm X and Fannie Lou Hamer. Interestingly, this invocation is undertaken not to ask whether the inheritors measure up to the martyrs but to insinuate that America is not living up to the saints' sacrifice and hence that the societal debt has not been paid in full. Black worthiness of continued societal attention and turmoil is assumed, regardless of the state of black America, as if the moral high ground could be bequeathed like a hereditary title or a trust fund. Even a black deadbeat dad, a neglectful teacher, or a drug dealer can crack the whip of white racism.

But what is the individual black person's *responsibility* to the movement and to the marchers and the conscience-stricken voters and the policemen who defended a status quo that increasingly sickened them? What does the individual black person owe those four little girls murdered in their Birmingham Sunday school? Or Viola Liuzzo, the white working-class Detroit housewife who came to Selma in her green Oldsmobile to ferry civil rights marchers around and died for America's sins? Did she die to make blacks citizens, fully realized persons free to make rational decisions, or to make them good "race men and women," ready to do battle with America indefinitely? The assumption has always been that those martyrs died to change America, but do blacks themselves require no attitude check, no modification, no critique? If the answer is no, then aren't blacks defining themselves out of America, supposedly their bitterest lament?

This rejectionist cadre ensnares many a gullible black with demonstrably false sentiments tearfully recited at Black Students Association meetings, sentiments like "I have never at any time felt like an American." Presumably these dissenters mean that their native land won't include blacks in the American identity, that blacks are excluded and treated differently from "real" Americans. There is merit to the latter contention, but it is rarely put that way. The dissenters do not say, "I have never at any time been *treated* like an American." They do not say that because in all honesty they cannot. Can it be that they *choose* not to feel like Americans because of bitterness over its unfinished racial business?

The Buffalo Soldiers and the black World War I and II fighting men chose instead to feel like Americans by *acting* like Americans: in the ultimate exhibition of civic commitment, they demanded and won the right to fight for their country. They did so at a time when lynchings were as common as tree branches, when the Allies treated European POWs better than they treated their black captors, when the democracy that black soldiers were making the world safe for didn't apply to them, when racially restrictive covenants were enshrined in law, when blacks had no rights that whites were bound to respect, and when blacks who weren't murdered during white riots were incarcerated. How dare blacks today not feel like Americans? Is it not their duty to do so? Did not their forebears otherwise labor and sacrifice in vain?

There is a suspicious relish in such disavowals of citizenship, a savoring of a slight that ought to rather sicken and galvanize. Before the civil rights movement blacks felt cheated when their rights were abrogated, a response that led to action, like lunch counter sit-ins; post-movement blacks feel vindicated, a response that leads to speechifying. They have not been left out of America; they affect rejecting it while availing themselves of every morsel of its benefits. But they are not hypocrites. They are liars acting out feelings of inferiority; they feel American to their core. The danger lies in their access to podiums from which they lead other blacks to join them in their civic insecurity, to ask for a refund on their American identity. They exhort them to make a mockery of their ancestors' triumphs. But who and what are blacks if not Americans? African? The notion is laughable. Forty years ago Albert Murray was already providing a counternarrative to what he termed this politics of unexamined slogans:

> [S]ince the negative aspects of black experience are constantly being overpublicized (and to little purpose except to obscure the positive), justice to U.S. Negroes, not only as American citizens but also as the fascinating human beings that they so obviously are, is best served by suggesting some of the affirmative implications of their history and culture. . . . [S]omeone must at least begin to try to do justice to what U.S. Negroes like about being black and to what they like about being *Americans*. Otherwise justice can hardly be done to the incontestable fact that not only do they choose to live rather than commit suicide, but that, poverty and injustice notwithstanding, far from simply struggling in despair, they live with gusto and a sense of elegance that has always been downright

enviable. . . . [T]he time for accentuating the positive and eliminating the negative is long overdue.[2]

Indeed. No black bus driver breathing gas fumes for thirty years as he makes endless loops through blizzards and drive-bys is ambivalent about his civic identity. Rather, he sees America quite clearly: it is the place that makes him work like a dog to live well but that allows him to work like a dog to live well, as opposed to a peasant in Afghanistan or much of Africa. It is the place where his children can realistically aspire to the Ivy League, Wall Street, or Capitol Hill. Yes, they will be out-numbered and disadvantaged at every step of the way, but they can nonetheless arrive there if they don't give up and aren't unduly unlucky. The black *folk,* submiddle-class and non–Ivy League blacks, see America clearly, its warts and beauty marks alike; they are comfortable, confident, and hopeful, if somewhat wary. It is the well-off Talented Tenth blacks who feel least at home. Carter G. Woodson, that son of slaves who left the coal mines at twenty to begin his education, had this in mind when he remarked that "Harvard has ruined more Negroes than bad whiskey."[3] The black community needs to unravel the mystery of why its most successful act like the most dispossessed. (Woodson would blame, in part, "[t]heir filled but undeveloped minds."[4]) Or maybe it just needs to reread E. Franklin Frazier's 1957 *The Black Bourgeoisie.*

While Frazier's critique of that group's neuroses is dated and overly harsh, it is true that bourgeois blacks' greater proximity to whites, who still reject them, can result in an inferiority com-plex that manifests as a constant need for white reassurance and approval. Observes Frazier:

The black bourgeoisie has been uprooted from its "racial" tradition and as a consequence has no cultural roots in either the Negro or the white world. In seeking to conform to bourgeois ideals and standards of behavior, this class in the Negro community has sloughed off the genteel tradition of the small upper class which had its roots among the Negroes who were free before the Civil War. But more important still, the black bourgeoisie has rejected the folk culture of the Negro masses. The artistic creations of the leaders of the Negro Renaissance in the nineteen twenties, who turned to the black masses for inspiration, were regarded largely with indifference by the increasing number of Negroes who were acquiring a middle-class outlook on life. As a consequence of their isolation, the majority of the black bourgeoisie live in a cultural vacuum and their lives are devoted largely to fatuities.[5]

Fatuities like pretending not to be Americans. According to Nicholas Lemann, former Senator Harris Wofford, who taught at Howard Law School in the 1950s, "was surprised to find that the prevailing style among his students was an especially pronounced version of the conformity of white students of the Silent Generation. All the men wore ties to class, and all the women dresses; the students called each other 'Mister' and 'Miss.' [E. Franklin] Frazier, who was teaching at Howard also, told Wofford that every year he asked whether anyone in his class was the descendant of slaves, and never a hand was raised."[6] Today these sufferers exhibit their neuroses by claiming to be descended from slaves whether they are or not, then insisting that all remaining class time be spent denouncing slavery rather than preparing for exams. Still, confused though they are, they are not completely to blame. America has made it its business to unman blacks; those who succumb to this civic siege should be rehabilitated and reeducated, not rejected.

Let us be clear: America is not a racial utopia. It can be painful to be black and love a country this difficult and that still gets so many things horribly wrong. America simultaneously gives then takes away so much; it ennobles, then debases; it inspires, then shames. That bus driver knows just how likely he is to be body-slammed against a police cruiser without cause, his patriotism notwithstanding; he knows exactly how obsequious he must seem if he is to reach his home without having had his body cavities publicly probed. He knows. Small comfort though it is, he can soothe himself with the knowledge that the police at least have to lie about what they did to him. Where else in the world, outside the West, would that be true?

For blacks, America is a complicated place to live and to love, especially given what Murray identifies as "the folklore of white supremacy and the fakelore of black pathology."[7] Picking up on Frazier's point about the absorption of idealized white norms as the unexamined baseline for all behavior, blacks need to free their minds, that last plantation, of misleading comparisons and focus instead on self-actualization. For the confused or the cowardly, it's perhaps better to pretend not to be playing the game at all. Best to pretend one is prevented from playing the game, when the reality is that no one can stop the American, black or blind, who is determined to succeed. He can stop, but he cannot *be* stopped. Blacks may not be loved, but they cannot be denied, and it is long past time that black nay-sayers stopped telling them otherwise. Blacks went to war when it was whites who stole their birthright; they should do no less when the thieves are their brethren, because black folk should know better than to participate in their own disenfranchisement, as Frazier argues:

[W]hile the Negro folk were exposed to a greater extent to the violence of the whites, the black bourgeoisie was more exposed in a spiritual sense. Except for the economic relations with whites, the Negro folk could retreat within their own world with its peculiar religious life, recreation, and family and sex life. Moreover, since the thinking of the Negro folk was not affected as that of the black bourgeoisie by the books and papers in which the Negro's inferiority was proclaimed, the black bourgeoisie suffered spiritually not only because they were affected by ideas concerning the Negro's inferiority, but perhaps even more because they had adopted the white man's values and patterns of behavior. Consequently, they developed an intense inferiority complex and because of this inferiority complex sought compensations.[8]

Compensations like Academy awards, Pulitzer prizes, Ivy League degrees, and sinecures from which to harangue whites into loving them. If an upheaval on the scale of the civil rights movement couldn't do it, it is hard to know what it will take to satisfy the "woe is me" race men that they are citizens; perhaps a giant Hallmark card signed by every Caucasian in America. What *is* clear is that their focus on racial grievances, however legitimate, keeps them from having to fashion a constructive way of viewing their role in American life. These rejectionists *do* feel like Americans; they are just afraid to say so and be spurned. More fundamentally, they are afraid to say so and then have nothing important left to think about, no other way to organize their lives, no mechanism by which to understand themselves except as always marginalized, the perpetual outsiders. Though he was a member of the black bourgeoisie, Ralph Ellison successfully labored his way through this thicket:

Some such effort was necessary . . . before I could identify the areas of my life and personality which claimed my mind beyond any limitations *apparently* imposed by my racial identity. . . . This was no matter of sudden insight but of slow and blundering discovery of a struggle to stare down the deadly and hypnotic temptation to interpret the world and all its devices in terms of race. . . .

[F]iction became the agency of my efforts to answer the questions: Who am I, what am I, how did I come to be? What should I make of the life around me, what celebrate, what reject, how confront the snarl of good and evil which is inevitable? What does American society *mean* when regarded out of my *own* eyes, when informed by my *own* sense of the past and viewed by my *own* complex sense of the present? . . . Too often they fear to leave the uneasy sanctuary of race to take their chances in the world.[9]

Ellison was speaking of black writers, but his observation holds true across the board. These sufferers struggle with a twofold racial fraud syndrome: on one level they merely lack civic confidence, but on another they are civic terrorists actively at war with America and fighting for their psychological life. For without their oppression they are no one special, run-of-the-mill Americans, bores until proven otherwise. And they alone are responsible for their own betterment and their own problems, with the resources of a largely benevolent nation behind them. They are average Joes with average lives to lead. Theirs is neither the victim's nor the hero's glamour.

Lacking civic confidence, however, they wait for an overture that will never come because it need not. The civil rights movement and its attendant societal upheavals are all the acknowledgment any black person needs of his place in the American family. That some whites don't like it is irrelevant, and dwelling on that fact keeps blacks from civic self-actualization. The second impulse, civic terrorism, is illegitimate and should be unmasked—as a mercy to the sufferers if for no other reason. However focused blacks had to be on whites a generation ago, it's long past time for them to redirect the spotlight inward to scrutinize and interrogate the communal decisions they make.

If blacks had nothing societally to answer for before the movement, they certainly do now. Scholastic achievement, crime, family breakdown, welfare reliance—all are now as bad as or worse than they were during Jim Crow. Why? These complicated realities certainly implicate racism and structural inequality, but the problems remain regardless and can only be addressed by blacks, not whites. Black infant mortality and venereal disease rates need addressing not because they exceed those of whites but because they exceed the levels that blacks ought to accept.

If a magic wand were to end white racism tomorrow at noon, the black community would not be very much changed at 12:01. White racism doesn't mug a neighbor at the bus stop; it doesn't have unprotected sex or drop out of high school. It doesn't underachieve, it doesn't give up on the troubled students, it doesn't give in to hopelessness and settle for a life behind a broom, it doesn't favor its boys over its girls. It doesn't refuse to breastfeed, it doesn't infect 50 percent of its young with herpes, it doesn't believe wacky conspiracy theories or that AIDS is a hoax. It doesn't watch endless hours of television instead of reading to its children or overseeing their homework or taking them to a cultural event. It matters not at all whether white rates of these same phenomena are higher or lower; all that matters is that they are too high for black comfort. This is not who blacks want to be. There is work to do, and it must be done by black people, regardless of how whites behave.

So the question is whether blacks will repay that debt to Viola and those four little girls by being the best Americans and human beings possible or by being the best African Americans. How *should* the tumult of a nation affect the lives of an inheriting generation? How are blacks today to decide what to do with their freedom, how to conduct themselves, and how to fulfill their responsibilities as well as enjoy their rights?

Blacks often ask what their country can do for them, but never the converse—even to pose the question is scandalous, given to understand as we are that black worthiness of continued societal attention is never to be questioned. But by definition, wouldn't a focus on good citizenship, a mental working backward from the common good, result in black progress, at once individually and nationally? A focus on ending racism is unlikely to produce results that are more than masturbatorily symbolic. But a focus on improving one's neighborhood through self-help projects or service on a city council, a decision to enlist in the armed forces, to excel academically, to adopt neglected children, to organize and educate voters—such plans could not help but improve conditions in the locality, the state, and the country, as well as the individual so involved. (As an added bonus, it would shame the devil, the nation that ignores and burdens a straggling group except to incarcerate or be entertained by it.) But from whence would such a mindset even come?

One of the most fundamental revelations a black person can come to in analyzing his past and claiming his future is that pressures and expectations arising from within the black community are usually more life-affecting than those from without. Whites have at least theoretically accepted that they do not have the right to question black choices or limit their options. But blacks recognize no such boundaries.

It is blacks who critique other blacks' choices—from styles of dress, to relationship partners, to careers, to political affiliations. It is blacks who tell other blacks what they must think about affirmative action and O. J. Simpson. It is blacks who tell other blacks that they have to belong to certain organizations and not others. It is blacks who try to control the political, intellectual, and social discourse of other blacks. It is blacks who ostracize and denounce their brethren for disagreeing with them and who can understand disagreement only as opportunism, self-hatred, or insanity. It is other blacks whom blacks spend their lives trying to please, not whites. Sister Viola and the four little girls in that church mostly took care of that.

"The race will free itself from exploiters just as soon as it decides to do so. No one else can accomplish this task for the race. It must plan and do for itself."[10] Carter G. Woodson wrote that admonition eighty years ago, at a time when whites were making life unimaginably difficult for blacks. While he certainly mentioned white exploiters, his focus was on the black ones, the ones who used their skins as camouflage to hijack the black program either for their own ego gratification or for position and money or simply because they were bad leaders. *The Mis-Education of the Negro,* often invoked but rarely read, is an *intra-communal* critique. As bad as things were racially in his day, Woodson knew that poor leadership was as bad for the community as was white racism. Unfortunately, his message is still relevant today because the exploiters and the racial hysterics are still leading their flock in circles. Rather than focus, as they do most often, on what happens politically and socially between blacks and whites, blacks must focus on what happens between black people—more specifically, on what should and should not happen.

The final phase of the civil rights movement has yet to be undertaken. In some ways facing it will be more difficult than facing fire hoses and attack dogs because no outsiders can help blacks with it or share responsibility for its conduct or outcome.

Now that blacks are free from whites[11] (that is, of the societal understanding of blacks as a caste that can be oppressed and exploited at will), *The End of Blackness* will argue that the time has come for black people to free one another.

Blacks cannot effectuate their collective will, unmediated by outsiders or exploiters, until they trust themselves and one another to effectuate their individual wills. What else do derogatory labels like "Uncle Tom" and "incog-negro" mean except that the individual so derogated cannot be trusted to be black? That he cannot be trusted to be neutral, let alone biased, toward his tribe? Frederick Douglass understood the role of the individual in community uplift: "Society is a hardhearted affair. With it the helpless may expect no higher dignity than that of paupers. The individual must lay society under obligation to him or society will honor him only as a stranger and sojourner."[12] He did not mean white society alone.

So confused are blacks by the lies they've been told, so shell-shocked are they by the horrors they've suffered, that they can at once accept that blackness is rightfully inescapable—no one believes as fervently in the "one drop" rule as blacks do—but that some blacks are "not really" black because of their politics. Are they then white? No, they are "Oreos," black on the outside, white on the inside. Voting Republican can accomplish what blue eyes, blond hair, and three white grandparents cannot.

The way out of this enemy-created quagmire is for blacks to locate and embrace the selves they've not known since 1619 when the first twenty captives were brought to America. Only by daring to live as autonomous individuals with *voluntary* group identification, only by charting a course unconcerned with the existence of white people, only by taking responsibility for their comportment and decisions—only then will blacks be able to achieve collective goals, assess collective penalties, award collective benefits, and jockey for sociopolitical position like fully entitled citizens.

So far, blacks have been social weaklings, buffeted about and informed of their boundaries by the first-class citizens, both their protectors and their enemies; racial profiling, real estate and credit redlining, and even refusals to deliver pizzas to black areas all are just kinder, gentler Jim Crow. It must end. The time has come for blacks to engender passivity in others, to inform outsiders of who they are and what will and won't happen in black communities. Blacks must stop screaming and start speaking with quiet authority, the authority of the fully entitled, the authority of the calmly confident, the authority of the self-legitimized citizen who has no intention of being silenced or marginalized ever again *and does not expect anyone to try to silence or marginalize them again.*

The first step in freeing one another is for black people, collectively, to surrender. Blacks must consciously give up on achieving racial justice. They must renounce any notion of achieving justice that is meant to even the historical score or to bring about full racial integration.

The problem with the goal of integration is that to whites it has meant only the absence of tangible oppression. It has not meant a willingness to live or educate all children together. It has not meant the acceptance of equal police scrutiny and treatment; it has not meant dismantling structural inequalities. It just means no lynchings, no de jure back-of-the-bus treatment. The more fundamental problem with integration as a post-movement goal is that its focus is on white behavior and largesse—on whites allowing blacks to live nearby, to eat with them, to send their children to the same schools. But black autonomy is not whites' to bestow—it is blacks' to exercise.

A free person does not live with integration as a goal but rather focuses on living, eating, and schooling his children as he chooses. If he is interfered with, he takes appropriate action, be it a restraining order or a backyard barbecue, a fence or a loaned power tool, a friendly phone call or a lawsuit. Sometimes he walks away and chooses a different battle, something that all grown-ups eventually have to do. He focuses not on what whites do or do not want, what they will or will not do, but on requiring his society to treat him like a citizen.

The Civil War did not end with Robert E. Lee's surrender at Appomattox. Nor did it end with the passage of the Civil Rights Act one hundred years later. It continues to this day. But that war—over the social and political position of black people— must end, and it can end only with black surrender.

What blacks must surrender is the notion that they can be made whole for the centuries of loss and degradation they endured, that whites can be made to suffer guilt and shame equal to the portion they have dealt blacks, that white America will ever see itself the way its black citizens do. White America will never feel blacks' ambivalence for the Founding Fathers,[13] it will never waver from nostalgia for that much-vaunted "age of innocence" that the black experience alone proves never existed. It can't. If it did, it would have to come up with another, less glorious definition of itself, because its "innocence" is that of the criminal whose victim lies mute, buried in an unmarked grave and lost to history. Whites will never cringe with the shame blacks feel appropriate; they will never welcome blacks nonchalantly into their neighborhoods and schools—or at least blacks should assume so. Practically speaking, as both intermarriage and black uplift continue, whites will passively participate in integration, but blacks still should not list it among their goals. They should ignore whites qua whites and focus on being prime movers.

Blacks must abandon their quest to gain whites' respect, settling instead for their acceptance, however grudging, of the fact that interference will not be tolerated. Blacks must cease clutching the fetters of humiliation and self-elimination that, although now unlocked, still chain them to a view of the present that is shrink-wrapped to the circumscribed past.

Alas, too few blacks even have their faces pressed up against the plate-glass window of the future. In trying to convince black kids to consider applying to Ivy League and challenging colleges, one is routinely met, especially from their parents, with a disgusted pause, followed by a variant of this conversation-stopper: "I don't want her to lose her identity." Her identity as what— a graduate of a mediocre school? Why must blacks, to remain black, avoid prolonged contact with whites and the societal goodies that follow them wherever they go? This is know-nothingness, petulance, and self-elimination; who does one hurt in ceding Harvard to the haves? Who does one help? Why did James Meredith risk his life to integrate Ole Miss, if enrolling his granddaughter there now means harming her in some way? Why is it that when blacks get what they ask for, they don't want it anymore?

Where segregation exists, voluntarily or involuntarily, blacks should be working to turn it on its head—toward the day when whites clamor for admittance to black schools, black medical staffs, and black social groups and businesses. Historically Black Colleges and Universities (HBCUs) like Spelman, Morehouse, Florida A&M University, and Fisk were "discovered" by whites after mainstream news outlets took note of their low tuition and high standards. HBCUs, resultantly, are now navigating a white influx sustained enough to have created an identity crisis for themselves, with students, alumni, and administration choosing sides for or against integration. That's progress on black terms— societal goodies for which whites have to follow blacks. That's getting even.

Why not use segregation to end segregation, as with HBCUs? Or at least to ensure that separate is better, let alone equal. Blacks should be focused on producing the caliber of doctors and teachers and investment bankers and neighborhoods that *anyone* would wait in line for (so that they can become fully realized humans and citizens, *not* so that whites will approve of them). Woodson quotes Frederick Douglass as saying in 1852:

> It is vain that we talk of being men, if we do not the work of men. We must become valuable to society in other departments of industry than those servile ones from which we are rapidly being excluded. We must show that we can do as well as they. When we can build as well as live in houses; when we can make as well as wear shoes; when we can produce as well as consume wheat, corn and rye—then we shall become valuable to society.[14]

Then—if one may be so bold as to edit the master—blacks shall become valuable to *themselves*. Though he was writing at a time when life was terribly hard for blacks, Douglass nonetheless assumed the possibility of black leadership and a black choice to take charge, to make themselves valuable to society, not to whites. Until blacks today chart such a course for themselves, they will remain the annoying kid brother Mom forces you to tolerate.

This surrender must also acknowledge that blacks are Americans living in a Eurocentric culture, but one that could not have been built without them and that they profoundly shaped. Count Basie was conservatory trained. Ralph Ellison, originally a music man and a stalwart of the jazz/blues movement, said of his 1920s elementary school band:

> [W]e played military music, the classical marches, . . . symphonic music, overtures, snatches of opera and so on, and we sang classical sacred music and the Negro spirituals. . . . [O]n May Day we filled the Western League Ball Park, wrapping maypoles and dancing European folk dances. You really

should see a field of little Negro kids dancing an Irish jig or a Scottish fling . . . for us the dance was the thing.[15]

In parts of the South most slaves were owned by Scots- and Irishmen (like Scarlett *O'Hara* and like *the Klan,* named in homage to the Scottish clans from which they claimed descent); of course blacks would have been influenced by the dominant culture, especially since African culture was suppressed; the dominant culture, in turn, was influenced by them. According to Amiri Baraka, the Charleston, unbeknownst to the segregationists who danced it, was derived from an Ashanti ancestor dance transmitted to America through blacks who knew not why they moved as they did, just that they had to.[16] Martin Luther King Jr. fought for *inclusion* in the dominant culture, not to have his culture made parallel. (It already was.) His writings and speeches are liberally strewn with besotted references to Ovid, Cicero, Paul Tillich, and a host of dead white males. He saw no problem with blacks having two cultures from which they could draw as needed. "I sit with Shakespeare and he winces not," wrote W.E.B. DuBois, perhaps a tad too eagerly.[17] (Better if he had said, "I sit with Shakespeare, who welcomes me, and it excuses racism not.") There's no reason blacks should not feel free to consciously adopt Western culture, reject it, or meld it with some desired level of Afro- (or other) centrism. But they should make that choice while aware of its consequences and free of coercion from gatekeeping blacks and their apologists. This is a journey that each must make alone, as Ellison wholeheartedly did. James Baldwin's trek was somewhat more grudging, if equally successful:

I was forced to recognize that I was a kind of bastard of the West. . . . I brought to Shakespeare, Bach, Rembrandt, to the stones of Paris, to the cathedral at Chartres, and to the Empire State Building, a special attitude. These were not really my creations, they did not contain my history; I might search in them in vain forever for any reflection of myself. I was an interloper; this was not my heritage. At the same time I had no other heritage which I could possibly hope to use—I had certainly been unfitted for the jungle or the tribe. I would have to appropriate these white centuries, I would have to make them mine—I would have to accept my special attitude, my special place in this scheme—otherwise I would have no place in *any* scheme.[18]

Baldwin wept as he danced the Charleston and thought it made him less African, or any more Western than he already was. His brilliance notwithstanding, he bought the lie that the slaves came empty-handed and that, once here, they somehow managed to stand outside the forward sweep of Western civilization in which even the most debased white was automatically included. Baldwin is as responsible for the Empire State Building as any Larson from Minnesota. Still, he made his peace, however unnecessary, with Western civilization and made a place for himself within it. As Ellison remarked, only the West could have produced James Baldwin.

As proof of Baldwin's formulation, in a nonfiction work called *A Hope in the Unseen*, a striving black youngster claws his way to Brown University, only to find that the Afrocentrism of his neighborhood education left him knowing all the words to "Lift Every Voice and Sing" but clueless as to the identities of Winston Churchill and Sigmund Freud. He was also lacking in the academic basics, though he'd committed himself to the available advanced coursework. That youngster aspired to greatness, but his well-meaning black teachers impeded him from availing himself of that to which his citizenship entitled him and for which he had worked so hard. Poorly funded inner-city schools were only part of his problem.

In *Riches for the Poor,* author, anthropologist, and educator Earl Shorris cites a similar example. A white social worker, he explains, dissuaded her clients from participating in Shorris's college bridge program because the curriculum didn't include African history. "You're indoctrinating people in Western culture" she objected. In the end, "[t]he social worker convinced her clients that no education was better than an education in the humanities; not one of them applied for admission to the course."[19] Many of Shorris's poverty-stricken, poorly educated students have gone on to selective colleges. Probably they encountered few, if any, of that social worker's charges there, except as cafeteria workers or janitors. Albert Murray would say of such a woman that she either "do[es] not know what education is, or [she] knows only too well."[20]

Aside from its instrumental value for blacks in preparing themselves to thrive, an education in Western literary, artistic, and scientific culture is valuable also because the truth of white oppression doesn't diminish its grandeur. Shakespeare's sonnets are no less mellifluous because he was an imperialist; the elevator and the air conditioner revolutionized the entire planet. Blacks needn't deify whites, or hate themselves, to give the devil his due.

It is undeniable, however, that whites' narcissism and xenophobia require them to diminish and deny African and black culture and learning. Carter G. Woodson was much more charitable than they and made a sensible, bracing point in admonishing blacks to embrace their own history without dismissing that of others:

> We do not mean to suggest here, however, that any people should ignore the record of the progress of other races. . . . We say, hold on to the real facts of history as they are, but complete such knowledge by studying also the history of races and nations which have been purposely ignored. We should not underrate the achievements of Mesopotamia,

Greece, and Rome; but we should give equally as much attention to the internal African kingdoms, the Songhay empire, and Ethiopia, which through Egypt decidedly influenced the civilization of the Mediterranean World.[21]

True knowledge can know no boundaries. (Propaganda, by contrast, must be very selective with the facts.) Blacks must accept that they are a numerical and political minority and must master the dominant bodies of knowledge even as they fight for the inclusion of worthy black knowledge. As rational adults, they should concede that, forced to choose as the young man in *A Hope in the Unseen* was, it must be Winston Churchill before Patrice Lumumba, the Inchon landing before the Zulus' defeat of the British. Of course, they shouldn't have to make such choices at all; the goal should be to expand the base of cultural literacy, one sinew of a strong nation, not to play a zero-sum game in which one nugget of Western civilization must be jettisoned for every multicultural nugget included. If an education is to be lacking, it should lack that which is least likely to help the student get ahead. For the same reason that all schoolchildren need to master algebra whether they think they'll ever use it or not, blacks must master the master's world. They needn't embrace it or even believe it; they must simply render unto Caesar the things that are Caesar's. And then subvert it from within if they are so inclined, something they can do precisely because they *are* within. Only the black nay-sayers and paternalistic whites, like that social worker, say otherwise:

One of the great destructive shibboleths of modern literary studies insists that the canon is the exclusive preserve, the self-perpetuating creation, of Dead White Men. Of course, this shibboleth also happens, by and large, to be true, but as a result of historical and social happenstance rather than some sort of conspiracy. Once upon a time, indeed, the restrictions went even further, permitting only Dead White Well-Born Christian Men into the literary parlor. Who would have thought a poor, spottily educated, rustic glover's apprentice from Warwickshire might have something to contribute, for example? Well, he managed it, and with a vengeance. . . . Who would have guessed that a lower-middle-class spinster from Hampshire would become one of the greatest novelists in the English language? Who would have thought the great-grandson of a black African would become the national poet of *Russia,* for God's sake? Who would have imagined the great-grandson and the grandson of a Haitian slave would become two of France's most popular novelists? Who could have foreseen that the despised Irish were going to produce so many world-class poets, playwrights, and novelists? And who knew 20th-century American letters were going to witness the noisy emergence of that rambunctious throng William Styron has styled "the Jewish mafia"?

Dead white well-born Christian men dominate the canon because, for much of written history, they dominated *everything*. But the glory of the tradition is precisely that anyone ambitious enough, talented enough, and clamorous enough is free to elbow the aristocrats out of the way, seize the baton, and run with it. That's part of what gives the tradition its great ongoing vitality. Western literature, since perhaps Homer himself, celebrates individual experience and individual consciousness. It exults in the particular over the generic. It thrives on messy human variety. Which is why it isn't mere bleeding-heart sentimentality to embrace a liberal, expansive vision of multiculturalism; the Western tradition— the canon—requires it. The tradition *embodies* such a vision.[22]

Can it be that blacks are not ambitious enough, talented enough, or brazen enough to elbow the aristocrats out of the way, seize the baton, and run with it? Instead of refusing to acknowledge the grandeur of Western civilization, the better strategy would likely be to study it and give credit where credit is due while also picking it apart for its flaws and its apologists' misinterpretations. Those who want to prove non-Western civilization its equal must also study it on its own terms, because they have to master both. But Shakespeare sucketh not; why fight the majesty of white culture? Why shouldn't blacks make a comfortable place for themselves within that which cannot, and need not, be avoided? If blacks cannot retain an appreciation for Africa's cultures simultaneously with appreciation for the West's, then Africa's cultures don't merit appreciation. Further, as a matter of morality and logical consistency, blacks cannot criticize Western civilization for dismissing worthy non-Western contributions and then dismiss Western civilization.

Blacks must surrender themselves to America. Why not? Their enslaved ancestors did. Historian Constance Rourke argues that elements of the black personality have been embedded in America's national character almost from the moment of blacks' arrival. Three generations before Emancipation "[t]he Negro . . . was to be seen everywhere in the South and in the new Southwest, on small farms and great plantations, on roads and levees. He was often an all but equal member of many a pioneering expedition. He became, in short, a dominant figure in spite of his condition, and commanded a definite portraiture."[23] Rourke argues that every American is part Yankee, part backwoodsman and Indian, and part Negro. We are all mulattoes now. In fact, we always have been.

This is why blacks must give themselves permission to be happy Yanks and well-adjusted Westerners. They also have to shoulder the adult's full responsibility as a member of the polity—no longer can standards of conduct and morality be lower for blacks than for whites: crime is crime, sloth is sloth, and merit is mostly measurable. Blacks debase themselves pretending to believe otherwise.

The black problem child wants nothing so much as to feel confident in his membership in the American family. To do that, he will have to be brave and give up the malcontent's chair at Thanksgiving Dinner, pretending he doesn't care, even though he bothered to show up. He will have to stop nyah-nyahing that, though Mom has lost two hundred pounds, she still has ten to go. He will have to stop believing that the only power he has, and the only way to matter, is to create and prolong turmoil. He will have to learn to trust in the power of self-determination and in the riveted foundation of his rich birthright. They *will* support him.

This black surrender is not defeat. It is not an admission that the racists and the conservatives were right all along. It is the mature acknowledgment that, right or wrong, the past is as rectified as it's ever going to be and that the future is blacks' to claim. Black surrender is both honorable and justified because it is a response to whites' surrender of the right to exploit and oppress them or to appease those who do. What else but the forfeiture of those rights could have caused all the white complaints about becoming second-class citizens? Even the rise of skinhead groups is a reflection of this new white inability to oppress at will, just as the Klan arose with Emancipation. White polls, if not white hearts, concede the basic tenets of antiracism. White hearts know that the status quo is racist; white hands are just having a hard time giving up all the goodies. Anyone would.

Even so, it's clear that they're surrendering their right to a whiteness defined as control over nonwhites, as a preordained spot at the top of every pile, be it character, intellect, beauty, or talent. Together the two surrenders constitute a truce. All that's left is to formulate a strategy for the peace.

In order to make progress possible, blacks have to give up on the past. Tomorrow is their only option.

PROLOGUE:

Blackness Before the Dawn

"[B]y 1470, 83 percent of the slaves in Naples were [sub-Saharan] Africans. There were also African slaves in Sicily. . . . [Their] perceived inferiority [was] becoming part of the cultural folklore of Europe. Italian (and emerging European) racism was examined by William Shakespeare in *Othello,* written in 1604. That racism was a topic of this major work indicates that racist ideas concerning Africans must already have spread to England. Elizabethan literature abounded with lecherous and degenerate black men. The presentation of Moors in Elizabethan drama before *Othello* consisted of only foolish or wicked characters. . . . These characters were used to fulfill the dramatic expectations of this period, whereby a man's color revealed his villainy."

— JOSEPH L. GRAVES[1]

"Nothing is more certainly written in the book of fate than that these people are to be free. Nor is it less certain that the two races, equally free, cannot live in the same government."

— THOMAS JEFFERSON, *AUTOBIOGRAPHY*, 1821[2]

"Good gracious. Anybody hurt?"
"No'm. Killed a nigger."
"Well, it's lucky because sometimes people do get hurt."
— MARK TWAIN, *HUCKLEBERRY FINN*, 1884[3]

"Do you really think a nigger's a human being?"
— CLAY HOPPER, DISGUSTED MANAGER OF THE
BROOKLYN DODGERS' TOP MINOR LEAGUE FARM TEAM,
TO THE GENERAL MANAGER WHO ORDERED HIM TO
TRAIN JACKIE ROBINSON, THE FIRST BLACK MAJOR
LEAGUE BASEBALL PLAYER, 1946[4]

Americans, black and white, have forgotten just how America thought of blacks before the civil rights movement. They have lost the understanding of how widely and deeply held was whites' disbelief in black humanity or equality, let alone the extent to which that disbelief was enshrined not just in custom but in law. Some version of Clay Hopper's question has ricocheted through American religious, civic, scientific, artistic, political, and jurisprudential discourse ever since some nameless colonist first realized that African indentured servants, being without protectors, could be transformed into slaves for longer and longer terms, eventually for life. There was no way to achieve that goal without defining, and treating, blacks in direct opposition to the way whites defined and treated one another. Four centuries later, where is America to begin unraveling the twisted entrails of race that ensnare them all, white, black, red, yellow, and brown?

"[C]urrent ways of talking about race," explains philosopher K. Anthony Appiah, "are the residue, the detritus, so to speak, of earlier ways of thinking about race; so that it turns out to be easiest to understand contemporary talk about 'race' as the pale reflection of a more full-blooded race discourse that flourished in the [twentieth] century."[5] That discourse also flourished, without much of the pseudo-scientific varnish, in the seventeenth-, eighteenth-, and nineteenth-century West as well. (Otherwise there would have been no need for America's Civil War, for instance, to end the controversy.) Any talk of race today certainly takes place on ground packed hard by many generations of assumptions, apologies, wishful thinking, lies, fallacies, and insights of which no American can be completely free, especially so long as he denies or remains unaware of them.

For centuries, it was often illegal to treat blacks like human beings, let alone citizens—a fact often underplayed in the nation's American history curricula. In the early 1990s a civil rights attorney was astonished to learn that the U.S. Naval Academy cadets to whom she taught civil rights history had not known and refused to believe that Jim Crow was a system of laws and staunchly enforced custom, not just quixotic white rudeness to blacks. The nation's best and brightest, including the blacks among them, had no understanding that racism, every bit as much as democracy, was the way America thought. But America didn't start out that way, even though slavery predates it. Whether it makes blacks feel better or worse, and whites more guilty or less, the fact is that racism was a choice, a largely economic one. Thomas Sowell writes:

[E]xcept for debt-bondage or bondage as punishment, the process . . . has generally been one of enslaving outsiders. . . . For centuries . . . it was . . . legitimate for the Christians of Western Europe to enslave "pagans" from . . . Eastern Europe, and it was long after all of Europe became Christian that the Catholic Church finally [ended] the pretense. . . . [W]hich outsiders to enslave was not a matter of racial ideology, but was based on pragmatic considerations as to availability, . . . both the military and legal obstacles. . . . [C]ontinued enslavement of particular populations became less common with the rise of powerful nation-states [because] to attempt mass enslavement of subjects of [a powerful empire] was to risk war. The consolidation of nation-states . . . reduced the number of places from which people could be captured and enslaved. . . .

[Globally], the slave trade was conducted by merchant peoples, such as the Venetians, Greeks, and Jews in Europe, the overseas Chinese in Southeast Asia, or by the Arabs who played both the merchant and marauder roles in Africa. . . . Neither a national policy nor a racial ideology was necessary . . . [only] the existence of a vulnerable people. . . . Slavery flourished in ancient Greece and Rome without any racial ideology. . . . Enslavement was based on self-interest and opportunity, not ideology. . . .

Peoples regularly [enslaved] might indeed be despised, and treated with contempt . . . , but that was not what caused them to be enslaved. . . . Although there was no religious basis for racism in the Islamic world, the massive enslavement of sub-Saharan Africans . . . was *followed* [emphasis added] by a racial disdain toward black people in the Middle East . . . [that] had not been apparent in the Arabs' previous dealings with Ethiopians. In the West as well, racism was promoted by slavery, rather than vice versa. Both in North America and in South Africa, racist rationales for slavery were resorted to only after religious rationales were tried and found wanting. . . . [Often], no rationale was . . . necessary.[6]

Africa, then and now the least urbanized continent, remained prey to mass enslavement when other countries no longer were, simply because it remained defenseless,[7] not because Africans were thought a priori to be lesser beings. One of Moses' wives was an "Ethiopian," the ancient Greek word for an African.[8] Logistics (sub-Saharan Africa is the only convenient place to obtain slaves) became ideology (blacks are slaves by nature, the weaklings). Antiblack racism was the by-product, not the cause, of slavery. Racism was an upgrade that made the basic model more valuable as a commodity because it made it less valuable as a human being.

Americans tend not to know that Europeans, especially southern Europeans, constructed the template for the structure that North American slavery and racist attitudes would take, especially the seafaring, mercantilist, slave-trading Italians and Portuguese. Before there was science, early Christians had only "natural law" to analyze their world and saw "all things as created by God with a purpose in the hierarchy of nature," Joseph L. Graves writes. "Was not the African, a beast of burden, delivered by divine Providence to labor for the benefit of the noble and Christian European?" he asks rhetorically on their behalf.[9] Seeking a religious explanation for the glaring differences between Europeans and non-Europeans as well as a justification for their treatment of blacks, between about 1520 and 1655 southern Europeans promulgated and refined the theory of "polygenism," a belief in the entirely separate origin of each race (race being denoted by physiognomy and skin color).

Cain, having been cast out by God, had to have married a woman who was not descended from Adam and Eve, no? As repulsion grew among Italians at the presence of so many Africans in their country, thinkers like Giordano Bruno surmised either that God had created separate Adams (it being impossible for Aethiopes and Jews to have a common origin) or that Africans were pre-Adamite, with all the baseness that would entail. Naturally, such thinking would give rise to attempts to ban race-mingling and to the emergence of the first notions of racial separatism as natural, godly. Toward the end of this period the disgusted but prescient Italian Lucilio Vanini argued that Africans had to be descended from apes and were previously quadripedal. As xenophobia spread north and west, in 1655 the French Protestant Isaac de la Peyrère closed the logical loop by positing that pre-Adamites peopled Africa, Asia, and the New World. All of which, of course, begs the question of the very existence of "races," these mutually exclusive, nonoverlapping, biologically determined separate strands of very different and hierarchically arranged peoples. Instead, these thinkers assumed the existence of races and worked backward to "prove" it. Confronted with "others" so visibly different from themselves, whites became trapped in the tar pits of their own imaginations, even as they stood astride the Age of (Western) Discovery and on the brink of the Enlightenment.

As Europeans, and slavery, spread to the New World, racist thinking spread with them. This is not to say that there was ever unanimity of opinion on the subject. The problem was that "[i]n trying to answer these questions [regarding the humanity and morality of blacks], whites of the [colonial] day did what they always did when dealing with the status and definition of black people: they consulted one another (a practice that remains all too prevalent today)."[10] It should not be construed, however, that blacks were passive, merely praying to their God (Jesus) and their god (whites) for deliverance. They engaged in active resistance—espionage, sabotage, arson, subterfuge (future revolt leader Denmark Vesey feigned epilepsy for years), aiding and abetting all manner of proscribed activities, work slowdowns, open defiance, murder, lawsuits, lobbying, and of course open revolt. In the ultimate act of defiance, they escaped, or sought to, in droves *à la* Frederick Douglass, Harriet Tubman, and Sojourner Truth.[11] For seven years Harriet Jacobs hid in an attic space too small to stand up in right over her lascivious master's head. Several enslaved blacks had themselves nailed into crates and mailed north to freedom, spending days upside down. Two female slaves hid in plain sight in head-to-toe widows' weeds and took a leisurely train ride North. In 1848 Ellen Craft, a white-looking mulatto, dressed up like a man whose head injury necessitated silence and a face swathed in bandages; the faithful slave attending "him" was in fact her husband. There would have been no need for the Fugitive Slave Act (which required the entire nation to participate in slavery) had there been no fugitives. Politically, free and fugitive blacks formed self-help and lobbying societies as early as 1787, when two former slaves founded the Free African Society in Philadelphia "from a love of people of their complexion whom they beheld with sorrow."[12] As well, the history of slave revolts has been widely downplayed; how many know that slaves burned down Dallas in 1860? Whites, via the Civil War, take credit for freeing blacks, just as they would hijack the history of the civil rights movement a century later. Blacks always knew they were human, and they always said so. Still, blinded by narcissism, xenophobia, and greed, the sharpest eyes in revolutionary America could see only what they wanted to.

As any schoolchild knows, the slaveowning Jefferson nonetheless had the vision to prophesy: "Nothing is more certainly written in the book of fate than that these people are to be free."[13] They are probably less familiar with the sentence that follows: "Nor is it less certain that the two races, equally free, cannot live in the same government."[14] Jefferson explained the reasons for this conclusion in his *Notes on the State of Virginia:*

Deep rooted prejudices entertained by the whites; ten thousand recollections, by the blacks, of the injuries they have sustained; new provocations; *the real distinctions which nature has made* [emphasis added]; and many other circumstances, will divide us . . . , and produce convulsions which will probably never end but in the extermination of the one or the other race. To these objections, which are political, may be added others, which are physical and moral. The first difference which strikes us is that of colour. [Whatever the source of his color], the difference is fixed in nature, and is as real as if its seat and cause were better known to us. And is this difference of no importance? Is it not the foundation of a greater or less share of beauty in the two races? Are not the fine mixtures of red and white, the expressions of every passion by greater or less suffusions of colour in the one, preferable to that external monotony, which reigns in the countenances, that immoveable veil of black which covers all the emotions of the other race? Add to these, flowing hair, a more elegant symmetry of form, their own judgment in favour of the whites, declared by their preference for them, as uniformly as is the preference of the Oranootan for the black woman over those of his own species. The circumstance of superior beauty, is thought worthy attention in the propagation of our horses, dogs, and other domestic animals; why not in that of man?[15]

There is lots more. Blacks have:

a very strong and disagreeable odour . . . require less sleep . . . [are] at least as brave and more adventuresome. But this may perhaps proceed from a want of forethought. . . . [They are] more ardent after their female; but love seems with them to be more an eager desire, than a tender delicate mixture of sentiment and sensation. Their griefs are transient . . . one could scarcely be found capable of tracing and comprehending the investigations of Euclid; and that in imagination they are dull, tasteless, and anomalous . . . never yet could I find that a black had uttered a thought above the level of plain narration; never see even an elementary trait of painting or sculpture. Misery is often the parent of the most affecting touches in poetry. Among the blacks is misery enough, God knows, but no poetry. . . . This unfortunate difference of colour, and perhaps of faculty, is a powerful obstacle to the emancipation of these people.[16]

Thankfully, Jefferson was not a polygenist; he was a natural historian (biology's precursor) and versed in Carolus Linnaeus's classification scheme. While he believed blacks to be mentally and aesthetically inferior to whites, he did believe that both were of the same species and that therefore whites had no right to rule blacks. Whites did, however, have a right to be free of their inferiors.

With this idea, he provided the most thoughtful, most humane thinking of his day on the complicated, still incoherent subject of race, that "running together of biology and politics, science and morals, fact and value, ethics and aesthetics. . . . [I]f we query [Jefferson's] conflations, we are querying not so much an individual as the thinking of a whole [Enlightenment] culture," Appiah notes.[17] "Not only, then, is race, for Jefferson, *a concept that is invoked to explain cultural and social phenomena,* it is also grounded in the physical and the psychological natures of the different races; it is, in other words, what we could call a *biological concept.*"[18] And biology, of course, is neither right nor wrong, neither racist nor color blind. Biology is inescapable. Biology is not white people's fault.

With this idea coming from a bona-fide genius, imagine the racial analysis of the average eighteenth-century tavern keep or the average manual laborer whose pay was kept low by wage pressure from the unpaid. Pity, history tells us, was not the white workingman's dominant emotion toward slaves.

The question of how to treat the helpless outsiders that were among them threw into sharp relief the demands the colonists were making for their own freedom as the Revolution loomed, then was won. Those rights to life, liberty, and the pursuit of happiness (or as John Locke originally proclaimed, "property") weren't quite so self-evident or inalienable when it came to blacks, not when both greed and white supremacy were involved. The philosophical loophole to the notion that *all* men were created equal was the idea that *some* men failed to "enter into a state of society." Blacks failed either to be white and civilized by definition or to have successfully defended themselves against whites.

Having dispensed with questions about slavery and the humanity of blacks, the Founding Fathers went on to important matters: "the voting power and property rights of the slaveholding South, and a favorable trade regime for the international shippers of the North."[19] Knowing enough to be ashamed but too weak to control their base instincts, the Founding Fathers could not bring themselves to inscribe the word *slave* in America's founding documents. Blacks were buried alive in the Constitution beneath a wall of euphemisms—"all other persons," and "such Persons," and "person held to Service or Labour"—and were assigned three-fifths the value of a white person for purposes of taxation and representation.

Fifty years after Jefferson, the landscape of Western thought had incorporated rudimentary biology and Linnaeus's taxonomies into its ideology of race as an explanation of a group's perceived morals, educability, and aesthetic orientation. Though the naturalist approach for the most part replaced polygenism and scientists thought blacks human, they nonetheless considered them inferior and assumed whites to be the baseline, of which all other phenotypes were corruptions. White researchers spent centuries measuring the heads, limbs, and privates of the grave-robbed to prove blacks' closer relationship to the ape and the yawning chasm between them and whites.

Appiah labels this new and improved thinking "racialism," the notion that human beings can be divided into "races" whose members share "fundamental, heritable, physical, moral, intellectual, and cultural characteristics with one another that they did not share" with members of other races and that were not related to environmental factors—white men can't jump and black men just don't want to work.[20] These characteristics form the "essence" of each race. "By the end of the nineteenth century most Western scientists (indeed, most educated Westerners) believed that racialism was correct, and theorists sought to explain many characteristics . . . by supposing that they were inherited along with (or were in fact part of) a person's racial essence."[21] Racialism defined groups by what separated them.

That mode of thinking came to dominate the popular imagination as well as the academic. Blacks were essentialized in ways that justified white oppression. (For example, they were said to be childlike and lazy and would starve to death without white oversight.) Black suffering was minimized. (Their griefs were said to be transient, their emotions animalistic: they didn't love their wives and children as whites did, so it wasn't inhumane to sell them; the women were wanton, like monkeys in heat, so no sexual relations with them could be rape.)

Over the centuries before Emancipation, the colonies, territories, and states promulgated Black Codes that governed every aspect of black life, free or slave. In everything from manner of dress to crime to curfews to court testimony to marriage to employment to travel to church attendance, blacks were regulated and controlled by whites, even in free states, and they had only the recourse to legal protection that whites saw fit. "Southern colonies were already outlawing interracial marriage in the 1690's. Wyoming was the last state to prohibit it, in 1913, joining 41 others—every state where the black population reached 5 percent. Though some had repealed their anti-miscegenation laws before the Civil War, 16 still had them on the books by the time the United States Supreme Court finally declared them unconstitutional in 1967."[22] Nationally, until the Civil War and the passage of the Thirteenth, Fourteenth, and Fifteenth Amendments, no federal court had held slavery, let alone de jure racism, to violate American ideals. On the state level, things were only marginally better.[23] Internationally, Europe—and especially England, given its centrality to both America and the issues of slavery—was embroiled in debates over the status and humanity of blacks. As nation-states solidified and advanced enough to oversee more closely their holdings, debates raged as to government's role in alleviating suffering and investing in its human capital.

In America in 1857, the patchwork of varying territorial and state laws, in free and unfree states, grew too unwieldy, so the Supreme Court settled the matter of blacks' civil rights in the Dred Scott case. Scott's owner had taken him to Illinois, a free state, where they remained for five years. When his owner returned him to Missouri, a slave state, Scott petitioned the court for his freedom. Amid the climate of moral agitation stirred up by blacks and the abolitionists and the turmoil surrounding whether nearby Kansas would enter the Union a slave state or free, Scott's case made it all the way to the Supreme Court. It ruled that "the African race [was] not intended to be included in the Constitution for the enjoyment of any personal rights" and that blacks had no rights that whites needed to respect.[24] Blacks were not Americans. They were not whites' equals. Rights were not imbued in them by the Creator they were required to worship; whatever ragtag rights they possessed were bestowed upon them by whites. But in reality the Dred Scott decision settled nothing—America couldn't keep slavery and couldn't give it up—and the course was laid for civil war.

Just as Emancipation took place, a scientific revolution—

Darwinism—seemed to settle the question of the unity of humanity. Charles Darwin's proof that natural selection, and not innate worth, explained human biological diversity, and that all humans derived from the same primal cupboard, revolutionized human understanding. Finally, the humanity and family membership of blacks was established beyond dispute. For Creationist white supremacy, however, the Darwinist threat had to be either smothered in its cradle or else kidnapped and issued a new identity. Hence the ideology of Social Darwinism.

Writing just before *The Origin of Species* was published, English philosopher Herbert Spencer had coined the term "survival of the fittest" as part of his theory of progressive social evolution. He argued that "human progress resulted from the triumph of more-advanced individuals and cultures over their inferior competitors. Thus, . . . wealth and power [were] evidence of inherent 'fitness,' and poverty [was] evidence of natural inferiority."[25] The Social Darwinists, following Spencer, molded Darwinism to their own purposes with great success, though Darwin himself denounced them, detested Spencer, and was an abolitionist. Nonetheless, according to Graves, "[v]irtually every major Euro-American thinker of the latter portion of the nineteenth century was profoundly influenced" by Spencer's perversion.[26] Blacks were worse off because, though equally human, they were inferior; it was by definition unnatural to interfere with natural selection by assisting them. Africa, essentialized as warm and effortlessly banana-filled, simply hadn't required blacks either to work as hard or to be as resourceful as Europeans, with their inhospitable climes, choppy waters, and uncertain harvests. When dumb, lazy Englishmen failed to hoard enough grain for the lean times, they died of exposure or starved to death, their low-wattage genes forever obliterated by an indifferent Mother Nature. Dumb, lazy Africans, however, danced naked in the ever-present sun, clenching with both fists a natural bounty that they'd never had to tend, and they died only in avoidable, boneheaded accidents; scores of equally dumb and lazy children attended their funerals. But when blacks were taken out of their own no-brainer environment and were forced to compete with hardscrabble Westerners, they were ninety-eight-pound weaklings. Their plight—disassociated from either past slavery or present discrimination—was attributed to their inability to compete with the better-endowed groups. Any perusal of an American op-ed page today will show that this view is still deeply embedded in the Western psyche.

America had been roused to rid itself of the evil of slavery, but that was as far as it was prepared to go; indeed, much of the opposition to slavery had had nothing to do with a belief in the equality of blacks, as Spencer's popularity proves. Many abolitionists, including Presidents Jefferson and Lincoln, preferred that blacks return, or be returned, to Africa. Blacks were seen as foreign bodies that needed to be purged from the American bloodstream. Many whites objected on supposedly humane grounds, believing that blacks could never be assimilated in America, that the two races could never live in harmony, let alone in equality, because of blacks' allegedly degraded morals, intellect, and aesthetics. Why else would blacks have to be so carefully controlled and kept in line? The Emancipation Proclamation justified itself in terms of "military necessity," not blacks' humanity, civil rights, or access to the ballot; it admonished *blacks* to refrain from violence (that is, vengeance). Slavery had to go, not because of its inhumanity, but because conflict over it was destroying the Union.

After the Civil War whites were disinclined to discipline one another for blacks' sake, so Reconstruction ended by 1877, and the counterrevolution began. Abandoned by the North and again defenseless, blacks were stripped of the protections of the Thirteenth, Fourteenth, and Fifteenth Amendments. They found themselves technically free but, in reality, despised serfs to their former masters. Jim Crow—racial segregation and exploitation in everything from housing to employment to the criminal justice system to the tax system—was instituted both as a system of laws and as a matter of custom that was nearly impossible for either whites or blacks to flout. As in the Constitution, blacks were taxed without representation and were stripped of every civil right, especially that to vote, even though whites did not use the words *Negro* and *former slave* in their state constitutions and statutes—Jim Crow was maintained through grandfather clauses, poll taxes, and selective enforcement or nonenforcement of laws (for example, vagrancy laws might be enforced against blacks so as to exploit them as prison labor, while laws against murder were not invoked when whites killed blacks). Most of all, black subjugation was cemented by whites' commonplace use of terror and violence against the black population. Blacks were buried alive again. White oppression in the isolated South was such that Jim Crow–era blacks "joked" of being from Hehunghigh, Mississippi, or Stringhimup, Louisiana. Blacks could not serve on juries; they could not hold public office; they could not realistically sue whites or have them prosecuted; they could not join political parties; the schools were segregated, with the black ones severely substandard; they could not join professional organizations; they were barred from public facilities; and most of all, they could not vote. There were exceptions, of course, but they only proved the rule. Otherwise, why would an upheaval on the scale of the civil rights movement have been needed?

After Emancipation ninety percent of blacks lived in the South; by 1940 seventy-seven percent did, of whom forty-nine percent lived in rural areas. Many escaped north; those who didn't were left at the mercy of their unrepentant former owners, who immediately invented the sharecropping system as the best way to reinstate slavery—unpaid, involuntary, brute labor—but without the need to provide any support for their peons. According to Nicholas Lemann,

[I]t turned out to be nearly impossible to make any money sharecropping. The sharecropper's family would move, early in the year, to a rough two- or three-room cabin on a plantation. The plumbing [was,] at most, a washbasin. . . . The only heat came from a wood burning stove. . . . no electricity and no insulation. . . . Usually the roof leaked. The families often slept two and three to a bed.

Every big plantation was a fiefdom. . . . Sharecroppers traded at a plantation-owned commissary, often in scrip. . . . (Martin Luther King, Jr., [was amazed to meet Alabama sharecroppers in 1965 who had never seen United States currency].) They prayed at plantation-owned Baptist churches. Their children walked, sometimes miles, to plantation-owned schools, usually one- or two-room buildings without heating or plumbing. Education ended with the eighth grade and was extremely casual. . . . All the grades were taught together, and most of the students were far behind. . . . The textbooks were tattered hand-me-downs from the white schools. The planter could and did shut down the schools whenever there was [field work,] so the school year for [them] usually amounted to only four or five months, frequently interrupted. Many . . . remember going to school only when it rained. In 1938 the average American teacher's salary was $1,374, and the average value of a school district's buildings and equipment per student was $274. For blacks in Mississippi, the figures were $144 and $11.

Each family had a plot of land [from fifteen to forty acres]. . . . In March, the planter would begin [providing] a "furnish," a monthly stipend [from fifteen to fifty dollars] that was supposed to cover their living expenses until the

crop came in in the fall. . . . The standard of living provided
by the furnish was extremely low . . . the money often ran out
before the end of the month, in which case the family would
have to "take up" (borrow) at the commissary.

The cotton was picked in October and November and then
was taken to the plantation's gin. . . . The planter packed it
into bales and sold it. . . . Then, just before Christmas, each
sharecropper would be summoned to the plantation office
for . . . "the settle." The manager would hand him a piece of
paper showing how much money he had cleared . . . and pay
him his share.

For most sharecroppers, the settle was a moment of bit-
terly dashed hope, because usually the sharecropper would
learn that he had cleared only a few dollars, or nothing at all,
or that he owed the planter money. . . . [The planters levied a
series of fees] over the course of the year. [Commissary goods
were marked up.] . . . [Planters] charged exorbitant interest
on credit at the commissary, and sometimes on the furnish
as well—20 per cent [typically]. . . . None of these charges
were spelled out clearly as they were made, and usually they
appeared on the sharecropper's annual statement as a single
unitemized line, "Plantation Expense.". . .

There was no brake on dishonest behavior by a planter
towards a sharecropper. For a sharecropper to sue a planter
was unthinkable. Even to ask for a more detailed accounting
was known to be an action with the potential to endanger
your life. The most established plantations were literally
above the law. . . . The sheriff would call the planter when a
matter of criminal justice concerning one of his sharecroppers
arose, and if the planter said he preferred to handle it on his
own (meaning, often, that he would administer a beating
himself), the sheriff would stay off the place. . . . If a planter
chose to falsify a sharecropper's gin receipt, lowering the

weight of cotton in his crop, there was nothing the sharecropper could do about it; . . . a sharecropper was not
allowed to receive and sign for a gin receipt on his own. If a
planter wanted to "soak" a sharecropper, by adding a lot of
imaginary equipment repairs . . . the sharecropper had no
way of knowing about it. . . .

Hortense Powdermaker, an anthropologist from Yale who
spent a year in the 1930s studying the town of Indianola,
Mississippi, . . . estimated that only a quarter of the planters
were honest in their accounting.[27]

Southern whites saw to it that blacks had no alternative to
the brutal reality of sharecropping. Their control extended to
every area of life; white rape of black women was endemic, like
heat and humidity, and victims had no recourse to the justice
system. Winson Hudson, a movement leader born in Harmony,
Mississippi, in the 1920s, recalls:

Back then, white boys would rape you and then come and
destroy the family if you said anything about it. You would
just have to accept it. They were liable to come in and run the
whole family off. I couldn't walk the roads at anytime alone
for fear I might meet a white man or boy. I couldn't walk the
street without some white man winking his eye or making
some sort of sound. It made me so angry because I had five
brothers, and I heard my father almost daily warning them
against even walking near a white girl or looking at them or
going near a house unless they knew that white men were
there too.[28]

While the women were raped, the men faced death for the
slightest offense. Between 1882 and 1968 approximately 4,742

black men were lynched. "As many if not more blacks were victims of legal lynchings (speedy trials and executions), private white violence, and *'nigger hunts,'* murdered by a variety of means in isolated rural sections and dumped into rivers and creeks."[29] Not infrequently, entire black towns or neighborhoods were lynched. The Tulsa (Oklahoma) and Rosewood (Florida) white pogroms against blacks in the early part of the century are among the best known, but such pogroms took place all over the country, the North included, and are too numerous to catalog. Usually some offense to a white woman was alleged, but the true reason was jealousy over black success or "uppityness"; Ralph Ellison writes of a jaunty black man being lynched merely for painting his house a vibrant blue. Very often lynching was a subterfuge for stealing black property, especially land. With legislative and judicial collusion, perhaps hundreds of thousands of acres of land were stolen from blacks.[30] Police and soldiers often took part in the riots. Rarely were any whites punished. Park Day, for example, is a celebration that takes place in Springfield, Missouri; it reunites the families and friends of blacks who fled the small town after public lynchings in 1906, for which no whites were ever prosecuted.

The 1955 murder of fifteen-year-old Emmett Till is among the most notorious individual lynchings. On a visit from Chicago to his mother's Mississippi hometown, he was accused of whistling at a white woman. He was found beaten beyond recognition (save for his father's ring) and lashed to an eighty-pound cotton gin fan in the Tallahatchie River. The sheriff included, white Mississippians told jokes ("ain't it just like a nigger to go swimming with a cotton gin fan around his neck?") and collected $10,000 for the defense of the two suspects. The defendants were acquitted by an all-white jury that deliberated less than an hour. Soon afterward the cleared defendants confessed what everyone already knew and what many whites didn't consider a crime. Jefferson was right—blacks and whites could not live together in peace—at least not yet.

There was no area of life in which blacks were not neglected (in municipal services), exploited (in employment—they were forced into the lowest-paying, least enjoyable, most closely overseen jobs, like maids and manual labor), or brutalized. For instance, from the 1920s to the 1980s thirty-three states participated in the eugenics movement (a spawn of Social Darwinism), which believed that the "cure" for mental illness, social pathologies, and genetic defects was sterilization. As many as 65,000 people were so "treated." During its last twenty years the eugenics program focused primarily on sterilizing black women.[31] Medical training was carried out on involuntarily obtained black specimens with great disrespect.[32] Of course, the most infamous and most telling example of white fascination, disgust, and need for violence against the black body is the Tuskegee Experiment.[33] For forty years black subjects were left with untreated syphilis so scientists could chart the disease's devastating progress.

Darwin be damned, there just had to be something wrong with black folks. If it wasn't biology, then it had to be culture. Appiah notes that "the legacy of the Holocaust and the old racist biology has led many to be wary of racial essences," such as the idea that blacks just don't want to work, "and to replace them with cultural essences," such as the idea that blacks' overreliance on welfare is due not to societal impediments to their participation in the workforce but to their cultural disdain for the dignity of work.[34] For the racist, all roads, be they scientific or cultural, lead to black depravity. Environment and social structures are irrelevant; black culture—with its unmarried mothers, its shabby neighborhoods, its materialism, and its criminal men—itself is the problem. Environment and societal structures are irrelevant.

Still, "in the absence of a biological basis for race, racism simply becomes ideology," notes Graves.[35]

Hence, the Great Migration.

In the sixty years leading up to 1970, six and a half million blacks fled the South. Five million of those refugees left after 1940, when cotton farming was mechanized and armies of oppressed cotton pickers were no longer trapped. The South was, for black people, hell; Nicholas Lemann tells us that this was likely the planet's largest and most rapid internal movement of people who were not facing immediate catastrophe. By the migration's end, America was a changed place: its northern cities teemed with hopeful blacks who were no longer serfs but were still far from equal. Black America was changed as well; a century after the end of official slavery, five minutes past share-cropping, they were only half southern and less than a quarter rural.[36] Finally, they were also something like free.

Certainly up north they were also segregated and brutalized by the police, the courts, and the employment system. Jesse Owens was allowed to represent the United States at the 1936 Berlin Olympics, where he bested the Aryans and humiliated Hitler (who refused the traditional schmooze with the winner). But instead of coming home to mainstream acclaim and inclusion, he was reduced to racing horses. W.E.B. DuBois, a brilliant historian with a Harvard doctorate and one of the top two or three intellectuals of his era, was never offered a position at a leading university. He spent the last bitter years of his life in exile in Africa. Public accommodations were segregated, albeit not as thoroughly or viciously as down south; there was lots of race mixing. Life up north, while difficult, was decidedly better. There blacks experienced a level of freedom and autonomy unprecedented in their three American centuries. Still, it was unimaginable what blacks were about to become.

In 1955 Rosa Parks was jailed for refusing to give up a bus

seat to a white. The teenage Stephens sisters went to jail for nearly fifty days simply for trying to eat at a dime-store lunch counter while black. College students throughout the South were beaten and jailed for trying to attend whites-only movie theaters and swimming pools. Interracial couples were jailed or run out of town. Enraged terrorist whites would maim and murder hundreds, if not thousands, of activists and innocents before the civil rights movement ended, so determined were they to keep blacks subservient.

Before the movement America was a very, very different place where blackness was concerned. Since the movement began, there has been a revolution in America's handling of blacks, if not in all of its thinking about them. Blacks may not be loved, but they are free. If they were not, then blacks—including those who deny there's been adequate racial progress—would still be strange fruit hanging from the poplar trees. Their houses would be bombed, as Martin Luther King's was. Before the movement, civil rights leaders were assassinated for critiquing whites. Now they are tenured at Ivy League universities and collect handsome speakers' fees to air their laments. Their very ability to make a living decrying racial progress proves them misguided.

Only the loss of understanding that blacks were once literally, officially second-class citizens and subject to the whim of any white anywhere in America can account for the fact that many blacks today claim that "nothing has changed" and equate the paucity of black faculty at Harvard Law School with Jim Crow. That charge is an obscenity. Jim Crow hanged black men for taking pride in their homes. Jim Crow cut fetuses from black women's bellies when they protested the lynching of their husbands for acting like men. Jim Crow taxed the black population but refused to pave or police or educate the black part of town. Jim Crow required a black part of town. Jim Crow had white parents chuckling while their children threw rocks from their school bus windows at black children trudging to bookless, one-room shanty schools. Jim Crow had mounted Cossacks riding down peaceful marchers on the Edmund Pettus Bridge in Selma. Jim Crow had cops in Philadelphia and New York and Chicago openly beating confessions from innocent blacks. It meant segregated churches throughout America. Jim Crow was active, pulsating evil that proudly detested blacks. Today's Republican Party is merely uninterested in their fate, except insofar as money can be made off them.

Today, in the wake of the movement, blacks helm multibillion-dollar international conglomerates like Merrill Lynch, American Express, and AOL Time Warner, as well as Fannie Mae. A black man was chairman of the Joint Chiefs of Staff and is now secretary of state. A black woman is the national security adviser. There have been two black Supreme Court justices, as well as black Nobel Prize winners and thousands of black officeholders—governors, mayors, dog-catchers. Blacks achieve at the highest levels of every American endeavor—science and technology, education, sports, the arts, and the military. These things would have been *inconceivable* before the civil rights movement. The most optimistic person, black or white, would not have believed it possible.

Thanks to the civil rights movement, however, black Americans are free and thriving. No one, apparently, is more surprised by that than some black Americans. Nothing else can explain their need to continue believing that they are marginalized, that whites are all powerful and all evil, and that America wants to see them fail. Some blacks have absorbed white supremacist notions and cannot give up perpetual protest, their only avenue to receiving Caucasian attention. Some blacks are simply addicted to having a spotlight on them to make them feel relevant. Primarily, however, these blacks simply do not know how to step into the limitless, frightening future they worked so hard to bring about, that future without a safety net and where you have no one to blame for your failures but you.

Black or white, those who deny how terrible things were for blacks before the movement, and those who deny the movement's overwhelming success, announce themselves as unfit to speak, let alone lead.

TAKING THE WORDS
OUT OF BLACK MOUTHS:

Narcissism, Know-Nothingness, and White Intransigence

"Priscilla and I, and nine others, had been charged with 'disturbing the peace,' among other charges, because we tried to order food at Woolworth. If not for segregation, and the fact that we were all Negroes, we would have been served without incident. At our trial on March 17, 1960, Judge John Rudd ruled that our lawyers should 'get off that race question.' "
—PATRICIA STEPHENS DUE[1]

"[I]n 1955, that's when the gruesome murder of Emmett Till came up in Mississippi. I remember how the *Charlotte Observer,* which was supposed to be a liberal or moderate newspaper, condemned the NAACP, saying it was just as bad as the Ku Klux Klan in raising 'racial' issues about this murder."
—JOHN DORSEY DUE JR.[2]

"Among the topics that the southern white man did not like to discuss with Negroes were the following: American white women; the Ku Klux Klan; France, and how Negro soldiers fared while there; French women; Jack Johnson;

the entire northern part of the United States; the civil war;
Abraham Lincoln; U.S. Grant; General Sherman; Catholics;
the Pope; Jews; the Republican Party; Slavery, Social
Equality, Communism; Socialism; the 13th, 14th,
and 15th Amendments to the Constitution; or any
topic calling for positive knowledge or manly
self-assertion on the part of the Negro."
— RICHARD WRIGHT[3]

*"All you need in this life is ignorance and confidence;
then success is sure."*
— MARK TWAIN

Black people are not crazy. They're not paranoid. They're punch-
drunk, or as Carter G. Woodson put it, "the Negro's mind has
been brought under the control of his oppressor. The problem of
holding the Negro down, therefore, is easily solved. When you
control a man's thinking you do not have to worry about his
actions."[4]

White racism and white supremacist ideology, however denied, however subconscious, continue to exist. To believe otherwise, one would truly have to believe that blacks are genetically
and morally deficient. Of course some believe exactly that, but
the rest of America understands that the disproportionately
lower status of blacks is at least in some measure a result of
group interactions. Blacks are neither blameless nor helpless,
but they are certainly not operating in a societal vacuum. Still,
blacks can be complicit in maintaining white supremacy by
playing the game on the master's terms—that is, by vying for
white approval or a white apology rather than for their own
autonomy, by giving in to nihilism and immorality in the face of

the endless struggle to surmount inequality. "Careless ignorance and laziness here, fierce hate and vindictiveness there; these are the extremes of the Negro problem which we met [while doing sociological research] that day," said W.E.B. DuBois, "and we scarce knew which we preferred."[5] Surely blacks reject both propositions, even knowing that white racism still exists and that, like all self-serving rationalizations, it has adapted to fit the times.

Having collapsed under the weight of its own contradictions, an articulated white supremacy—whites-only signs, restrictive covenants, overt police brutality—is no more. But structuralized greed, entrenched privilege, and xenophobia, on the other hand, are alive, well, and mutating athletically to retard each new inroad that blacks make into skin or class privilege. If you can't keep something but you can't give it up, you have to render it unrecognizable; racism has been defined out of existence and repackaged so that whites could retain its perks, especially the psychological ones. It has undergone existential plastic surgery. To keep it buried alive in its unholy grave, a host of Strangelovean anti-intellectualisms have been developed and honed.

For some whites, racism means nothing less than police attack dogs, George Wallace standing in the school-house door, and gentle seamstresses being carted off to jail for sitting in the front of the bus. Racism, thus, is now history. All that is left are isolated acts of individual bigotry, which probably, albeit regrettably, can be explained by some past run-in with black pathology.

For some blacks, racism means a societal infrastructure organized and operated so as to distribute benefits, burdens, and resources according to a racial hierarchy, however unspoken. The education and criminal justice systems are the most obvious examples.[6]

Modern white racism insists that the races remain separate, even if only psychologically, so that whites get to think of themselves as "America," as better, as the judge of every other race, and that whites get to remain on top. As Albert Murray noted, whites do not take their privilege for granted—they work at it. "They leave little to nature and what they inherit is the full-time obligation to keep up social appearances without ever seeming to do so."[7] Being the master race is a full-time job.

Regardless of the civic havoc that white racism wreaks, it is important for blacks to remind themselves that whites are no more innately evil than others. History has simply situated them to dominate in this era. Greed and power imbalances are at the root of the problem; racism is merely a by-product, but such a virulent one as to eclipse its progenitors. Given the success of the civil rights movement, however, these sociopathologies need be dispositive of nothing. Still, it is important for blacks to monitor the forms that white supremacy takes, even though it no longer dare speak its name. On a practical note, this is also a useful way for cowed blacks to demystify the all-mighty Caucasian, because there is nothing to be proud of in the current form to which white racism and denial, crazily clutching their pile of perks with ever more wizened fingers, has been reduced to sustain itself.

Second, it must be said that black racism, while largely masturbatory because largely powerless, is equally ignoble, sinful, and simian. There is little doubt that blacks would behave as badly as whites if they were the ones on top. We know this because of how badly blacks have treated one another. Rapidly falling under whites' racist sway, from nearly the beginning of their time in America, they practiced the same racism among themselves that they decried in whites. American-born slaves derided the Africa-born, while light-skinned and house slaves despised the dark field hands. Some free mulattoes distanced themselves politically as far as possible from slaves and even opposed their enfranchisement. Immediately after Emancipation, Brahmin blacks apishly erected a social structure patterned on that of whites, especially their disgust for low-class blacks. When southern blacks arrived up north during the Great Migration, their contemptuous brothers called them "Cornbread," wouldn't let them join their churches, and thought the problem of racism was whites' refusal to differentiate them from "the niggers." Now it is the ghetto blacks who are despised.

Franz Fanon aptly defined the "native" as "an oppressed person whose permanent dream is to become the persecutor."[8] We may say the same about "the African American." Even more relevantly, Fanon defined a "settler," in his 1950s colonial context, as "an exhibitionist" who "pits brute force against the weight of numbers." We may say the same about "the unreconstructed white." Far too little thought has been given to an examination of the exhibitionism attendant upon white predation. It is best described as *narcissistic know-nothingness.*

NARCISSISM

What is racism but a fascination with oneself?

Why, a seventeenth-century European newly arrived in Africa must have mused, *are these odd creatures not pale, not straight-haired, not freckled, not wearing filthy pantaloons, and not praying to two pieces of wood nailed at a right angle? Why are they so unlike* me? *What's the matter with them?* Whites couldn't have been white until they saw someone who wasn't.

Fundamentally, racism and xenophobia are more about self-exaltation than about exploiting others, more about filling the human need to feel special, set apart, and touched by grace, than about hatred. A sixteenth-century European genius perfectly illustrates this need and the ripple effects that ethnocentrism can set in motion across the centuries. Gerardus Mercator

solved an age-old navigational problem by devising the map
that every schoolchild has grown up with for nearly five centuries. The trouble is, partly for practical reasons but mostly for
reasons of cultural narcissism, he built huge distortions into "the
world." To better showcase his native Flanders and Europe generally, Mercator inflated and situated the northern hemisphere
so as to dominate the map. Africa is dwarfed by Greenland,
though it is twelve times larger. South America was pygmy-
ized. Those smart enough to figure out the world were arrogant
enough to try to make it over in their own image.

But has there ever been a society that didn't think itself
naturally superior to every other? Anthropologist Earl Shorris
explains:

> Ethnocentrism was not . . . a European invention. Most of the
> cultures native to the Americas named themselves "the Peo-
> ple," as if no others could even be described as human beings.
> The practice was not limited to any language group. . . . We
> know [Native American tribes] . . . by the names given them
> by their adversaries. The Lakotas, Dakotas, and Nakotas are
> known to us as "Sioux," . . . it means "snake" or "enemy."
> Similarly, the word "Apache" . . . meant "enemy," while the
> word the Apaches . . . used for themselves, "Diné," means
> "the People." [Just as whites had no respect for the native
> American cultures they encountered, the natives had no re-
> gard for whites' culture.] . . . [They] thought of the invaders
> as avaricious individualists who smelled bad; the word for a
> white in the Lakota language, for example, means greedy (lit-
> erally, he-who-eats-the-fat).[9]

Early blacks also thought whites suffered from delusions of
grandeur and a preening self-importance. The cakewalk, a dance
performed while goose-stepping with arms stiffly outstretched

and parading as if observed by adoring millions, was created by Reconstruction-era blacks to send up white ostentation and pretension. Olaudah Equiano, in recounting his capture in Africa and arrival in Barbados, wrote, "We thought . . . we should be eaten by these ugly men."[10] Every group thinks itself exalted and all others debased. China considered itself the "Middle Kingdom" between heaven and earth. An American journalist visiting Japan noted,

> Whenever there are warning signs or warning ads in Japan, they always show white people doing whatever stupid activity is being warned about. At the Ueno Zoo, the pictures showing a child crawling into the lion's den shows a Caucasian. Dozens of Japanese kids have died because their moms left them in hot cars when they went to play pachinko. So the pachinko industry launched a huge ad campaign to remind parents not to leave their kids in the car. But all the ads show Caucasian kids! There probably are not 10 Caucasians who have ever played pachinko![11]

Unfortunately, the mix of narcissism, technological superiority, and greed spelled doom for that race most unlike, "most inferior to," whites. Centuries later, having refined their narcissism into high art, whites have learned to place themselves, however irrelevantly and distractingly, at the center of any discussion. They anoint themselves not simple citizens but judge and jury.

When confronted with a demand for redress or for a justice-based redirection of societal resources, whites invoke the royal prerogative of their race and change the subject. Like the Old West stagecoach robbers who flipped the road signs to point their victims into the wilderness to be fleeced, whites divert black complaint to the question of whether white approval of the complaint itself will be bestowed. Needless to say, if the complaint doesn't involve German shepherds or fire hoses, if the complainant isn't a saint, racism is unlikely to be considered the culprit. Most maddeningly for blacks, whites refuse to consider complaints on their merits but instead issue their opinion of a complaint, so that it can be dismissed unexamined.

Thus, black complaint becomes a subject-changing round robin of white criticism of blacks. In the 1930s Woodson noted that "few whites of today will listen to the [Negro's] tale of woe."[12] Imagine, then, how little patience whites in the twenty-first century have for black complaint. That impatience is frequently demonstrated. When blacks make demands after police kill unarmed civilians, whites respond by demanding to know what blacks have done to improve themselves.

Note the assumption that whites need no improvement and that they get to judge blacks' civic fitness to be allowed to complain. Second, *arguendo,* let us posit that blacks have done nothing toward self-improvement; is indolence then a police license to kill? This implies that while blacks are societally abused, until they surmount the Everest of white approval, their abuse will justifiably, if regrettably, continue. How else will blacks ever learn?

Blacks claim that their schools remain segregated and underfunded, leading to decreased educational opportunity, and they demand educational affirmative action. The white response: Why do all the black kids sit together in the cafeteria?

This question is really a denunciation of blacks as unworthy of societal effort, of blacks as the "real" racists. Access to the good things in life is wasted on them. Whites never notice the all-white tables that usually outnumber the all-black ones, because white behavior is beyond minority critique (and because, when it's them, the silliness of this "critique" is apparent). Black comment on white behavior is still uppity, but that these days uppityness will find blacks only dismissed rather than hanged is undeniable progress.

The velvet rope of white privilege dangling before their eyes fascinates too many post-movement bourgeois blacks; instead of finishing their rhetorical meal at the table of their choice, they make a mental shuffle off to the margin, where they dance for white approval and cringe whenever a black commits a crime or loses a job. No better are the bitter bullhorn blacks who fume and mutter from their assigned spot on the sidelines, the spot from which they can most closely monitor whites who preen in this way. Note that neither the bourgeois nor the bullhorn Negro is about his own business but is catering to any random white who cares to opine on that which doesn't concern him.

This is what Albert Murray would deem the white norm/black deviation dialectic, the main vehicle for white supremacy. Counterintuitively, white supremacists and black polemicists work together to implement this strategy, though we are most concerned with the black leaders who succumb to this gambit. The problem is both parties' adherence to the literalist, white supremacist notion that all that is necessary for the construction of social policy is a direct comparison of black social measures, like illegitimacy or crime, with those of whites. Odd bedfellows indeed, these seeming enemies hope for the same outcome—a showing of black "pathology," that is, worse statistics for blacks than for whites. For whites, with their behavior enshrined as the norm, insofar as blacks fail to meet "the standard," their problems are their own fault rather than the result of racism. From the point of view of the wailing-wall polemicists, any black lag is to be celebrated because it *must* result from racism. The worse blacks do, the better they both like it. The focus, Murray says,

is never placed on the failure of white Americans to measure up to the standards of the Constitution. The primary attention repeatedly is focused on Negroes as victims. . . . [T]he assumption . . . is that slavery and oppression have made Negroes *inferior* to other Americans and hence less American. . . . [H]owever, slavery and oppression may well have made black people more human and more American while it has made white people less human and less American.[13]

Talking about numbers keeps America from having to talk about people or its own behavior. Ralph Ellison shared that skepticism over the misuses of data:

I learned that nothing could go unchallenged, especially that feverish industry dedicated to telling Negroes who and what they are, and which can usually be counted upon to deprive both humanity and culture of their complexity. . . . [The Negro experience is] a relatively unexplored area of American experience simply because our knowledge of it has been distorted through the overemphasis of the sociological approach. Unfortunately many Negroes have been trying to define their own predicament in exclusively sociological terms. . . . Too many of us have accepted a statistical interpretation of our lives, and thus much of that which makes us a source of moral strength to America goes unappreciated and undefined. Now, when you try to trace American values as they find expression in the Negro community, where do you begin? To what books do you go? How do you account for Little Rock and the sit-ins? How do you account for the strength of those kids? You can find sociological descriptions of the conditions under which they live but few indications of their morale.[14]

Or their character. Or their dreams. Or their talents.

America should question the construction of white behavior

as the civic starting point because racists and apologists focus on merely assigning the blame for blacks' continued "failure." Both are concerned, not with fixing problems, just with convicting their enemy. So racism is compounded by black cooperation and by fruitless black jousts with white intransigence, while winnable victories are ignored because they do not center on whites and because they are unglamorous. As one historian put it, policymakers "manipulat[ed] the therapeutic ethos, [and] sought to obtain black equality on humanitarian grounds by presenting blacks as damaged objects of pity rather than citizens whose rights had been violated. . . . Again and again, contempt has proven to be the flip side of pity."[15]

The obfuscation results in a politics of nonsequiturs aimed at creating rush-hour traffic circles of discourse without an exit lane. This gambit, in addition to protecting the status quo, is most concerned with giving whites the appearance of cooperation without the dangers of actual cooperation. It also functions as a conduit for white contempt and rage; many whites believe that nonwhites have no right to criticize them since whites are superior and alone responsible for the success of America.

A reflexive Orwellian lexicon of doublespeak has evolved to effectuate this ending of racism and thus the end of white tolerance for black complaint. It is comprised of code words and ways to ridicule and express contempt and condescension for blacks without appearing to do so, especially to themselves. All proceed from the white point of view while appearing to be objective, because all are designed to convince the world of white rationality and blamelessness while retaining white pride of place at the center of everything.

Assimilation:
the process of jettisoning any artifact of minority culture to which whites have attached a negative or derisive connotation.

Assimilation can be legitimate; for instance, immigrants need to learn English and relinquish customs that conflict with core American values or that retard their progress overmuch. But it is a short trip from *assimilation* to *self-hatred* and *appeasement,* a short trip on a poorly marked road. *Assimilation,* therefore, is most often used as a code word or at least as a word fraught with unacknowledged problematics and power dynamics. (See also *Transcending race.*)

Balkanizing, divisive, polarizing:
adjectives condemning critiques, complaints, demands, or policies that would require whites to change, be inconvenienced, admit guilt, or relinquish resources. Whites deem these things punitive, and since they are America, anything that punishes them is anti-American and hence balkanizing. This worldview is not new—whites attacked the proposed Freedmen's Bureau Act of 1866 as unnecessary and as "promot[ing] strife and conflict between the white and black races." Nothing on the white agenda, whatever its impact on blacks—however much blacks oppose and resent it—can ever be described as *divisive.* These three cover terms convey that blacks can never be seen to legitimately disagree or offer policy proposals but instead to be attempting to destroy America, something they are not part of. For example:

> The rush to judgment [that is, opposition to the confirmation of a conservative white Christian with suspect racial ideas as attorney general] is the latest evidence that the civil-rights community . . . is isolating itself from the American project, from self-governance, from a stake in our democracy . . . to the point of weakening not only themselves but our country too.[16]

It's not politics when blacks disagree, it's treason. Witness this Freudian slip of a headline on the Thomas Jefferson/Sally Hemings controversy: *Abolishing America: The Jefferson Anti-Myth Debunked*. It doesn't abolish America to accept that Jefferson owned a human, but it does to accept that he might have loved or raped one.

Politically correct:
doctrinaire, knee-jerk, pseudo-Marxist, apologetic. Only leftists, feminists, and blacks are described in this pejorative way. There is no rhetorical equivalent on the right, though the right has an equally rigidly defined orthodoxy of allowed opinions and thought processes. A term coined by the left as a critique of racist language, imagery, and the like, it has been corrupted both by martinet adherents of the original critique and by the politically unscrupulous such that it now connotes leftist thought control and civic oppression itself. Its invocation changes the subject and the power dynamic from one player to the other.

Politically incorrect:
the rhetorical cul-de-sac where white hate went—in goes racism, out comes political incorrectness. Use of this phrase is a tactic designed to derail discourse by disguising racism as defiance of far-left, pseudo-Communist attempts at enforcing behavior and speech codes. However vicious, brainless, knee-jerk, or crudely racist a sentiment may be, once it is repackaged as merely "un-PC" it becomes heroic, brave, free-thinking, and best of all, victimized.

Transcending race:
the process by which blacks become acceptable to whites; the process by which a black is deemed worthy of white approval or

respect. It is the ultimate white compliment; blacks who would have once been credits to their race have been reassigned to this category. No whites are ever required to "transcend race" because the term really means one is forgiven one's nonwhiteness. (See also *Assimilation.*)

Certainly being confronted with denial and subterfuge, especially when they result in the unjust distribution of societal resources, is frustrating. What it is not, however, is determinative of anything. Is it any wonder that it is those whites with nothing but their whiteness to sustain them who most ardently defend the dying notion that it is only and always white regard that matters and that they have a God-given right to pass judgment on nonwhites?

The ever-analytical Woodson summarized this point most aptly:

> It does not matter how often a Negro washes his hands, then, he cannot clean them, and it does not matter how often a white man uses his hands he cannot soil them.[17]

This is narcissism. It is something much worse as well, but narcissism it also most definitely is.

> "They say we're 'crossing over.' . . . But I'm just as American
> as the next guy. Crossing over from what?"
> —NEW YORK–BORN MARC ANTHONY,
> THE WORLD'S TOP-SELLING SALSA ARTIST[18]

> "Toy Company Making Hispanic G.I. Joe Doll"
> —*TAMPA TRIBUNE*[19]

Whites view such phenomena as identity politics and multiculturalism and bemoan that "Americans are drifting away from
the concept of belonging to a single nation."[20] Multiculturalism,
at best, is an ideology that promotes the coexistence of separate
but equal cultures and the belief that there are no absolute standards for measuring the respective worth of cultures. But if
America is not multicultural, what is it? Must every American
be white, male, Judeo-Christian, and a native English speaker?

Amiri Baraka has noted that "one of the most persistent traits
of the Western white man has always been his fanatical and
almost instinctive assumption that his systems and ideals about
the world are the most desirable, and further, that people who
do not aspire to them, or at least think them admirable, are *savages* or *enemies*."[21] The greatest entitlement of all is whites'
continued refusal to see America as inherently, organically multiracial and multicultural (though not so as to contradict a core
set of principles such as democracy and majority rule) and com-
prising only equal citizens. They insist on seeing themselves
as America and as entitled, therefore, to equate their good with
the common good, their preferences with justice. Deviation
from their preferences is inherently dangerous, fragmentary, and
wrong.[22] But Marc Anthony and the makers of Hispanic G.I.
Joe are *participating,* they're opting in. They are completing
America. How can they be expected to do so without Spanish
accents? W.E.B. DuBois had the vision to see:

> Work, culture, liberty—all these we need, not singly but
> together, not successively but together, each growing and aid-
> ing each, and all striving toward that vaster ideal that swims
> before the Negro people, the ideal of human brotherhood,

gained through the unifying ideal of Race; the ideal of foster-
ing and developing the traits and talents of the Negro, not in
opposition to or contempt for races, but rather in large conformity to the greater ideals of the American Republic, in
order that some day on American soil two world-races may
give each to each those characteristics both so sadly lack.[23]

Minorities assume they have something to add to the country
they love; whites assume their own perfection. A Che Guevara
doll ought to concern patriots, not a Hispanic face on America's
military might. That's the reality—Hispanics, like blacks, have
long been overrepresented in the U.S. armed forces. It's just that
that reality has been whitewashed for so long. Hispanics are
coming out of the civic closet, and they want to share what they
love with the country they love. They're adding to, not subtract-
ing from.

This nation cannot pride itself on its immigrant moxie, then
resist the benign cultural changes those immigrants unleash.
Becoming American does not mean becoming white, if only
because whites have always been affected to the core by minority
influence. What white wedding reception is complete without a
rendition of Kool and the Gang's "Celebrate!" and a sad attempt
at the Electric Slide? Slaves built the U.S. Capitol and helped
"tame" the West (mainly by helping to exterminate the Native
Americans who stood in the way). Had they not absorbed
Native American knowledge, the Pilgrims would never have
survived their first winter in the New World; Indian place names
were so perfectly apt, white settlers rarely bothered to rename
the mountains and lakes they annexed.

At its best, the antimulticulturalist stance is one that recog-
nizes that America is a multiracial nation united by language
and an acceptance of core Western values such as democracy,

the rule of law, secularism, and individual freedom. Anything that doesn't contradict those values, goes. At its worst, *multiculturalism* is a crude code word for anything outside the Western tradition politically, artistically, religiously, or philosophically. When used thusly, it is a pejorative and is often conflated with *identity politics,* a phrase that has only negative connotations.

In one illustrative example, journalist Franklin Foer derisively analyzed the rise of identity politics among heretofore docile Asian Americans through the prism of a riveting debate in one community over which Asian luminary to name an elementary school after.[24] The battle was fought among Chinese, Japanese, and Vietnamese Americans; in the end, deceased Hawaiian senator Spark M. Matsunaga won the honor. Foer ended his article with this gleeful taunt: "Live by multiculturalism, die by multiculturalism."

Since when has a fight over political pork been seen as dangerous? And why is a Hawaiian senator a multicultural—that is, fragmenting—choice? He wasn't some obscure medieval samurai with a hundred concubines and no idea of democracy. He was a great American. So why is he Asian before he's a senator? Why are the combatants Asian before they are citizens jousting in all-too-American fashion for some goodie, like bare-knuckling to rename Washington National Airport, already bearing the name of one male WASP president, after Ronald Reagan, another male WASP president? But they're not male WASPS, are they? They're Americans. Why can't whites look up to a Japanese American in the same way that Japanese Americans look up to George Washington? Here's why, according to Herbert Stein:

[A] more pervasive, although less obvious, reason why white males feel threatened by blacks . . . [is that] Blacks have taken over what used to be the traditional symbols of manliness [sports]. . . . The white Walter Mitty who could get satisfaction out of imaging himself as Rocky Marciano or John Riggins cannot similarly fantasize about being George Foreman or Emmit Smith. And he has lost something as a result.[25]

Obviously, Stein meant "symbols of *white* manliness" because Foreman and Smith are plenty manly. Note that they have "taken over," not "joined." They can't join—whites won't let them. Where whites are manly, blacks are bestial; how can mere masculinity compete with that? It's unsporting—the deck is stacked against whites. But why can't Walter Mitty identify with Walter Payton or Senator Matsunaga? What is it that's been lost? "Whiteness," of course, the myth of white superiority. As long as the black masculinity that so emasculates white masculinity was under lock and key, this ploy worked, but came the civil rights movement, and there went the neighborhood. Black athletes don't defeat the opposing team, they defeat white manhood. Why else castrate the black man you've just lynched?

As with the Asians naming the school, note the unacknowledged, unexamined implication that any public act of approval of anyone who isn't a WASP male is an act of identity politics and multiculturalism. Whites, lacking race, ethnicity, agenda, or preferences, float above the squall of politics, benign demigods who toss the odd bone here and there to the "multicultural" rabble. Why don't whites have race or ethnicity or agendas or preferences that are simply preferences? Because that would make them equal, not best. "Multiculturalism," in sneer quotes, with its built-in disapproval and contempt, is white nullification of the full citizenship of minorities. It is the back of the civic bus.

"After all," Franklin Foer points out, "the natural logic of identity politics is for people to define themselves in ever-narrower categories, rejecting the possibility of cultural assimilation." Like becoming a senator, like using the political process to bring home the pork for your constituency? Hispanic G.I. Joe is modeled after a blood-and-guts, red-white-and-blue Vietnam Congressional Medal of Honor winner who comes from a minority group overrepresented in the military, but to whites who lament their loss of hegemony, he's just Hispanic, not G.I.

For even the most seemingly enlightened, a Japanese American is Japanese before he's American; a native-born singer has to "cross over" to arrive where he's always been; and a hero's deeds play second fiddle to his nonwhiteness. Minorities are only partially American, revocably American, technically American, however many centuries their families might have parked their chopsticks here. In his *Oration in Memory of Abraham Lincoln,* given at the unveiling of the Freedmen's Monument in Washington in 1876, Frederick Douglass honored Lincoln but rejected the Great Emancipator myth: "Lincoln was not either our man or our model. He was preeminently the white man's president, entirely devoted to the welfare of white men. You, my white fellow citizens, are the children of Abraham Lincoln. We are at best only his step children."[26] Lincoln did the right thing, but not for the right reasons, and America is still using only its left hand with its minorities.

Minorities are always hyphenated Americans and racially profiled regardless of realm. Books written by blacks, regardless of subject matter, are placed in the Black Studies section. Without dream hampton's knowledge the Sundance Film Festival's publicity department changed the catalog description of her entry from "a schizophrenic" to "a black schizophrenic," though it had nothing to do with the plot; no doubt the good liberals there were flummoxed by her complaints. Striving blacks want what any human endeavoring to self-actualize wants: "To be a co-worker in the kingdom of culture, to escape both death and isolation, to husband and use his best powers and his latent genius. These powers of [the black] body and mind have in the past been strangely wasted, dispersed, or forgotten."[27] And, DuBois might have added, despised.

Most neurotic of all, Foer spends nearly four pages explaining how those docile Asian Americans were politicized by repeated doses of national-level institutional racism, with this result:

> As recently as 1992, they chose George Bush over Bill Clinton by a 27% margin. By the end of the decade, however, the situation had flipped. Al Gore won Asian American votes by 14 percent. . . . [Now] 57 percent of Asians . . . consider themselves Democrats. . . . Almost 30 years after other ethnic groups, Asian Americans have stopped worrying and learned to love identity politics.

Someone should have told him about "drapetomania," that baffling mental illness that made slaves run away; now it makes minorities organize politically around their race. Why chuckle at those silly Asian Americans and not at the whites who drove them to "define themselves in ever-narrower categories, rejecting the possibility of cultural assimilation"? Asians didn't reject assimilation, they were prevented from assimilating when they thought they had already accomplished it. So who plays identity politics, and who has to live it? Whites—not the Democrats or bad-element minorities—forced Asian Americans to think of themselves as Asian Americans. Identity politics is an entirely rational response to identity politics.

Thus blacks—indeed, all nonwhites—find themselves defined out of America except as afterthoughts. For proof, one need only consider the opponents' response to blacks' demand for reparations for slavery and Jim Crow. The problem is not the existence of white opposition, it's whites' view of their relationship to the nation and to their fellow citizens. A typical rejoinder to the call for reparations invariably includes a sneering restatement of the argument, something like, "All whites benefit to this day from the legacy of slavery, that is why we are given to understand that it is fair to demand reparations from all of them."[28] *L'état, c'est* white. Bereft of a unifying and legitimizing intellectual-moral framework, blacks rarely respond by pointing out that the reparations are demanded from *America,* not from the white residents of America, but from an America which includes blacks and is supported in large measure by the wealth created by blacks.

Another unstated notion is that blacks' civil rights come from whites. Blacks are frequently told they should show more gratitude, as in the well-worn complaint that blacks don't want civil rights, they want "special rights," a "critique" that Martin Luther King Jr. was often met with in the 1960s. As Malcolm X pointed out, sticking a knife in someone's back nine inches, then pulling it out six, isn't really progress, let alone a special right. Still, viewed from the point of view of those who see themselves as cleaning up a mess they didn't make, blacks should indeed cease their complaints. One might think that one generation of grudging change could hardly recompense centuries of slavery and Jim Crow. If one does, however, one wastes his time and retards progress because the maintenance of privilege allows for no logic, only a determined resistance to either sharing America's resources or accepting responsibility.

Simply put, whites held hands across generations to hold blacks down long enough to ensure that their own heirs would ascend to as much privilege as possible while simultaneously keeping their hands clean. Blacks need to accept this and then get over it—and get even. But instead blacks have been sidetracked on a fruitless, enervating quest for vindication and restoration. The know-nothingness required to keep blacks tilting at the windmill of white approval is no less odious than whites' determination to remain first among purported equals.[29]

That Strangelovean confidence born of whites' politico-intellectual thuggery has led to a social intransigence that blacks will not be able to overcome. They should stop trying. No group can live with a negative self-image, however well deserved; counterproductive behaviors in the black ghetto alone prove that proposition. Blacks must surrender that part of their political offensive that is concerned with gaining white admissions of guilt. It is a waste of time. Whites have accepted as much blame, however passive-voiced and twice-removed, as they intend to, and blacks must move on.

Blacks should, however, thoroughly dissect and document the strategies that have stalemated them (as with the above discussion), if only as a reminder that they're not imagining things—and out of respect for a formidable adversary. If Woodson is correct and whites are to be commended for their stewardship of themselves, then perhaps blacks should study their example in case it ever comes in handy. Regardless, every community is responsible for telling its version of events, especially if it doesn't get to write the history books. Even though whites will slip into the little denial comas discussed below, the black community has the intellectual and moral duty to count its dead and memorialize its campaigns. It must maintain primers like this one to catalog and rebut as necessary the strategies at play against blacks in the public arena. Catharsis can only come with confrontation.

THE DEVIL'S DUE: A PRIVILEGE PRIMER

Know-Nothingness

> "When Alexandra Ripley wrote her authorized sequel
> [to *Gone With the Wind*] *Scarlett* in 1991,
> the Margaret Mitchell estate imposed two conditions:
> no explicit sex and no miscegenation."
> —*WASHINGTON POST*[30]

The easy way to deal with whites' colorful history and compli-cated present is to muffle, ignore, or rationalize the bad while extolling the good. It helps (and may not be entirely coinciden-tal) that Americans have such a poor grasp of history.

Every American schoolchild learns about the Shot Heard Round the World and what it symbolizes. What they do not learn is that a black soldier who appears with white rebels in a famous 1786 painting of the Battle of Bunker Hill widely used in history books was erased in later editions. As America deter-mined to unknow its true nature, this practice became common. Henry O. Flipper, America's first black West Point cadet, was not allowed into the group graduation photo in 1877. (He was also given the silent treatment for his entire four years of school-ing, framed for embezzlement, and cashiered.) Forty percent of the Old West's cowboys were black—five thousand in Texas alone after the Civil War—including famous ones like Dead Eye Dick and Bill Pickett, the inventor of "bulldogging."[31] Pickett's white assistants, Tom Mix and Will Rogers, became famous Hollywood cowboys. The Negro Pickett did not. Thirteen of the fifteen jockeys in the first Kentucky Derby (1875), including the winner, were black. The sport was also dominated by expert black grooms until it became respectable. "Ask any Southerner why lawn jockeys are black," writes John Jeremiah Crown, Kentucky Derby expert, "They have no idea."[32]

Why does America need to "see" and "remember" its heroes, itself, as white?

Such instances of hysterical amnesia and re-rememberings of American history are legion. The thought of having to share the holy heroic founding of America makes those-who-must-eat-the-fat capable of any flight of dementia, so long as they don't have to minimize themselves by granting others their full humanity and the place they earned in the American family. Why?

Here's why: white America is a fiction, and fictions require comprehensive rewrites. From its founding America has been multicultural; indeed, Native Americans and Africans in America predate America itself, yet white hubris drives them to steep the nation in blood and sin "proving" otherwise. More is the pity, because the black experience encapsulates the best of America. Murray makes an overlooked but crucial point:

> [T]he Underground Railroad was not only an innovation, it was also an extension of the American quest for democracy brought to its highest level of epic heroism. Nobody tried to sabotage the *Mayflower*. There was no bounty on the heads of its captain, crew, or voyagers as was the case with all the conductors, stationmasters, and passengers on the northbound freedom train. Given the differences in circumstances, equipment, and, above all, motives, the legendary exploits of white U.S. backwoodsmen, keelboatmen, and prairie schoonermen, for example, become relatively safe when one sets them beside the breathtaking escapes of the fugitive slave beating his way south to Florida, west to the Indians, and north to far away

Canada through swamp and town alike seeking freedom—nobody was chasing Daniel Boone![33]

America should thank blacks for teaching it how to be truly brave, free, heroic, and democratic. Instead, whites have monopolized the American identity because their narcissism and greed require that they own everything, especially the right to America. They must be seen to dispense every societal resource as a reward to those who have earned their approval.

"A group of people united by a mistaken view of the past and a hatred of its neighbors." That's how French historian and philosopher Ernest Renan defined *nation*. James Baldwin made the point more specifically in *The Fire Next Time*:

> The American Negro has the great advantage of having never believed that collection of myths to which white Americans cling: that their ancestors were all freedom-loving heroes, that they were born in the greatest country the world has ever seen, or that Americans are invincible in battle and wise in peace, that Americans have always dealt honorably with Mexicans and Indians and all other neighbors or inferiors, that American men are the world's most direct and virile, that American women are pure.[34]

Blacks have access to the director's cut.

Whites will claim that these white-outs and names left off the honor rolls are mere threads separated from an American tapestry of democracy and equality, signifying nothing. But these seminal examples of the airbrushing of the American identity show that to separate blacks from any importance or contribution to America is to separate them from any right to blame, make demands, benefit, or participate, except as charity cases at white sufferance. Blacks may be mostly Christians, but they can never be white men, so they will never have made America great. We know this because North Carolina state representative Don Davis tells us so. He sent this triumphalist e-mail to every member of his statehouse contingent in 2001:

> Two things made this country great: white men and Christianity. Every problem that has arisen can be directly traced back to our departure from God's Law and the disenfranchisement of white men.[35]

White men disenfranchised? When challenged on this remark, the representative of millions of nonwhites initially insisted that there was "nothing racist about it."

Woodson, as usual, provides a succinct explanation of such phenomena:

> The same educational process which inspires and stimulates the oppressor with the thought that he is everything and has accomplished everything worthwhile, depresses and crushes at the same time the spark of genius in the Negro by making him feel that his race does not amount to much and never will measure up to the standard of other peoples.[36]

The lowliest white snake-oil salesman hustling quack cures one step ahead of the constable in seventeenth-century Boston, the babbling white woman soiling herself in an eighteenth-century madhouse, the nineteenth-century syphilitic white drunkard shtupping dockside whores in alleyways—*they* are automatically included in the transcendent glory that is Western civilization and American history. But not the slave woman forced to mix the snake oil for her master and endure nightly rape. Not the bondsman who delivered supplies to the madhouse. Not the freemen whom the drunkard, between binges, made his living shanghaiing and fraudulently selling into slavery. Blacks cannot clean their hands, and whites cannot dirty theirs.

What is this mechanism by which blacks remain outside the sweep of Western civilization while the white butcher's boy is enfolded? Whites, however unproductive or immoral, are born vested with Americanness. The most uncomprehending (European) immigrant donned that mantle by simply arriving at Ellis Island. But blacks must strive to earn that which can never be earned, not as long as they remain unwhite and certainly not as long as they disagree, complain, or critique. Blacks must resist this unfairness in the strongest possible terms. They must claim the Empire State Building. "Your country?" demanded DuBois. "How came it yours?"

Before the Pilgrims landed we were here. Here we have brought our three gifts and mingled them with yours: a gift of story and song-soft, stirring melody in an ill-harmonized and unmelodious land; the gift of sweat and brawn to beat back the wilderness, conquer the soil, and lay the foundations of this vast economic empire two hundred years earlier than your weak hands could have done it; the third, a gift of the Spirit. Around us the history of the land has centred for thrice a hundred years; out of the nation's heart we have called all that was best to throttle and subdue all that was worst; fire and blood, prayer and sacrifice, have billowed over this people, and they have found peace only in the altars of the God of Right. Nor has our gift of the Spirit been merely passive. Actively we have woven ourselves with the very warp and woof of this nation—we fought their battles, shared their sorrow, mingled our blood with theirs, and generation after generation have pleaded with a headstrong, careless people to despise not Justice, Mercy, and Truth, lest the nation be smit-

ten with a curse. Our song, our toil, our cheer, and warning
have been given to this nation in blood-brotherhood. Are
not these gifts worth the giving? Is not this work and striving? Would America have been America without her Negro
people?[37]

It would not. This is why blacks are the omni-Americans, as
Murray called them, and this is why whites cannot allow themselves to know their unbowdlerized, unexpurgated history. They
weaken themselves, not blacks, by trying to stand apart; this is
America, not Caucasia. This is a land that has never not been
multicultural. Like POW camp guard Sergeant Schultz in the
1960s sitcom *Hogan's Heroes* who witnessed and accommo-
dated everything, whites "know nut-ting!" when it comes to
black achievement or competence or, heaven forbid, excellence.
If they erase blacks from history, then they don't have to share
it with them. More, they don't have to share the fruits of that
history.

When instances of white racism or sociopathology or simple
injustice and misallocation of resources are undeniably shown
and nonsequiturs won't provide an adequate diversion, whites
slip into little walking comas, playing dead on the battlefield until the undeniable truth has passed, ostensibly unable to process
or respond to the information. When Senator John McCain,
a 2000 presidential candidate, was publicly confronted with his
family's slave-owning Mississippi history, he froze mentally,
though his vocal cords continued to function. Surprised, surprised, surprised—he heard the journalists out and thanked
them for educating him. He hadn't known, you see, even though
he'd read a family history that stated the obvious. He hadn't
known, even though he'd publicly declared that he had ancestors who had fought honorably in the Civil War, "none of whom
owned slaves." He hadn't known, even though his best-selling

memoir chronicled the lives and military careers of his father and grandfather, but not that of the slave-owning ancestor who'd died defending his property as a Civil War cavalryman. Indeed, he spares only four pages for his Mississippi roots.

One can almost hear the gears grinding as the bona fide hero who'd had the fortitude to survive five POW years tried to process eighth-grade history:

> I guess when you think about it logically, it shouldn't be a surprise. They owned a [two-thousand-acre] plantation [with fifty-two slaves] and they fought in the Civil War so I guess that it makes sense. . . . [M]aybe their sharecroppers that were on the plantation were descendants of those slaves.[38]

He mused in wonderment at two and two resulting in four. How rose-festooned the mental highway that led to his ancestors' heroic deeds, how frayed and torturous the rope ladder that led toward a whip in Mississippi, the worst place in America to have been a slave. Out with the bad, extreme close-up on the good. The otherwise truly admirable senator spoke for the privileged everywhere when he wondered, no doubt in sincere confusion, "why didn't I think about that before?" Because he didn't want to. Who would?

Confronted with the reality of who they are and who they have been, whites become deer in the headlights, but deer who know that the car will swerve at the last minute if they just gut it out.

Activists from drug havens in the ghetto of Hartford, Connecticut, took their protests to the white suburbs from which the majority of drug buyers verifiably come: the reaction from local whites was nothing but angry bewilderment. One waits in vain for their demands of stepped-up police enforcement against the drug users among them, in vain for their approval of "what blacks are doing to improve" their neighborhood by fighting crime. Black housing testers routinely document discrimination in the rental, real estate sales, and mortgage lending markets: from whites comes only silence, not the outrage they express over the racism of affirmative action or black crime. Hidden cameras record unrelenting discrimination against black testers in employment, housing, public spaces, and access to social services; white America changes the channel and the oft-invoked American love of justice yawns. "Urban" police forces are credibly accused of arresting and holding witnesses for days on end without obtaining a court order or filing charges, an illegal Jim Crow practice meant to coerce information about their "urban" friends or loved ones. Where are the whites who were incensed to near insurrection over Waco and Ruby Ridge?

Faced with the undeniable truth, whites just close down. They cannot face their own malevolence and pathology, so it cannot be allowed to register. That's why they want the police to racially profile blacks but didn't want them to be required to collect and publish the relevant statistics or justify the outcomes. That is why they are process-oriented on affirmative action but outcome-oriented on crime. If the depredations are not happening to whites or anyone with whom they can identify, if the crimes are not charged against an entity they disapprove of, the complaints merely annoy. If the accusation cannot be turned around to damn the accuser and if the subject cannot be changed, only one tactic remains to keep inconvenient facts from mattering: white misbehavior that cannot be denied must be ignored. Bored with other people's problems, insulted by black critique, insulated by privilege, whites simply choose not to know.

———

These are the most benign, most easily rebutted forms of white know-nothingness: to airbrush history or to stand mute is to concede your opponent's argument, even if nothing will be done about it. Unfortunately for the progress of racial justice, whites usually respond with a great deal more cunning and intransigence.

Active know-nothingness—the kind that keeps racism and structural disadvantage alive, the kind that wraps the past in a gauzy haze of unearned acquittal—requires an anti-intellectual arsenal of lies, distractions, distortions, sleights-of-hand, brazenness, and brutal frontal attacks all designed to make rational discussion impossible. It also functions as a diversion. It stalls for time so that whites can distance themselves far enough from their past that no one can remember or reliably prove how anything came to be the way it is. So long after the fact, it seems unfair for present-day whites to be required to make any sacrifices, unfair to make harsh judgments about what happened "so long ago." They have to run the clock out until America loses track of what happened when, of who did what to whom. To apply this historical gauze of half-truths, they slip into the passive voice, they whisper watery sentence fragments without subjects, without direct objects, without active verbs, without present tenses: "Slavery existed briefly in America" but it was "not unique and its effects are not permanent." "Virtually every American probably is a descendant of slaves."[39] Blame must be shared, avoided, or muted at all costs. Why?

Not because whites hate blacks per se; they don't really. They ostentatiously fear and feel superior to blacks, both of which feelings have to do with how precious whites think themselves, both of which feelings they'll get over as they come to accept their nondivinity and as blacks continue their rise. They are prepared, even eager to love and nurture those blacks they deem worthy, those bourgie blacks who have "assimilated" and "transcended race" and registered Republican. It is not even that they don't want to share America's resources. All they really want is not to have to feel badly about themselves and their protoselves, their ancestors. They are racists of convenience.

Whatever its source, whites' determination that blacks stop blaming them and dredging up their inglorious past requires a toxic know-nothingness so effective as to have become quite bracing. What should shame them, or at least silence them, they've decided to be proud of. They have to; the past won't stay buried, and they're too weak, too human, to accept its full dimensions.

WHO, ME?

With white supremacy as both the goal and the premise, whites' main strategy rests on a frenzied *plausible deniability*. No matter how damning the charge, how obvious the bias, how lasting the damage, how high the body count, how low the motivation, how legible the records, a robust rebuttal will be offered and more stridently proffered with every utterance. The rebuttal must be robust because it has to reverberate through white America and tell each what to say, let alone what to think, when confronted with the identity-destroying truth. Examples of this bracing tactic abound:

> [T]he Anglo-Saxon world has taken leave of its senses. The campaign to ban racial profiling is . . . a part of that large, broad-fronted assault on common sense that our over-educated, over-lawyered society has been enduring for some forty years now and whose roots are in a fanatical egalitarianism, a grim determination not to face up to the realities of

group differences, a theological attachment to the doctrine that the sole and sufficient explanation for all such differences is "racism"—which is to say, the malice and cruelty of white people—and a nursed and petted guilt towards the behavior of our ancestors.[40]

How comforting: no refutation, just attitude. Not only have they "proven" that blacks are not victims, they have "proven" that whites are! Note the "forty years American society has endured." The civil rights movement and black equality are the problem, not the racial injustice the movement overturned. Note the shift of blame onto whites' ancestors with no responsibility for modern whites.

Such whites function as high-priced political courtesans. They tell ashamed and angry whites that blacks just don't understand them, that blacks don't deserve them, that—their sagging political pecs notwithstanding—they are civic men among men. No one gives citizenship like they do. They're not racist, they're not privileged, they're misunderstood. Blacks don't deserve to shine your shoes. Though they should.

In 2001, for example, a Southern Heritage group announced plans to seek payback from the United States for war crimes committed against the South during the Civil War. Regrettably, their evidence will prove that Lincoln was not the Great Emancipator but a "war criminal,"[41] that the Confederacy was victim, not victimizer. At the turn of the century W.E.B. DuBois reported that blacks resented both the absentee landlords they sharecropped for as near slaves and the store owners who kept them mired in debt. " 'Why, you niggers have an easier time than I do,' said a puzzled Albany [Georgia] merchant to his [complaining] black customer. 'Yes,' he replied, 'and so does yo' hogs.' "[42] No one believes a lie more than its utterer, because no one needs to more; hence white vehemence.

The main objective of their plausible deniability is this: whites by and large accept that the status quo must change. But they're desperate to find a way to silence blacks so that they can cease their depredations (a) as slowly as possible; (b) when they deem blacks have earned it; and (c) when they can do so without losing face. It is crucial that (c) be accomplished without criticizing whites' ancestors with any specificity. This impulse pops up again and again as modern whites try to reconcile the past with the present. In a challenge to Virginia's racist, Confederate-era state song, a judicial decision took pains to note that a finding in favor of the challengers should in no way be understood as a condemnation of whites' ancestors. So the song is racist, but those who chose it were not. Denial is double-jointed. It has to be.

PLAUSIBLE DENIABILITY REQUIRES:
Aversion Therapy
Literalism
Ahistoricism, Decontextualism
Knee-jerk Defiance
Cunning Defiance
Africa-Bashing
Divide and Conquer

The mental gyrations necessary to perform these measures are so exhausting, they've made whites societally short-tempered and rage-filled. In the past, even whites at the bottom of the socioeconomic ladder had the currency of their whiteness to sustain them: they might have had thankless jobs, but at least the jobs were better than any blacks could obtain, and they were allowed to mistreat their black co-workers; whites' tenements surpassed any to which blacks might aspire or at least were off limits to them. DuBois dubbed such currency the "public and psychological wages of whiteness." More recently, law professor Cheryl Harris has argued that whiteness *is* property.[43] *Black* was defined as innately negative so that its "opposite" could be innately positive.

Accordingly, it is no accident that mass, random killings are disproportionately perpetrated by whites; that white males between thirty and sixty hold a near monopoly on serial, random, workplace, and intrafamilial killings, while young white males bring up the rear with schoolyard shootings and drug use—all the earmarks of extreme crisis, yet not at all who whites think they are. According to the Centers for Disease Control and the U.S. Department of Health and Human Services:

> [W]hite high school students are seven times more likely than blacks to have used cocaine; eight times more likely to have smoked crack; ten times more likely to have used LSD; and seven times more likely to have used heroin. In fact, there are more white high school students who have used crystal methamphetamine (the most addictive drug on the streets) than there are black students who smoke cigarettes. What's more, white youth ages 12–17 are more likely to sell drugs: 34% more likely. . . . [W]hite youth . . . are twice as likely to binge drink, and nearly twice as likely as blacks to drive drunk. And young white males are twice as likely to bring a weapon to school as are black males.[44]

Why do we not learn these facts from the same evening news that never misses a chance to show a young black man perp-walking from the jailhouse to the courthouse with his jacket over his face?

In early 2001, after yet another young white boy shot his classmates for no apparent reason, the mayor of his 82 percent white suburb—Santee, California—expressed his shock on CNN. Things like that just "don't happen here." Yet in 1999 police there logged "231 weapons-related domestic violence reports, along with arrests of 300 adults for felony property, drug, and violent crimes (including homicides) and 600 more adults for other offenses."[45] Major drunken white riots have occurred at colleges in Boulder, Colorado; Carbondale, Illinois; East Lansing, Michigan; Eugene, Oregon; State College, Pennsylvania; Storrs, Connecticut; Pullman, Washington; and Tucson, Arizona—at least twenty since 1995—mostly over restrictions on underage drinking. Have you heard about them? Ten thousand rioted at Michigan State in 1999. Is anybody scared of young whites now? In several of the white college riots locals and police reached out to the rioters, "adopting" dorms and inviting them to community events so as "to understand their frustrations." In 2003 senior girls at a wealthy white suburban Chicago high school went on a drunken rampage, seriously injuring some younger girls. The school moved promptly to suspend the attackers but were immediately met by parental lawsuits and an unwavering refusal to see white children subjected to any punishment, let alone criminal punishment. One girl suffered a broken ankle, while another received ten stitches. Officials attempting to gather evidence in the case have been met with a code of silence, making their job extremely difficult. The parents seem to believe that the embarrassment of the home video of the attack that aired nationally in May 2003 is all the punishment their precious children deserve.

White male baby boomers and their spawn are the true American danger, yet you could never tell it from the nightly news or from white America's self-descriptions.

When black folk look at the would-be master race they still know so intimately, they see something far different from the model of sound mental health, good social adjustment, and personal fulfillment that they are expected to look up to. Blacks may be disproportionately emptying trash cans, but there are trash cans in corner suites, too; somebody's taking all that Prozac, and it isn't working-class blacks. Ellison notes that even pre-movement poor southern blacks had no illusions about their supposed betters. He provides two children's rhymes of the period:

> These white folks think they so fine
> But their raggedy drawers
> Stink just like mine

and

> My name is Ran
> I work in the sand, but
> I'd rather be a nigger
> Than a poor white man.[46]

"Prisoners," Murray noted, "sleep better than jailers."[47] The reason is that prisoners have no illusions about what's going on; fantasies are taxing. Speaking of the 1965 Moynihan Report's disquisition on black pathology, Murray asserted that it

> insists that Negro men are victims of a matriarchal family structure, [but] makes no mention at all of the incontestable fact that aggressiveness of white American women is such that they are regarded as veritable amazons not only in the Orient but also by many Europeans and not a few people at home. But then the Moynihan Report also implies without so much as a blush that all of the repressions, frustrations, and neuroses of the white Organization Man add up to an enviable patriarchal father image rather than the frightened,

insomniac, bootlicking conformist, "The Square," which even those who are too illiterate to read the [comic strips] can see in the movies and on television.[48]

Think of modern white self-expression—art, literature, music—and who it is telling the world whites are. It bespeaks not superiority, not mastery, not sanity, but pathology. Think for a moment of Shakespeare's, Arthur Miller's, or Eugene O'Neill's plays; they're not exactly archetypes of sound white mental health, yet they're considered universal by whites. Du-Bois was actually moved to pity for them; "I should be the last to withhold sympathy from [whites in their] efforts to solve [their] intricate social problems," he wrote.[49] Yet America never speaks of its Caucasian Problem. Brilliantly but taxingly, whites circumvent all this neurosis by establishing themselves as the measure, not the measured. But the pressure of keeping up appearances is straining its seams.

Certainly, many whites have accepted that racial justice requires a fair redirection of resources, if only in the future. Most of those who have not, of course, confine themselves to supporting reactionary politicians, writing incoherent letters to the editor, or building careers as right-wing pundits. The marginal few who can't cope with their straitened (i.e., less privileged) position in life are the ones who take hostages, shoot up schools, or support brutal cops.

Two rational options remain for whites. They can either accept responsibility for the past and its effects on the present, or they can simply accept that an identifiable population is lagging behind to everyone's detriment. The nation could then proceed to do what's best for itself. But that's a thought too many whites cannot bear to countenance (because they're human, not because they're white); hence the need for the foregoing unproductive schemes.

Historical white supremacy was a proactive, unabashed policy, in dealing both with Africa and with Africans in America. No one bothered to deny it. Indeed, it was wearily invoked as a sigh-inducing duty: the white man's burden. Today whites deny the continuing effects of their past racism as well as the privilege they yet retain, simply because they are too stiff-necked, too embarrassed, and too sickened to follow these truths to their logical and moral conclusions. They simply cannot live with the truth of how they came to be who they are, so they choose not to know. This explains why decent, sensible whites ignore, defend, and rationalize slavery, Jim Crow, and their badges and signifiers. Most significantly, it explains how they justify, rationalize, or deny their continuing privilege.

AVERSION THERAPY

There is a children's ghost story that if you look into a mirror in a spooky house and call on Bloody Mary three times, the demon will appear and mutilate . . . someone. Only a few are brave enough to invoke the demon, even though they're almost positive nothing will happen; the remote possibility of her arising is simply too frightening to risk. Modern whites, their backs against the wall due to black attacks, have come to understand, however counterintuitively, that they cannot afford not to look. They must invoke the beast of their own racism and spit in its eye. Blacks having gained a social voice post-movement, whites have been confronted with pictures of themselves that contradict everything they tell themselves they are. But the pictures don't go away. What can they do but dissect them stoically and declare that the pictures don't mean what blacks say they do?

Aversion therapy is what allows whites to watch samizdat videos of police hordes beating an unarmed black man and believe that the black man "was in charge the whole time"; they have to watch with the understanding that their entire self-image, everything they've built their beliefs on, rests on the black man's deserving the beating. It's how they hear the list of blacks killed by the police and know the blacks "asked for it." The paranoid exists in a perpetual state of anxiety; whites live in constant fear of the bestial blacks. Hence their purse-hugging and car-door-locking, however benign the circumstances. It's always Nat Turner time for them. That explains the police's hair-trigger mayhem at the least black resistance.

The therapy for mental patients who fear filth is to stare at garbage until it loses its power to disgust; the same therapy is needed for those being confronted with their role in a crime with which they have hitherto safely gotten away. The hard part is not flinching at the crime scene photos, and not crumbling when the victim tracks you down and rings your doorbell. This gets easier with practice.

Often, with aversion therapy, "talking" has to be added to "walking" in those little comas of denial. When a white person is charged with being a racist and has no defense, yet it cannot possibly be that she is a racist, the person will simply deride the charge or render it with *so-called* in front of it, as in "*so-called* skin privilege" or "*so-called* civil rights leaders" or "*so-called* diversity," or the person will say: "I *suppose* it's 'racist' to . . ." The speaker appears to be grappling bravely with a charge but is merely repeating it with a beleaguered scorn meant to discredit it by the sheer weight of his holy white derision.

That which you most fear you have to confront most directly, to rob it of its power to pursue you. Crucially, aversion therapy requires that whites rhetorically invoke the specter of their own racism repeatedly in order to steel themselves against the sting of it. They have to court the oppressor tar baby early and often so that it can be drained of all meaning, for themselves and for society. But when whites let a sneering repetition of an accusation pass for a manful response, they actually clamor to be deemed racist, feigning despondent fortitude at the prospect. In the same way that stuck-in-the-past blacks like to experience racism, whites like to be called racist; in both cases each enjoys the supposedly worst of all things.

Many whites are actually relieved to be called racist—it is the fulfillment of their worst fear. But they defang it by constructing "racist," something they think no longer exists, as merely a loser's taunt. Blacks are given to believe that calling a bullwhipless white a racist is like calling the girl who won't date you ugly—you both know it's a pathetic admission of defeat. Whites' counterintuitive quest to be wrongfully, heroically slurred as racists is a vindication of a deep-seated belief in their own fitness to rule and in their own suffering in maintaining that rule, the new-millennium white man's burden.

This stratagem confirms the racist belief that blacks are dumdums who barely understand what's happening to them, who debase whatever legitimate claims they might have by failing to distinguish mere disagreement or opposition from oppression. It plays to the cynically effective unspoken notion that if any one claim of racism can be portrayed as bogus, all such claims are suspect. That if blacks knowingly accuse whites of nonexistent racism, then *blacks* are really the racists. So whites send in Trojan horses of racism and wait for the diversion to be attacked in morally wasteful force. As regularly as clockwork, knee-jerk blacks and liberals oblige them, throwing around, as a drunk scatters his money, the charge that should be made only sparingly, and falling into the same trap again and again. These blacks are too vengeance-obsessed to husband the moral high ground, too undisciplined to take the long way around the banana peel on the freshly waxed floor, and too fascinated with whites and too desperate for their attention to note the neon whoopee cushions upon which they are about to sit.

With full black cooperation, whites are on the verge of successfully gnawing the notion of racism to Jabberwockian meaninglessness when uttered by blacks. *"Everything is race with them,"* whites complain now, just as they have since Emancipation. This from the people who gave the world the one-drop rule and scientific gradations like mulatto, octoroon, and quadroon, segregated swimming pools, and fingernail inspections to detect black blood. This from those who in 1851 first diagnosed the baffling mental illness "drapetomania," the disorder that caused slaves to run away, and "dysaesthesia aethiopis," whose symptoms were sloth and a tendency to break things. (The recommended treatment for both forms of insanity was whipping.)

Whites worshiped at the cathedral of race-obsession when it worked in their favor, and they taught an entire nation's mind to work that way. Now that overt racism must be denied, blacks are blamed for thinking as they have long been trained to think. For centuries, race affected every aspect of American life; now we are to believe it affects nothing.

LITERALISM

In 1949 Senator Lyndon Baines Johnson arranged an Arlington National Cemetery space for Felix Longoria, a Mexican American war hero who had been denied a funeral at a white mortuary in segregated Three Rivers, Texas. The contretemps became national news, and the town exerted itself to prove that it was the family's fault that the vet wasn't buried there; it also tried very hard to derail Johnson's budding political career in revenge. The town was covered in whites-only signs and restrictive covenants, yet the truth of this incident had to be disproved. In their heyday, white southerners would pick slave narratives apart for minute inaccuracies—the fugitive's need for obfuscation notwithstanding—ostensibly on the assumption that if they found one untrue word, they had proven that slavery was not inhumane. In 1955 white southerners refused to believe that the body that authorities identified by his dead father's ring was Emmett Till's. A Negro pummeled beyond recognition *and* dumped in the Tallahatchie River with an eighty-pound cotton gin fan barbed-wired to his neck embarrassed them not, as long as he had no name.

Slaveowners were embarrassed, not by the inherent inhumanity of slavery, just by being *known* as inhumane. Segregationists were embarrassed, not by segregation, just by being *known* as segregationists. Murderers and their accomplices were embarrassed, not by being murderers and accomplices, just by being *known* as such. It was, and is, the particularization of their racism with which they cannot live.

Because white privilege no longer exists de jure, whites employ literalism to deny its obvious de facto existence. They deny the undeniable with round-eyed questions like "Who is it that's discriminating against black people in the ghettoes?"

If George Wallace is not standing in an Alabama schoolhouse door, they seem to ask, if no German shepherds are mauling black mothers, if no fire hoses are breaking black bones, and no Cossack cops are on horseback in Selma, then where, pray, is the privilege, where's the oppression? Examples of this tactic abound.

Poor minority students sued California in 2001 alleging that the abysmal conditions—out-of-date and insufficient textbooks, fainting from the lack of air conditioning, rodent infestation—impeded their ability to learn. In court the state's blue-chip lawyers reduced them to tears with questions like "How did the mouse droppings you saw on the floor affect your ability to learn in U.S. history?" and "You got an A, even though there were a number of unfair conditions in this class, right?"

Blacks allege that they are systematically charged more for cars than whites ($420 on average). Whites do not deny the charge but rather defend the practice, responding with subject-changing nonsequiturs and aversion therapy. They argue that sometimes blacks are the overchargers, as if that justified the practice, as if those blacks weren't either self-hating, following orders, or heartless opportunists (like antebellum whites who hid behind lynchings to steal black land). Or perhaps, they argue, it's only natural to overcharge blacks, the dummies; whites must just be savvier, the proof being their better car deals. When it is pointed out that women and minorities who buy cars online get the same deals as white men, the only response is the silence of the coma.

AHISTORICISM, DECONTEXTUALISM

Whites often supplement literalism with ahistoricism and decon-textualism, thereby achieving the double jackpot of white exoneration and black guilt. One history-challenged white opined:

> Do blacks understand how deluded they seem by rejecting the GOP, party of the Great Emancipator, and instead voting 93 percent for the party of the slave owners, the Klan, Jim Crow, and Bull Connor—the Democratic Party?[50]

This ploy has become a popular Republican gambit for simultaneously expressing contempt for blacks and distancing themselves from the racist obstructionism of their own modern party. Neither the Democratic nor the Republican Party is what it was in Lincoln's day, as he must surely know.

The day after slavery ended, whites were already busy decontextualizing it so that they could continue it. Decontextualizing allowed them to believe they were upholding transcendent values rather than warping them for their own benefit. Legislative history unearthed in the 1960s in support of civil rights movement legal strategies makes clear that whites' determination to remain on top immediately after Emancipation differed little from that same determination now. Jack Greenberg, Thurgood Marshall's successor at the NAACP Legal Defense and Education Fund, writes:

> Opponents in Congress had attacked the Freedmen's bill which extended such preferences [for example lands, hospitals, and educational programs], in terms used to assail affirmative action today: "A proposition to establish a bureau of Irishmen's affairs, a bureau of Dutchmen's affairs, or one for the affairs of those of Caucasian descent generally, who are incapable of properly managing or taking care of their own interests by reason of a neglected or deficient education, would . . . be looked upon as the vagary of a diseased brain." One congressman of that era said, "We used to talk about having a white man's chance; it seems to me now that a man may be very happy if he can get a negro's chance."
>
> President Andrew Johnson vetoed the Freedmen's Bureau bill with a message that might have been written by contemporary opponents of affirmative action. When the bill was enacted once more, Johnson vetoed it again, writing that the bill established "for the security of the colored race safeguards which go infinitely beyond any that the General Government has ever provided for the white race. In fact, the

distinction of race and color is by the bill made to operate in favor of the colored and against the white race."[51]

The freed slaves' problem was a neglected or deficient education? Whites were happy to have a Negro's chance in 1870?

In addition to ahistoricism and decontextualism, identity politics—the pure, original version, in which whites reduce a minority to one disfavored feature—was also required. Former slaves had to be essentialized to their blackness, and their oppression had to be airbrushed out. Whites had to be essentialized to their whiteness, with their hegemony and oppression airbrushed out. Blacks, now officially "equal," attempted to discriminate against blameless whites.

Eriq La Salle, a popular black TV actor, played a character who had an interracial relationship as well as relationships with black women. On his insistence, his show ended the interracial relationship because it was an emotionally well-adjusted one, while his character's relationships with black women were invariably dysfunctional. He said, "If the only time you show a balanced relationship is in an interracial relationship, whether it's conscious or subconscious, it sends a message I'm not comfortable with."

He was criticized by whites who willfully reinterpreted his comment, and all such critiques of black representations in white media, to mean that he was simply opposed to interracial relationships. Critic Charles Taylor painted blacks as the real racists while simultaneously indulging in self-congratulation: "The difference today [from groundbreaking movies about interracial relationships like *Guess Who's Coming to Dinner*] is that black actors and audiences may be just as turned off by miscegenation as white ones."[52] Blacks are the true bigots, while white racism went out with the 1960s.

In a 2001 case where two white Florida boys, Derek and Alex King, were accused of bludgeoning their father to death and then setting a cover blaze, the *New York Times* wrote:

> The fact that the two earlier cases involved black boys and [these] boys are white may put pressure on prosecutors to try [them] as adults to avoid appearing to apply different standards based on race, said [a juvenile law professor].[53]

Wouldn't it actually *be* racist? Note the smooth donning of the victim's mantle: white boys will be punished because of black stupidity and oppression of whites, not because they deserve it as much as any other kids convicted of beating their father to death. (Neither of the black boys had acted with premeditation or killed a parent.)

Looking at black responses to racism in a vacuum, separated from the circumstances that gave rise to those responses, is a tried and true method for "proving" blacks' stupidity, racism, and unfitness to handle their own affairs, let alone America's.

In perhaps the ultimate decontextualization, white apologists often point out that blacks owned slaves. What they fail to mention is that the people whom the historical record calls "slaves" the purchasers called parents. Unless manumitted, relatives could be legally returned to their families in no other way.

Art, as well as history, does its part to whitewash America's sins. The epic 2002 movie *Gangs of New York* glorifies Irish immigrants as standing up to anti-Irish racism and the classism that sent the poor off to fight the Civil War while the rich bought their way out. The reality was that the Irish didn't want to fight for the blacks they loathed. They rioted for days, lynching blacks by the score and burning their neighborhoods. Yet in this film they are portrayed as heroic victims standing up to tyranny.

The 2000 Revolutionary War epic *The Patriot* depicted a vast plantation that was run only with paid Negro labor, no slaves. Whites defended this cinematic whitewash on the grounds that there were freemen in South Carolina at the time; apparently they all worked on this one plantation. Ignored was the fact that such a plantation could not possibly have competed with plantations that used slave labor. Also, if teaching a slave to read was illegal and even freemen could not move about without stringent social controls, wouldn't such a plantation owner as depicted in the movie have been run out of town by his peers? Much more important, what of the affront to the slaves' descendants to have bondsmen revivified as contented capitalists trading their free labor for enlightened treatment and equality? How reminiscent of the white tour guide at President James Madison's plantation in 2000 who sniffed delicately, "I call them servants, *not* slaves," as if her doing so rewrote history, made whites pick their own cotton, and bestowed upon the millions gone their freedom and dignity. As if she was doing *them* a favor rather than deodorizing her own past.

Whites are determined to relive their revolutionary glory— picture President Madison riding his beloved horse Liberty among his hundreds of slaves—without having to "own" the slave system that made it possible. So they airbrush slavery out of the picture, magnify the barbarism of the oppressive British overlords, and turn up the volume on the oppression of the true victims, the colonists. Worst of all in *The Patriot* was the apologia defending a slave who at first was forced to take his master's place in the fighting, then later soldiered on for the promise of his freedom. ("He understood the ideals of American freedom better than today's so-called 'civil rights leaders.' ") Both *The Patriot* and its defenders failed to acknowledge that those slaves never received their promised freedom. Blacks have never had a problem understanding the *ideals* of American freedom. Why else struggle so hard to attain them? It's the *reality* of freedom that long proved so elusive.

Saving Private Ryan, another contemporary megamovie meant to hearken back to a time of simple-hearted American glory and heroism, managed to avoid showing even one visible minority among the thousands of actors onscreen. Thousands of blacks served. None in the D-Day invasion, true, but thousands served elsewhere. Why no symbolism? Why show hundreds of free Negroes happily toiling on an eighteenth-century tobacco plantation, but not even one tanned-looking extra in a World War II movie? Why did whites crow when blacks and liberals opposed casting a white man as a Vietnamese in the Broadway musical *Miss Saigon* in 1991 but defend the exclusion of black Americans from a movie meant to restore America's sense of comity, joint endeavor, and high moral purpose? Why omit black Americans from a event meant to critique and chastise the selfish, moribund pass that America's culture has come to? No other group has so embodied the ideals of the Constitution or contributed so much to a nation that burdened them so much. Why leave them, or force them, out?

When a September 11 memorial was proposed that depicted the three white firemen who raised the flag over the rubble as multiracial, no such symbolic argument (it was, after all, an attack on America, not on the fire department) was raised by those defenders of *The Patriot*'s whitewash. As well, those who pointed out the exclusion of minorities from New York City's fire department (it's 97.3 percent white) were attacked as unpatriotic abettors of terrorism. The three white men in their segregated fire department who raised the flag "are disappointed that this historic moment has become something that's more political than historical," said [Bill] Kelly, their lawyer. "History should be told as it happened, rather than someone's interpretation of history. History should be recorded according to the facts."[54]

Who can blame blacks for wondering what algorithm dictates when the literal truth will suffice and when a metaphor is necessary?

Now that overt oppression has buckled under the weight of its own contradictions, whites accept that they must subsist on their windfall of skin privilege, their inheritance of entrenched socioeconomic advantage, a status quo that enshrines that privilege, and most important, their indissoluble sense of entitlement. Much as the flatulent saunter nonchalantly away from their stench, whites now try to back away from their crimes, if not their booty.

They require reverence for the Founding Fathers and the pioneers and the imputation of their positive values to the present day, but they consider blasphemous the logical notion that negative values made the crossing as well. We are given to believe that America absorbed from history's heroes the ethos of hard work, entrepreneurship, and self-sacrifice but not selfish hypocrisy, gleeful expropriation, and hegemonic tendencies. The most outrageous is whites' newfound repulsion for identity politics. But who invented identity politics? Who required and enforced it with the lash and the law book until yesterday? Gender, race, sexual orientation, physical ability, national origin, religion—these aspects of identity were how whites determined who could do what kind of work and at what pay, who could live where, who could marry whom, who could sue whom, who could murder or rape whom. But now that it no longer works for them, now that they have a four-century head start, whites want it scraped from the American psyche—as if they don't still practice it—like gum from a table leg. But this is how they taught America to think and to organize itself. They can't now just tell the jury to disregard centuries of evidence and expect the world to "un-know" what's been the enforced mode of thought until yesterday. They made the black hysterics see themselves and the world the way they do; they thought it was fine when that myopia functioned to keep blacks in their place, but it is unacceptable now that it emboldens and animates them. Changing the subject from legitimate black critique to a debate over identity politics is just another in their bottomless bag of tricks.

This sleight of hand is especially resorted to insofar as those crimes affect the present. Hence the common tactic of delegitimizing accusations of inequality and privilege by uncoupling them from the relevant past and analyzing events in a vacuum. It is especially true when those crimes give rise to any notion of reparation or acceptance of the past. When, one wonders, oh when will whites accept that Thomas Jefferson could both own humans and bone the humans he owned?

In an illuminative volley aimed at Sally Hemings's descendants' demands to be included in the Monticello Association (which admits only legitimate white descendants), a former association president circulated a drawing of a black with a zipped zipper for a mouth. Attacked, he said the color was irrelevant— he was "just advising discretion." He eventually apologized to the association members, but not to the black distant cousins before whom he'd dangled the noose.

The important question that the Jefferson "defenders" beg, though, is this one: why are these accusations considered slander (which any perusal of the right wing's discourse on the subject will confirm)? Why is nephew Randolph Jefferson's "character" deemed more likely to have resulted in a liaison with Hemings than Thomas's? Is it that whites also assume that most such dalliances were rapes? Or is it that a love affair with a nigger was beneath the great man? Which is the slander?

For once, whites want a variant of what blacks have. They are voluntary amnesiacs demanding that the day they come to in the defendant's chair, vehemently innocent as to how they got there, be the first day of a new, blank-slate existence. What could reasonable people, in such a situation, do but leave the past in the past? "Why pick at old scars?" said one white woman who passed on seeing a film version of *Uncle Tom's Cabin* in 1927, while thousands of former slaves were still alive, still oppressed. "I don't think we need to . . . start scratching these sores," said a white Mississippi state senator in 1998 when payments for the survivors of those lynched for civil rights work was proposed; the proposition was voted down along racial lines. Yet America never tires of picking at the sores of Pearl Harbor or southerners at the "war crimes" of the Yankees during the Civil War. One southern writer observed that when his father died in 1998, his obituary noted that General Sherman had burned his great-grandfather's home.[55]

It is blacks who want to endlessly relive their degradation and who refuse to get over their trauma until every last white person has had a turn at the self-criticism microphone, gotten down on his knees, and absolved blacks of their humiliating failure by begging their forgiveness. Since that will never happen, blacks will never have to take full responsibility for themselves and for formulating a plan of action that does not revolve around refurbishing the hearts and minds of whites.

KNEE-JERK DEFIANCE

The University of Alabama, which grooms the state's best and brightest for future leadership in all facets of Alabama life, has thirty-seven white fraternities and sororities. None of them have ever knowingly accepted a black member. These organizations have low-cost leases (usually a hundred dollars per year) on lush mansions on prime real estate on expansive grounds. Alabama public and university life is dominated by these organizations. As criticism of their segregation grows, they respond only with tight-lipped refusals. Certainly, some of the intransigence is due to racism. More is simply knee-jerk defiance. Their spokesman said, "It's one of those things where if your mom and dad tell you not to play in the street, what's the first thing you're going to do? You're going to run out in the street."

Among the many abrogated and illegal treaties with Native Americans, New York State's with the Cayuga Indians ranks among the most nefarious. Although it was opposed by George Washington himself for its blatant theft, it has taken centuries for the obvious judicial determination of its illegality to be made and a remedy assessed. Mounting no argument that the treaty was in fact legal, New York State whites (none of whom will lose land) are nonetheless violently opposed to paying damages and returning the land to the Indians. White violence is expected when the judgment is enforced. Their rhetoric of "filthy Indians" and "bloodthirsty savages" is right out of an old Western.

This stupid schoolyard defiance is why whites defend the Confederate flag and the other noxious, anachronistic remnants of the slave South and its determination to hold on to its "way of life." They are simply too embarrassed, self-absorbed, and stiff-necked to acquiesce. So they keep a straight face and insist (Bloody Mary! Bloody Mary! Bloody Mary!) that the Stars and Bars can be exorcised of all inconvenient symbolism and be made to signify nothing except benign regional sentimentality.

In November 2000 Alabama became the last state in the union to excise its antimiscegenation statute. Forty percent of Alabamans voted to retain it. One who did so, Michael Chap-pell, who heads a Confederate Heritage political action committee, explained himself as motivated by the desire to preserve southern heritage:

> It's to protect our monuments, symbols, the history of the South, whites or blacks. It ain't all good, but it ain't all bad. People that try to take our monuments, change their names, we're fightin' against that, like a hundred years down the road when they start wantin' to change Martin Luther King things.[56]

So he doesn't oppose interracial marriage, just admitting that his ancestors did. In his childish refusal to let the past speak for itself, he and his ilk help to hold America hostage to the past. But at least he did us the favor of letting slip his true motivations rather than repeating the plausible denials of the more intelligent.

But all of this begs the most fundamental question of all: why couldn't southern whites give slavery up? Thinking it absolves them, whites like to point out that slavery was about to end even without the Civil War. According to historians, the slave system was a major impediment to the South's development. Says Joseph L. Graves:

> The North had more manufacturing and capital, far greater value in farmlands, and vastly more railroad mileage. New York State had more real and personal wealth than Virginia, North Carolina, Tennessee, Missouri, Arkansas, Florida, and Texas combined (even when slaves were counted as wealth). The slave system benefited only the large slaveholders, but the mass of poor whites suffered from poverty, ignorance, and superstition.[57]

Thomas Sowell says that the American South

> was by no means the most economically dynamic region of
> the country, either during or after the era of slavery. It was in
> fact the poorest. . . . In the United States, it is also question-
> able whether all the profits from slavery exceeded the enor-
> mous cost of fighting the Civil War—a war that would not
> have had to be fought if there were no slavery.[58]

Slavery's effect on the southern economy was common knowledge, but whites couldn't let go of slavery because it was too
fundamental an admission of wrongdoing and miscalculation.
Making war was easier than confronting themselves.

CUNNING DEFIANCE

The more intelligent white opponents of black complaint have
adopted a radical, extremely effective, and bracing strategy.
They don't deny their racism—they defend it.

Honed in the academy, "stereotype accuracy" defends the
proposition that stereotypes are not pernicious but should in
fact be honored. Their production is hardwired into the human
psyche as an evolutionary defense mechanism; Darwin makes us
do it. The apolitical powers of human observation note and
associate certain characteristics with certain groups of people,
just as the invisible hand of the marketplace neutrally deter-
mines relative value. Stereotypes are neither good nor bad, they
simply *are,* deny them though one may. The cave man had no
a priori opinion of snakes, but he came to know that they should
either be avoided or killed. Today whites know that blacks
should either be Republican or jailed. It's simple, if unfortunate,

common sense. Stereotypes, we are told, are like clichés; one hates to admit it, but they're true. They're downright scientific.

So deeply held is whites' belief in their own infallibility that when blacks don't fit the stereotypes, reality has to be altered to restore the balance of the universe—they have to build their own Frankensteins to fear and loathe. Just as blacks seek out racism, whites seek out blacks to flee. This is why white women flagrantly grasp their purses when even the most innocuous, ninety-eight-pound-weakling black man passes. This is why the police target black families, complete with wives and small children, and even the black elderly for invasive drug searches. This is why whites who find themselves in all-black settings, no matter how assiduously the blacks ignore them, tremble and later recount their close call to other whites. This is why being mugged by a black justifies fearing all blacks, when being mugged by a white does not lead to a fear of all whites. This is a performed whiteness, a whiteness defined by its reaction to a phenomenon arbitrarily defined as nonwhiteness. Comedienne Cheryl Underwood understood perfectly this minstrelsy when she pointed out on Def Comedy Jam in 1998 that whites couldn't possibly be afraid of blacks "because every time they want some sex or some drugs, they head right for our neighborhoods."

An excellent example of whites' need to experience their own wonderfulness as a function of black baseness is two articles by white journalist Stephen Glass who was found to have invented myriad characters, events, and dialogue to fit his reportorial needs from 1996 to 1998. Since he didn't think he'd be discovered, he said what whites actually think. Posing as a phone psychic, he wrote of foolish, near bestial black callers ("Dis be Lowell") to vivify white stereotypes. They squandered their money on two-hundred-dollar phone calls even though they were poor; "Lowell" had seven kids by five women. He couldn't feed them because he was saving his welfare money for a VCR. That's why he called the psychic, fo' his lucky lottery numbers. ("Ain't you the man who be able to tell what lucky numbers I be able to pick at the Illinois lottery?"[59]) Most important, the black callers attributed the direction of their lives to a destiny they could never master and had long since stopped trying to affect: "Believing that their lives are completely ruled by fate, callers hope I can tell them a little about what fate has in store for them. They're resigned to the notion that they can't affect their own lives." That hopeless nihilism is what necessitates the anesthetic of too much sex, too much shopping, too much substance abuse, and too much blaming of white people for all their problems.

Glass's second article examined why blacks, who used to happily drive D.C.'s taxicabs, no longer did so and had been replaced by God-fearing immigrants. He wrote of an elderly black cabbie who wore three-piece suits, smoked English cigarettes, kept calling cards on his dashboard, scrubbed his cab and his shoes spotless every day, and had nothing but contempt for the young black men of today who confused "respect and the dignity in working hard." He juxtaposed Super Negro with a ne'er-do-well young black man who used to drive a cab but quit to chauffeur for a limousine service. " 'I was sick of smelling all those curry people,' " he sneered. " 'It is low class.' . . . [C]aressing the hood with one hand and point[ing] at a beautiful woman with the other, [he says,] '[Now] I can get that babe. Wanna see me try?' "[60] The coup de grâce was the comparison with today's immigrant, religious corps of drivers who work long hours for low pay, only to be disrespected and robbed by the lazy, shiftless blacks who should have been driving those cabs in the first place.

Stereotype accuracy allows whites to hold on to their contempt and even feel good about it. But however seductive, it has two flaws. First, it looks at black behavior in a vacuum, firewalled from any societal context. There is only black crime, as evidenced by the large numbers of the black incarcerated; there is no police or prosecutorial treachery or even the lack of opportunity that makes crime a viable option. There is only black carnality and immorality as evidenced by high rates of illegitimacy and venereal disease; there is no hopelessness and the low expectations for your life that make children and orgasms the only rays of sunshine. Snakes bite because it's their nature; is their "nature" really why there are so many blacks in prison and poverty?

Second, narcissistic to the end, stereotype accuracy remains just another ventriloquistic code word translating as "stereotypes about blacks."

We have yet to see this chic new analytic tool leveled at whites. If stereotypes about blacks are true, then aren't also blacks' of whites?

So it must be true that whites would deal with the devil were there a dollar in it.

That whites are neurotic and mentally weak, and that the women especially are prone to insanity.

That white men are sexual wimps. (This accounts in part for their cruelty and for the women's proclivity to go insane.)

White children are spoiled; this is how they learn to grow up to be white.

Whites are so jaded, they can't feel anything. That's why they have to jump out of airplanes and climb mountains. And they just have to force themselves on every thing, every one, and every place.

Whites are sexually kinky, prone to perversions like incest, kiddie porn, and extreme masochism.

Whites have to take credit for everything. No one else can have, or be, anything good. No matter what's going on or for how long, whites have to take everything over and then rearrange it all.

One could go on; blacks have a great many stereotypes about whites. But it is unlikely that they would be deemed a valid basis upon which to construct social policy—nor should they be.

AFRICA-BASHING

"The silently growing assumption of this age is that the probation of races is past, and that the backward races of today are of proven inefficiency and not worth the saving. Such an assumption is the arrogance of peoples irreverent toward Time and ignorant of the deeds of men. A thousand years ago such an assumption, easily possible, would have made it difficult for the Teuton to prove his right to life. Two thousand years ago such dogmatism, readily welcome, would have scouted the idea of blonde races ever reaching civilization."
—W.E.B. DUBOIS[61]

Toronto's mayor Mel Lastman was "scared" to visit Kenya in 2001 because "I just see myself in a pot of boiling water with all these natives dancing around me." At the press conference he called to apologize, he entered a walking-talking coma and would only repeat robotically that he was sorry. He wouldn't grapple with his underlying thoughts; he wouldn't even claim to be joking.

Africa-bashing provides another conduit for white contempt and rage at blacks. Europe adopted nothing from Africa "but slavery," these whites opine, saying that Africa had no culture, no art, no learning, and has added nothing to civilization. They need to believe that for tens of thousands of years Africans ran about naked, surviving on larvae and mud, letting hyenas and monkeys rear their young, incapable of communicating with one another or making records of any kind or repeating behaviors until traditions were ritualized. They can believe that as man migrated from Africa to populate the planet, he left home a blank slate, taking no knowledge with him, no technology, to sully what would become holy Europe and requiring the white man, even before he existed, to do the black man's job. Apparently, at no time in history has there ever *not* been a White Man's Burden. But how would man have survived, either before or after leaving Africa, with no knowledge, no culture of any kind?

Tens of thousands of years—but the black man developed no birth or death rituals. No literature. No dance(!). No systems of justice. No repetitive processes for the creation of necessary items. No politics. No trade. No philosophy, theology, or science. It is the cradle of life, yet the know-nothings take their lack of knowledge about Africa as proof that there is none. One wonders what they think it is that keeps archaeologists so busy over there.

Such was their disgust at the black man that early, "scholarly" whites actually suppressed evidence of literacy in Sudanic Africa. The first American slave narratives were written in Arabic, the Latin of Africa; whites went to great pains to establish literate Africans as Moors, explaining that, contrary to the evidence of their own eyes, these individuals weren't black—they were dirty. In the same way that constructing black women as wantons made them responsible for their own sexual exploitation, constructing Africa as an intellectual void made it permissible to dismiss and obscure Sudanic Africa's intellectual traditions as nonexistent while absconding with its knowledge. In distancing themselves from having played an active role in the slave trade, whites argue that they knew nothing of the African interior, so how did they know what knowledge was or was not to be found in that interior?

Nowhere is this need to lobotomize Africa more evident than

in medicine and agriculture. Traditional healers led whites to 75 percent of the ingredients involved in pharmacological research, yet virtually none of the global drug research funds are focused to benefit Africa. Neither have the natural pesticides and growth enhancers it shared with the West been used to aid famine-stricken Africa. The West steals from Africa, then denies that Africa had ever had anything to steal.

Corruption, political violence, post-apartheid crime, and modern slavery in Africa have given whites real, albeit grim, pleasure. These phenomena "prove" that what whites did wasn't really so bad. Africa being devoid of any culture or learning, blacks weren't missing out on much by being enslaved; indeed, many whites then and now believe that Africans were better off as American slaves. Modern African depredations prove that blacks are worse than whites because their misdeeds are current—they prove that blacks are incapable of governing themselves or anyone else.

Heartfelt or not, whites' antislavery efforts now provide them with another chance to show Africa how to conduct its affairs, another opportunity to condescend to blacks, a chance to even the historical score by working to end African slave trading now when it's no longer useful. In this way they believe they undo their own slave-mongering and bring it full circle to blame on blacks.

"I do not feel responsible for [slavery]," went one letter to the editor of the *Washington Post* in 2002. "The slave trade was initiated in Africa and continues today on that continent." Yet Americans jail the purchasers as well as the suppliers of narcotics, stolen property, and kiddie porn. More important (and leaving aside oversimplifications about white control of the African slave trade),[62] the African slave traders did not require their customers to brutalize their purchases or to enslave them for life. Every culture that whites have ever identified with practiced one form of slavery or another, yet no other slave-owning culture constructed its slaves as subhuman—that was a white invention. White brutality to the defenseless was a choice. As W.E.B. DuBois noted, "many have suffered as much as Black people . . . but none of them was real estate."[63]

Blacks are given to believe that their contributions have been equally negligible in the United States, that only in their crime and their welfare reliance are they remarkable. But besides basketball and jazz, what else are they good for? The aim is always to make blacks believe that their African core is rotten, that slavery and Jim Crow were the price of proximity to whites and their institutions, and those institutions are the world's only worthy ones. "Reparations?" writes another *Washington Post* reader. "If any are due, you and yours are greatly indebted to those who altered the base of your lineage and shifted it from its base in Africa to its new homeland in America."[64] Note the convoluted passive voice in this perfect morsel of denial and blame shifting. Why could she not write, "You blacks are greatly indebted to us whites for enslaving you"? For the same reason the Founding Fathers couldn't bring themselves to use the word *slave* in the founding documents. Shame.

DIVIDE AND CONQUER

As whites squirm for a way out of black demands, they turn to other minorities as guilt- and concessions-buffers. Maintaining good relations with those groups proves that whites aren't racist and also allows them to make amends by proxy insofar as their remorse is genuine. No other group was singled out for torture the way blacks were, so no other group causes whites much guilt. Partially to assuage that guilt over their treatment of blacks, whites fawn (politically) over Asians and Hispanics.

Sociologist Andrew Hacker has written about Asians, with their unthreatening physiques, strong family structures, low crime rates, and high academic achievement rates, as being "prepared for whiteness."[65] By this he means that they have almost transcended race; whites do not object to them living in their neighborhoods or attending school with their children. Intermarriage rates (Asian woman, white man) are increasing; more children are born to couples with an Asian partner than to those with two Asians. In other words, whites are seriously considering thinking almost as well of Asians as they do of themselves. Soon after that will come treating them as well.

Here's a typical example of fawning over the industrious, well-mannered Koreans and a passive-voice, plausibly deniable denunciation of blacks:

> One reason Koreans have been so successful . . . is that many Koreans were well-educated with experience in professional jobs. Immigrants from Latin America and the Caribbean have tended to come from poor backgrounds, and they often settled in low-income African-American communities. They were more likely to assimilate into the youth culture of those neighborhoods, that [Pyong Gap] Min [a sociologist at Queens College in New York] says sociologists theorize, "tends to be more oppositional" and can lead to feelings of powerlessness. Most Korean-Americans grow up in largely white, middle-class areas, where they learn mainstream values.[66]

Like contempt for blacks?

Note the careful phrasing of the racist insult; exactly who is it that thinks poor black neighborhoods are "oppositional"? Not the writer, not the named expert, just amorphous sociologists. And blacks' problem is "oppositionality"? Not "marginalization"? Not discrimination? Not structural disadvantage? Not an entirely rational defeatism? Not racism? Not ever? Whatever else might be said for such a pronouncement, it supports the proposition that Asians are on their way to whiteness.

Whites are toying with bestowing at least some vestiges of whiteness—that is, approval—on the large Hispanic population as well. Frequently Hispanics are compared to blacks, and blacks are found wanting. In particular, whites cosset (if only rhetorically) the hardscrabble Hispanic immigrant, he with lots of reason to be grateful, undemanding, and quiescent. In the antireparations discourse, especially, a well-worn tactic is to juxtapose "Juan," a five-dollar-per-hour dishwasher, with the offspring of black doctors and demand to know why the former owes the latter. But why does Juan get to opt out of the burdens but in to all the benefits that predate him? One suspects the reason is an attempt to keep minorities from coalition-building. More, it's a strategy to keep the racial hierarchy intact; whites remain on top, but they signal that Hispanics and Asians can outrank blacks while they work on their promotions to whiteness.

Hispanics generally tend to be conservative and traditional (except on immigration and affirmative action); handled properly, they are poised to become the "Republicans' minority" to counterweight blacks as the Democrats'. Not only are they a decisive voting bloc poised to stymie blacks at key state and local levels, they also assuage white racist guilt and provide an outlet for the amends that whites are too stiff-necked to make to blacks.

Whites, especially that know-nothing bloc that doesn't bother to learn the differences between Hispanic communities, expect Hispanics to be grateful, not vengeful, and the forward-thinking ones are poised to buy their loyalty, for instance, with amnesty for illegal aliens. Also, in some states with large Hispanic populations, Mexican government–issued documents are accepted as proof of identity, and plans are afoot to allow the undocumented to drive legally, since most already do so illegally. With the acquisition of the all-important driver's license, the undocumented become documented, a foretaste of full civic acceptance. Imagine America legalizing crimes most closely associated with blacks.

THE RIGHT KIND OF BLACKS

"I read in a poll taken by a top pollster, talking about how satisfied Negroes are. Maybe I haven't met the Negroes he met. Because I know he hasn't met the ones that I've met. The worst thing the white man can do is to take one of these kind of Negroes and ask him, 'How do your people feel, boy?' If he tells that white man we're satisfied, then he puts him up over the Negro community. He becomes the spokesman. But this is dangerous. This is where the white man does the most harm. *He invents statistics to create an image,* thinking that that image is going to hold things in check. For the man knows that *even Uncle Tom is dissatisfied,* he's just playing his part. Meanwhile, the masses of our people still have bad housing, bad schooling, and inferior jobs that don't compensate with sufficient salary for them to carry on their life in this world. So the problem has gone absolutely unsolved."

—MALCOLM X, FEBRUARY 14, 1965[67]

The main thrust of the divide-and-conquer strategy, however, has to do with the cosseting of black Republicans and conservatives. Policies they would have ignored or resisted, whites support when promulgated by the right kind of black. The race card rankles not at all when played for the right Spades team.

Clarence Thomas speaks of a "high-tech lynching for uppity blacks." Alan Keyes trumps pro-choice opponents with "as a black person I particularly feel it. . . . [M]y ancestors would not have been freed from slavery but for . . . the appeal to conscience that is based on the will of God." The black conservative Frances Edwards fired from her HBO publicist's job claims to be a "casualty of diversity run amok" and sues because "I guess this little nigger was too uppity for her masters." (HBO seems to think the reason was her performance.) All these stratagems disgust when wielded by liberal blacks, and yet those who deploy them successfully are all right-wing celebrities.

"Even today," writes white conservative Eric Cohen, "the most independent black thinkers, from Thomas Sowell to Shelby Steele, speak with a special courage, special voice, and special authority."[68] Ah yes. The "specialness" of white approval. Note also that these thinkers are said to be "independent," not conservative, right-wing, or Republican.

The 2000 Republican National Convention was indistinguishable from the Democrats' in its ostentatious diversity; an obscure black Republican and an obscure Hispanic were elevated to prime-time speaking slots, though they were far from the most qualified. Every recent Republican administration has been athletic at minority head-hunting and bean-counting among its appointments. With gleeful malice, Republicans accuse Democrats of racism for opposing minority Republican nominees when the opposition is actually ideological. Integrating their ranks, minuscule though it is, has made Republicans giddy. And calculating.

The Malcolm X quotation at the beginning of this section isn't offered to insult conservative or Republican blacks as opportunist Uncle Toms—an immature, manipulative slur that this work specifically rejects (and for which it forgives Malcolm)—but to consider the proposition that blacks who downplay racism speak with the "special courage, special voice, and special authority" of white approval. While their views need not be calculated to gain white approval, their critiques of movement-style maneuverings nonetheless make them useful operatives against their black brethren. This cannot be helped and should not be feared; acknowledgment and acceptance of intracommunal complexity is progress. Yet their support for vouchers or for privatizing Social Security no more means that they don't believe racism exists than whites' lack of knowledge about Africa means there's nothing to know. Blacks get to think about other things than being black—they also get to care about a strong national defense and the capital gains tax. One reads the right's fawning head-rubs for right-leaning blacks (special courage, special voice, special sauce) and hears black teeth gnashing; how frustrating it must be for black right-wingers to be used as foils.

Malcolm's real insight was in noting that "even Uncle Tom is dissatisfied." Writing as he was in 1965, when whites-only signs still appeared and truncheon-wielding policemen stood on every corner, Malcolm can be forgiven his failure to understand how any black could be a Republican without being irrational. Filtering his overheated rhetoric, we see that he meant that even moderate blacks, those transcended blacks who have assimilated race, know that things are harder than they should be for blacks because they're black. They know the special burdens they carried while they made their way, however successfully, up the ladder. They may not form their political personae around it, but they know that racism is real. That blacks rank education, the economy, crime, and the like as higher concerns than race in polls does not mean they don't think race is important; they're just being practical. Even the most blasé, bourgie, apolitical black just surfing the Net and living his life is confronted daily with the knowledge that blacks come in last in everything good, first in everything bad—even a corporate Negro is concerned. His own personal success, he knows, is insufficient to consider racism ended.

He likely thinks that "those folks" in the ghetto could do more to help themselves, that black criminals are a scourge on the community, and that the rap world should exercise more self-control—but he thinks structural disadvantage is at play as well. Blacks are capable of complex, layered thought. Black Republicans know that racism isn't dead; but they also know that it need define neither your life nor your politics. And they know, too, that the relative well-being of blacks is just that, relative. Appreciating that life is better for blacks in America than anywhere else in the world is not the same as believing that blacks have the same opportunities and freedoms as any other American. Even Secretary of State Colin Powell is dissatisfied at the state of black America, and even he does not believe that blacks have only themselves to blame.

Voluntarily or involuntarily, these Republican blacks are credits to their race, condescendingly set up in opposition to the ungrateful, unsavory, irrational blacks who criticize whites. Their presence in whites' political midst proves that whites aren't racist. (Note that this is not an argument against black Republicanism or conservativism; this is a critique of white attitudes toward such blacks.) The right kind of black, a Republican black, can—indeed, must—proffer de rigueur examples of racism from his own life. The National Security Adviser has obediently offered up the same tale—of being disrespected at a jewelry counter when she asked to see the expensive items—too often to tally. White Republicans spit up this nugget repeatedly, anxious to show that they can concern themselves with racism as long as the victim is a team player who is casual about it, as long as the incident was inconsequential. They can acknowledge nuisance-level racism, but only from a safe space.

So in love with their own opinions are whites, such is their condescension toward blacks who manage to get it right, that they shower these fellow travelers with far too much approval. The right-wing press fairly drenches the black right with the Holy Grail of white approval. Its "courage" is invoked so often that an extraterrestrial could imagine that the black Supreme Court justice wears a bulletproof vest under his judge's robes, or that the black Republican congressman J. C. Watts varied his daily route to Capitol Hill. Florida's Republican governor Jeb Bush actually wept on stage over the intracommunal travails of a black staffer. Claiming that her children had been teased because she worked for him, she actually had to bring him a tissue on stage. It's a good thing children only taunt each other over party politics. This unctuous praise is the political equivalent of the praise heaped on the "articulate Negro," though his Pulitzer Prize or Harvard Ph.D. might have hinted at a facility with words.

THE TRUTH SLIPS OUT

The blasé bourgie black just going to the gym, moving up the corporate ladder, and trying to enjoy his life surfs the Net, reads a magazine, or takes a class—and is tapped on the shoulder by a screeching litany of white venality and denial; no corner of the culture escapes it. He is made to know things that he'd rather not know, and knowing, he can't remain blasé. That's why black Republicans remain few; voting Democratic is a middle finger raised to American hypocrisy. It is an act of protest, and the hysterical black polemicist is the snarling German shepherd that blacks loose on racism; he serves no purpose except harassment and catharsis. That black folk voice poll support for the kente cloth–draped racial hysteric on television sputtering pseudo-Marxist doggerel is no reason to think they take him seriously. It is an act of protest and a veiled threat, a reminder that black good behavior is not a given. The black leaders whom the folk actually respect remain unknown to whites and even to nonlocal blacks because they are too busy building low-cost housing, tending to unwed mothers, and ministering to black boys on lockdown to bewail the lack of rich black youngsters in Ivy League professional schools. This rage that leads blacks to let hysterics speak for them is rational because even Uncle Tom is dissatisfied when he learns the following:

Magazine sales slump by 40 to 60 percent when blacks are on the cover.[69]

White study subjects feel the white college applicants should be admitted over higher-scoring Asians because the whites are "more well rounded."[70]

Psychologists found that 73 percent of subjects automatically favored white over black, linking blacks with nearly every negative attribute possible. Whites favored their own group to a much greater degree than admitted, while black subjects were close to neutral. Seventy percent of whites linked blacks with even anachronistic weapons like medieval axes and cannons, rarely doing so with whites.[71]

In a rough draft erroneously published, a white high school yearbook staffer identified an African American runner as "Blacky." Not "Speedy" or "Iron Man." Blacky. Suspended, he sued the school for $100,000 for spreading "false and malicious" information about him.

When members of two white Auburn University fraternities staged a pimp-themed Halloween party, partygoers wore blackface, Afro wigs, T-shirts with the logo of a well-known black fraternity, gold jewelry, and flashed gang signs. They published the party photos on the Web. Disciplined, they claim university officials defamed them by describing them as racists and sued for $100 million. Auburn caved; the unrepentant fraternity will remain on campus. The blackface/pimp theme resurfaced at white parties the following Halloween.

Five black students stayed at a chain hotel during the 1999 Black College Reunion in Daytona Beach, Florida. The students were denied services such as access to parking facilities and higher-quality rooms; they were also forced to wear color-coded wristbands and leave telephone deposits. They sued the Adams Mark hotel chain, which will pay millions to settle the suit. Black College Reunion generates $145 million in economic activity, $32 million more than on a nonevent weekend. More than 14,000 residents leave town during the festival, while only 5,300 flee during Bike Week and fewer than 3,000 during Speed Weeks.

An African American studies professor at Smith College, Kevin Quashie, had his introductory Afro Am literature class treated like "the social event of the season." Sixty-five nonblack students enrolled, many bringing friends. They believed that knowledge of the latest rap CDs and having black friends were all that was required to master black literature. Ninety percent failed the midterm, even though the professor undertook heroic measures to assist them. White students began coming to his office hours— not to ask for guidance on raising their grades, but to ask to be allowed to take the class pass/fail.

In a survey, 75 percent of white Americans agreed that "black and Hispanic people are more likely than whites to prefer living on welfare," and a majority believed that "black and Hispanic people are more likely than whites to be lazy, violence-prone, less intelligent, and less patriotic."

Leading white anti-abortion Christian right leader Pat Robertson defended China's birth control policies (which in-

clude forced abortion) because otherwise Chinese racial
purity would be diluted, "like the United States."

The parents at a white California high school fought to pre-
vent the school from being renamed for Martin Luther
King because the school, and therefore their children,
would be perceived as black. Knowing how other whites
think, these parents feared this would hurt their children's
college entrance prospects. They preferred that the school
be renamed for the city's citrus heritage, because "in some
parts of the country, [King is] not looked upon as somebody famous."[72]

The real disparities between whites and blacks in the health
care, mortgage, and insurance industries are so glaring, one cannot bear listing them. The reality is that even a moderately well-
informed black person cannot live without being pummeled
with constant reminders of the invisible target on his people's
chests. Whether put there by neglect, contempt, or persecution,
they are targets nonetheless. There is scarcely an area of American life in which blacks are not the worst off of all groups. More
to the point, they are worse off for reasons that have nothing to
do with either accident or simple black failure. For generations
insurance companies charged blacks more than whites for the
same coverage. Billions have been stripped from blacks in preda-
tory mortgage lending scams sanctioned by law. Blacks suffer
and die by the thousands while well-established medical treat-
ments are reserved for whites only.

Blacks have a right to be angry. So did Frederick Douglass,
but he never let his anger own him. He never let it excuse either
inaction or failure; instead he channeled his fury into excellence
and civic participation. He lived life on his own terms, never
accepting injustice though faced with death; he stood up to his
masters, then fled slavery. Though a hunted fugitive, he lived on

the world stage and helped deliver his people from bondage. He even married a white woman. Douglass refused to play the game on the master's terms. He didn't complain from safety, negotiating with whites for assurances that he wouldn't be punished—he acted and dealt with the consequences that befell him. He made the racists do their own dirty work. Douglass transcended *racism,* not race.

For all we know, racism may be eternal; it certainly seems so. But post-movement, white people's hearts are their own, and black people's lives their own to live. What good does it do blacks to leave race behind if they are still hated for the color of their skin? What they have to leave behind, though under guard, is racist whites. Hardest of all, blacks must work through their bitterness and join hands with nonracist Americans. They are plentiful.

Douglass did it; he transcended racism and worked for the betterment of his country, knowing that that was the best way to help his people. Modern blacks can do the same. It's a simple question of will. If a fugitive slave could make America respect him, so can a black MBA. The first step is admitting that it is time for the next phase of the plan. It is time to chart black life after the movement.

KENTE CLOTH POLITICS:

The White Man's Ice, Know-Nothingness, and Black Futility

"When you make men slaves, you compel them
to live with you in a state of war."
— OLAUDAH EQUIANO, ESCAPED SLAVE[1]

"Race was a handicap, sure . . . but, hell,
I didn't have to marry it."
— CHESTER HIMES[2]

Has there ever been a more defeated people than the American black?

They lost their family structure, their histories, their knowledge, their religions, their customs, their cultures, their countries, their continent. They even lost the understanding that there was more than one of each of those things.[3] They are a people without a return address; even the lowliest refugees know what they've lost and where it is to be found, but not the American black descended from slaves. It bears repeating that Africa is a continent, not a nation. Long gone is any notion of themselves as a proud, free people. But that is not the defeat of which we speak; the defeat is in not knowing how to be free. This knowledge will continue to elude American blacks as long as freedom is defined as concessions from whites. Slavery and race prejudice, W.E.B. DuBois knew, are potent but not sufficient causes of blacks' position.[4] Freedom can be accomplished only through self-assertion.

Internally, blacks position "nigger sticks" in their cars and under their beds, girded for attacks, the likely source of which they are all too aware. When they were less self-conscious, a "nigger mess" was how blacks ruefully described many a black-run event and the Colored Peoples' Time it ran on. Activists who conduct programs for disadvantaged youngsters express off-the-record relief at the abysmal black parental involvement rates; all too often parents only make things worse. Blacks watch more TV than any other group, but black parents oversee homework and breastfeed least. While the black political class focuses on the rare racist violence of extremist whites, nearly a thousand blacks a year are slain by a fellow "New Afrikan." Does anyone even tally the wounded? More black youth succumb to injury and death from their parents' failure to ensure seatbelt usage than from racial profiling or police brutality. If racism ended tomorrow, it still wouldn't be safe to walk through many black neighborhoods at night. The black family disintegrates before their very eyes—blacks have the highest rates of divorce and illegitimacy.[5] They have the lowest rates for marriage and home ownership. The intermarriage rate is mostly made up of black men marrying out. The percentages of black men who choose never to marry and of black women who involuntarily never marry far exceed those for any other group.[6] The black community is tearing itself apart.

But blacks' true problem is accepting the white supremacist notion that these conditions arise from and are exhibitions of black pathology. Their true problem is conceptualizing these conditions as bad because whites experience them, or appear to, less. A near total black failure to breastfeed needs remedying, however many white women do or do not breastfeed; black children need to watch less television however many hours white children spend supine on the carpet.[7]

Externally, successful blacks strolling with Fido in their upper-middle-class neighborhoods are reduced to bitter hypertension when whites mistake them for professional dog walkers. Their Ivy League professorships are incapable of providing them comfort, let alone a condescending magnanimity, in these exchanges. Security guards trail them, and their self-esteem evaporates; their sense of citizenship is reduced to bitter ashes in their mouths. Co-workers make ignorant remarks about the sudden appearance of several hundred dollars' worth of new hair, and the evil of it all makes blacks unable to function in the workplace without an attorney on retainer. One student had to drop out of college when a white cafeteria lady uttered "nigger" in his presence. Now on Wall Street, the wounded young man was jubilant at his $2,500 settlement (sensitivity training and her firing had been insufficient); presumably the cafeteria worker is once again shoveling mashed potatoes for the pampered for a pittance.

Harlem Renaissance poet Countee Cullen's poem "Incident" evocatively captures the psychic assault of the word *nigger*.

> Once riding in old Baltimore,
>   Heart-filled, head-filled with glee,
> I saw a Baltimorean
>   Keep looking straight at me.
>
> Now I was eight and very small,
>   And he was no whit bigger,
> And so I smiled, but he poked out
>   His tongue, and called me, "Nigger."

I saw the whole of Baltimore
  From May until December;
Of all the things that happened there
  That's all that I remember.

This poem perfectly encapsulates the horror that that epithet connoted; it was shorthand for white denial of black humanity and citizenship, and it telegraphed the barely veiled promise of violence to keep blacks in their place. Or at least it did in the 1920s. In 2003 it's a loser's taunt. It's an artifact, not a reality. It's an admission of defeat imbued only with the power that blacks ascribe to it. Whites will stop calling blacks "nigger" when it stops being effective. It isn't that the person who uses this word isn't racist; it's that he or she is impotent and trying to feel powerful. In any event, every day black women run the gauntlet of vulgar sexist insult and threat of violence from black men on the streets, while few blacks are called niggers to their faces.

Viola Liuzzo faced the Klan, but the blacks she died for can't roll their eyes at a minor bureaucrat with a swirl-pattern comb-over and no way to hurt them except through the continued withholding of his all-important, because white, respect. Zora Neale Hurston had the right attitude: "Sometimes, I feel discriminated against, but it does not make me angry. It merely astonishes me. How can anyone deny themselves the pleasure of my company? It's beyond me. . . . I do not belong to the sobbing school of Negrohood who hold that nature somehow has given them a lowdown dirty deal and whose feelings are all hurt about it."[8] Yet modern blacks who have it much easier than Hurston did cannot see that the nuisance-level behaviors that so discomfort them are born of that ill-gotten sense of entitlement and ownership of the world, let alone the country, that whites forged for themselves and their progeny through their world dominance.

The last plantation is the mind, and through those magnolias blacks can't see that they have the ultimate power in post-movement America—the power to disregard nonsense and to refuse to be sidetracked from accomplishing what's important, the power to make whites feel foolish when they behave foolishly, the power to reduce them to impotence when their attempts to undermine black confidence are thwarted, the power to render them invisible by giving a snarled "nigger!" no response save the swift loss of that troglodyte's job. If blacks refuse to acknowledge white superiority, or even relevance, in such situations, does it actually exist? The slave Harriet Jacobs didn't think so. She was with her free, entrepreneur grandmother in the aftermath of the Nat Turner revolt. Roving bands of rioting, poor militia whites burst in and were incensed by how well those niggers were living:

> My grandmother had a large trunk of bedding and table cloths. When that was opened, there was a great shout of surprise; and one exclaimed, "Where'd the damned niggers git all dis sheet an' table clarf?" My grandmother, emboldened by the presence of our white protector, said, "You may be sure we didn't pilfer 'em from your houses." "Look here, mammy," said a grim-looking fellow without any coat, "you seem to feel might gran' 'cause you got all them 'ere fixens. White folks oughter have 'em all."[9]

Coatless, illiterate, and penniless, the prosperity and self-sufficiency of these niggers lessened their whiteness. In fact, it disproved it. If they were so much better, why weren't they better off? Why didn't they already "have 'em all"? Good questions.

One can only feel superior where one encounters inferiors; hence the Jim Crow concern with "uppity Negroes," those Negroes who acted like sovereign humans, who acted free, who acted white. Ponder the largely white tennis world's hatred of Venus and Serena Williams. Unlike golfer Tiger Woods, whose biracial looks and transracial attitude comfort whites and make it acceptable for him to win at something "white," the Williams sisters are physically very Negroid and uninterested in whites' comfort. They think they're free. They think nothing matters but their awesome ability. Whites, those believers in merit, can't abide them; the Williamses are just too black, in every way. That's why whiteness, that preordained seat at the head of every social, economic, and political table, must be shorn of its privileges and its centrality to the universe, just as blackness must be shorn of its negatives, its limitations, and its forced inclusions.

It's not victimology that keeps blacks focused on the peripheral. It's something worse. Blacks can't claim their own power because, in their heart of hearts, they believe the white man's version of them as immoral. Ugly. Dumb. In their heart of hearts, they believe in the white man's version of himself as better, smarter, good at math. Since no one believes in white superiority more than blacks, when whites respect blacks, blacks will be able to respect themselves.

But freedom is not the absence of malice on the part of others; it is the impotence of that malice. It is not the guarantee that others will never deal with you on the basis of their own stupidity; it is the irrelevance, the pathos even, of that stupidity. Freedom is not given. It is taken. Acted upon. Assumed. Defended, on the increasingly rare occasions when it is challenged.

Instead of behaving in accordance with this concept of freedom, blacks are like soap opera amnesiacs, surrounded by the very ones whose blows placed them in the emotional dark. (But which ones? What if they're sorry now? Aren't some of my best friends white?) The same ones who stole her inheritance and bankrupted her. The same ones who now require her to digest whatever they tell her about her past. Worse, the history huck-sters come in all versions—kente cloth boxer shorts are only slightly less violative of a worthy black identity than a bigoted policeman's targeting of blacks.

Too many blacks have little notion of their identity apart from a history of oppression and a thoroughgoing self-hatred incul-cated by ruthless, narcissistic oppressors. This circumscribed, oppression-based self-notion, counterintuitively enough, is kept alive by the victims, as if it were helpful. In fact, it is merely fa-miliar and reinforcing of a belief in never-ending black oppres-sion born of never-ending white racism.

THE WHITE MAN'S ICE

" 'I like big fat white women,' Conway started, ' 'cause
there's so much of 'em that's white. An' I like old white
women 'cause they been white so long. An' I like young
white women 'cause they got so long to be white.
An' I like skinny white women 'cause . . .' "
— CHESTER HIMES[10]

A good two-pronged example of blacks' fascination with whites is their common fear that the perpetrator of a heinous, TV-splashed crime will turn out to be black. When Malcolm X's blood-soaked pocket diary was stolen and nearly auctioned off in 1999, a widely read black infotainment Web site worried in its coverage, "Please don't be black, please don't be black."[11] This fear of white disapproval is rationalized by reinterpreting black criminality as an expression of internalized oppression and thus an indictment of whites. There is truth to the latter proposition, but it still presupposes failure and reduces blacks to mere reactors (black crime ineluctably brought about by white racism). Second, it favors the black criminal over the black victim. As usual, blacks choose jousting with whites, and acquiring their all-important respect, to caring for each other, to protecting themselves, or to being morally accountable.

The black mugger will get a public defender and an Ivy League lawyer from the ACLU or the NAACP Legal Defense Fund if no one reads him his rights. But what of the black victim? He is worse than ignored; he is required to smother his feelings of victimization and redirect them toward whites. And the black political class? It is the symbolic but powerless Oz, signifying with bombastic impotence from behind a curtain long pulled back for all the world to see; it is only blacks who refuse to acknowledge the obvious. A mature black strategy—one aimed at black uplift and not white opinion—should be to minimize both categories at the black source and provide both victim and victimizer with the type of intervention they need. Martin Luther King Jr. claimed that crime in black Montgomery went down 65 percent during the yearlong bus boycott, a fact he attributed to the self-respect engendered in blacks when they acted to improve themselves and their community.

When Malcolm X said, "We need to stop airing our differences in front of the white man, put the white man out of our meetings, and then sit down and talk shop with each other," he meant that it was a diminution of black autonomy to be concerned with outsiders' agenda-stealing input.[12] "Talking shop" has to mean that dealing appropriately with black malfeasors will be both prerequisite and corollary to demanding redress for the racism that contributes to black underachievement and undesirable behaviors. It must be so, not to appease whites but because it is both moral and necessary for improving conditions for blacks. Blacks must develop an inward focus; an outward one merely highlights blacks' craving for the approval and guilt admissions of whites and for their much colder ice, their much hotter coal.

Blacks, and their supporters, create magazines, inaugurate academic departments, and publish bodies of critical theories devoted to the study and repudiation of "whiteness"—as morally, scientifically, and intellectually bogus an invention as ever existed. One has only to consider the fact that whites can have children of any race, while a person of color may produce only children of that color, to know that one is in the presence of nonsense. Whiteness, along with all the other "races" whites created, is no more than the codification of hierarchies of relative oppression and exploitation. "Black," these "whiteness" specialists tell us, has been arbitrarily formulated as the most depraved and degraded category of all. Yet it is blacks who fight hardest to maintain the tautology, to cram every possible "black" into the leaky lifeboat with them, to define the parameters of the category most narrowly. One cannot help snickering at the ridiculous nobility with which the Jefferson-Hemings heretofore "white" descendants nobly accepted their newly discovered blackness when presented with DNA evidence that there was once a black in their lineage, however many generations ago.

Blackness is existential Play-Doh: it's biology, it's ideology, it's sociology. Blacks are liberals and Democrats. Blacks support affirmative action and marry other blacks. Blacks never criticize other blacks "in front of" whites. Bill Clinton was the first "black" president because he had no daddy, poor nutritional habits, played the sax, and was sexually self-destructive. "Monster" Kody Scott, an L.A. gangbanger turned community leader, was headed for a body bag until, in Folsom, radical Muslims informed him that "the real battle is with the white oppressor."[13] Were whites not such villains, the Monster would have had no reason to stop dealing drugs and making his neighborhood a living hell. Why couldn't contemplation of his own evil reform him? By the way, against whom had he been fighting his "false" battle? Himself? Other blacks? Decency? "Obviously and unavoidably, the black American," Chester Himes observed, is "the most neurotic, complicated, schizophrenic, unanalyzed, anthropologically advanced specimen of mankind in the history of the world."[14] Amen.

In a women's magazine spread dedicated to the different parts of the body, most of the writers rhapsodized about the heart, the brain, the skin, and so on, on their own terms. Not black poet Nikki Giovanni, who was tasked to praise the feet. Her contribution was a lugubrious ode to black oppression (e.g., "Out ran the mob in Tulsa / Got caught in Philadelphia / And am still unreparated"). She ended her dirge thus:

> It is appropriate I sing
> The praise of the feet
> I am a Black Woman.[15]

Blacks simply do not know who and how to be absent oppression. To cease invoking racism and reveling in its continuance is to lose the power to haunt whites, the one tattered possession they'll fight for while their true freedom molders unclaimed. It is to lose the power to define themselves as the opposite of something evil, rather than on their own terms. Much more bravery is required to assert black power, set an autonomous agenda, and court the failure that too many blacks fear is all they're capable of. DuBois writes of this black quest to overcome the oppressor's voice within and to believe in oneself: blacks must overcome "the temptation of Hate, that stood out against the red dawn; the temptation of Despair, that darkened noonday; and the temptation of Doubt, that ever steals along twilight."[16] They must struggle with those temptations as they cross the Valley of Humiliation and the Valley of the Shadow of Death. It's melodramatic but, one hundred years later, still apt. It is progress that the only Shadow of Death that blacks face today is not the rope but the political death of questioning the knee-jerk black agenda. And, of course, that to be found in a direct confrontation with black crime. These foes are not as terrible as those that Martin Luther King and Ida B. Wells faced, but they are formidable nonetheless.

Indeed, much fortitude is required to redefine "black failure"—a white supremacist notion—as simply "black problems that need addressing, however much hooting whites may do." If blacks don't accept that high incarceration rates say more about white chicanery than about the black character, why should whites?

The legitimate demurral to transracialism is, of course, the valid argument that if blacks accept it, then whites will then have gotten away with their crimes. But blacks ought to accept this frustrating outcome. There's no way to define blacks as the group owed by "whites" without keeping whites at the center of black agenda-setting. It's a maddening but obvious choice.

What passes today for knowledge of a self-reliant, sovereign black past untainted by slavery and Jim Crow is the reinvention of carpetbagging Afrocentrists. Instead of carrying out substantive studies of African history, these charlatans imagine glorious achievements such as the Bronze Age African development of airplanes or routinized surgery. Another variant is "Yoruba priestesses," like the best-selling Iyanla Vanzant, who traffic in ancestor nostalgia. Draped in flowing "African" garb, Vanzant is given to pronouncements like:

The ancients knew the connection between man and the Divine. They knew that buried beneath the personality, perceptions and self-imposed limitations there [lies] a spirit of unlimited possibility. . . . "The ancient ones knew that only with diligent maintenance of the mind and emotions would man master his fate."[17]

But why couldn't these ancient wise ones master the fate that made their children disappear into the Middle Passage? If the ancients possessed wisdom, and Vanzant possesses it today, why don't modern black Africans possess it? Few emigrate to Africa these days. Also from Vanzant:

The ancient Africans knew that no matter what was going to happen, it would not happen until it happened. Therefore, they were prepared for all possibilities, the good and the bad.[18]

Like being colonized by Europe? Like falling prey to the worst Marxist and strongman excesses? Like being branded and shipped to the South Carolina rice fields? Did these ancient superbeings with perfect mind control suffer in their servitude? And if they didn't, wasn't Massa correct when he swore that his slaves were content?

What Vanzant and the Afrocentrist conjurers are doing is positing ancestors in a vacuum. Their world has no slave traders, no slaves. No oppressors, no victims. No tainted from contact with whites. Impossible ancestors. Given the regions that most blacks came from, few west coast Africans born after the late fifteenth century lived a life innocent of the lucre and danger, let alone knowledge, of whites and slavery. Certainly modern apologists fail to point out that whites left Africans little choice but to participate, and that whites were endless in their machinations to expand and transform the slave trade. Then as now, the powerful knew how to camouflage their trail and make the world their accomplice. Still, the fact remains that blacks' ancestors cannot be separated from slavery's stain or from the knowledge of whites and their effect on the continent.

What Vanzant and the other Afrocentric hustlers are invoking is mytho-ancestors, so far outside the past as to be in fables. These nearly deified creatures are capable of anything, as long as it's good. The ancestor nostalgists impute omniscient holiness to them, making modern blacks, by extraction, exalted, angels fallen through the treachery of the unscrupulous vandals, much as the unwashed hordes defeated glorious Rome, except that that actually happened. There is no difference between these believers and the Sons of the Confederacy; both seek to cleanse themselves—of humiliation in the first instance, and of evil in the second—by reinventing those who bequeathed those unholy legacies to them. Blacks feel the need to deify their forebears, make them float above and outside an inglorious reality. The children of the Confederacy and Jim Crow feel the need to humanize theirs, remove them from the realm of monsters. A North Carolina community college offered a class called "North Carolina's Role in the Southern War for Independence," taught by two members of a Confederate heritage group. They taught that the "slaves were happy in their captivity," that "tens of thousands of slaves fought patriotically for the South and that the Civil War was not a battle over slavery."[19] Those things had to be true, in their eyes, otherwise their ancestors were bad people basting now on spits in hell.

The black importunings, however, are nothing more than the fantasies of the unhappy child who imagines that her "real" parents—the handsome, wealthy, famous explorers—will soon come to rescue her and punish the subhumans who now hold her hostage to their mediocrity.

Most damning, most cunning, and perhaps most responsible for the inability of certain blacks to form a viable black identity has been whites' insatiable sexual desire for their chattel and, later, their serfs. This mongrelization of the American black, for better or worse, renders him incapable of truly separating from those who enslaved him. (Of course, whites are mongrels, too. They've just decided not to "know" it. At least five percent of whites have African roots, while as many as two-thirds of blacks have European ones and two-fifths have native American ones[20].) To truly separate from Massa, blacks would have to at least partially disown themselves, given the extensive mingling of the races and given whites' reluctance to identify themselves in black birth records. Hence the ingeniousness of keeping blacks illiterate and ignorant, of denying slave families the protections of the law and so readily severing them.[21] We have no way to know whose great-grandmothers were raped, whose were prostitutes, whose were love slaves as well as chattel slaves. We have no way to prove that Massa was also your daddy. But isn't it really better that way, having no way to know how to feel about the whites who may or may not be your relatives? It leaves you with nothing to do but make the mature choice and just move on, ensuring that you add no more injustice to the world's already full measure.

Instead, blacks have meekly accepted whites' cramped vision of themselves as always and only black, and of blackness as always and only something less than. This explains the current white push for the understanding of their children with blacks as bi- or multiracial, not as black. Now that they are ready to legitimize such unions and their offspring, they are tacitly acknowledging that "black" is bad, less than, or at least an amputation of healthy limbs. At a minimum they are acknowledging that "blackness" is meaningless. The impulse is the same as for the white parents who didn't want their kids' school named for Martin Luther King so their kids wouldn't be thought of as black.

Why do blacks accept white definitions of blackness, even

though they are so obviously meant to be a straitjacket, a "do not enter" sign, an invisible fence meant to confine beasts to the property? Ponder these pronouncements: "The mixed-race South African is one of a few Black classicists holding a full-time academic position at an American university."[22] Is he mixed-race, or is he black? Is he both? Why does it matter, as long as he's qualified to fill the niche for which he was selected? "Four historically black colleges are majority white." Are they still black? In announcing that the first historically black fraternity had been chartered at the University of Wyoming, it was noted that currently two Samoans and a Hispanic student were in the chapter and that the organization "encourages everyone to join."[23] So what makes it a black fraternity? One smells the same tar pits in which whites' racial imaginations have for so long been trapped.

Why did black comedians fill the airwaves and comedy clubs with bitter demands for half-Thai golfer Tiger Woods, who calls himself "cablinasian," to identify as black? "Let the police catch him with a white girl in his car," went one all-too-typical observation. "Then he'll know he's black." When a golf official joked that Woods would request fried chicken and watermelon as his celebration dinner, blacks were gleeful. "It wasn't 'fish heads and rice,' was it? Tiger know he black!" hooted another overjoyed comic. But if the comment was racist, why were they so happy? Why were they focused on Woods instead of the offending white? Misery never loved company more than among blacks.

Harry Houdini once famously struggled for hours picking a jail cell lock, only to lean against it in exhaustion and have the door swing open. It had never been locked at all. All that confined him was in his own head. That's blackness.

How can it be that blacks—with eyes, skin tones, hair textures, and facial features too numerous to catalog, who among them-

selves wistfully invoke their Indian and European ancestry[24]—
are not leading the way to a transracial future? Frederick Douglass said that a man painting him insisted that he show

> my full face, for that is Ethiopian. Take my side face, said I,
> for that is Caucasian. But should you try my quarter face you
> would find it Indian. I don't know that any race can claim
> me, but being identified with slaves as I am, I think I know
> the meaning of the inquiry.[25]

Like *el-hajj* Malcolm X, Douglass saw his mission as breaking down the walls between the races. He knew this was the
future of America. If you can't know exactly who you are and
where you come from, you can choose to be victimized by that
ignorance, or you can make some educated guesses and consider
yourself a citizen of the world, free to add and subtract from
your identity with what you're able to piece together. Why
should blacks not think of themselves as akin to the unidentifi-
ably mixed-race foundlings who are so hard to place but who
have no choice but to grow up? They might be descended from
knaves, but then again they might be kings. Either way, they're
born innocent. To steal someone's past is also to free him from
it; why allow the thief to aggravate his crime by defining your
new identity for you?

Instead, blacks rhetorically damn the oppressor to hell while
fetishizing every stray remnant of his DNA.[26] While the black
beauty image is certainly undergoing a much-needed redefinition,
light skin, light eyes, and nonnappy hair still make a black attractive, however else he looks. Seventy-five percent of black women
straighten their hair and spend hundreds of millions of dollars
on hair weaves and pieces, skin bleach, colored contacts, nose
jobs, and lightening hair dyes. Not all of them are self-hating—
but one or two must be. Why else would such women (espe-

cially Latinas, bi- and multiracial women) be overrepresented in music videos, on TV shows, in movies, and on runways? Generations ago blacks summed up this phenomenon thus:

If you white, you all right
If you brown, stick around
If you black, get back

Many black women argue that straightened hair is simply easier to manage, but how would they know? Most haven't seen their natural hair since starting school. Were they to stop straightening their hair, they'd have no idea what would sprout from their heads. It seems not to occur to them that they might even learn to love it or be more attractive au naturel. Black hair-straightening has come to be seen as a matter of personal hygiene; America's streets teem with black women with lifeless, ragged, helmet hair offgassing chemicals, hair that fights every aspect of their physiognomy.

The significance of such a seemingly unworthy topic for social discussion is the reality that most black women simply do not realize that *not* straightening their hair is an option. Yet if hair breakage and scalp reactions to the harsh chemicals are common and are accepted as natural, it can only be because straight hair is natural, even if achieving and maintaining it consumes your time, sends you to the dermatologist, and empties your wallet. If artificially straightened hair on a black person is natural, then what is unprocessed, nappy hair? With straightening products named African Natural, African Pride, and Nubian Natural, and with bleaching creams called Skin Success, the schizophrenia and self-hatred aren't even subconscious. As Carter G. Woodson wrote, "Along with this sum [that Blacks spend on studying other races instead of their own], of course should be considered the large amount paid for devices in trying not to be Negroes."[27] How little has changed in eighty years.

Black women nearly lost the ability to care for their hair in its natural state. There has lately been a resurgence in natural hair, which has brought about a rash of books and videos on how to comb, style, and care for it. But who else on the planet needs such things? A joke e-mail that makes the rounds of black computers is "You Know It's a Ghetto Salon when . . ." (see page 219). One way is, "You want your real hair styled, and no one knows how." This refers to the proliferation of extensions, wigs, and hairpieces but also to natural hair (though at an up-scale salon they are probably even less likely to know).

Still, blacks come by their color consciousness honestly. The income gap between light-skinned blacks and dark-skinned blacks is the same as the income gap between whites and blacks; more light-skinned blacks hold white-collar, professional jobs than darker-skinned ones. Pre-movement, black organizations played a role, using the "paper bag test" or combing applicants' hair to screen out the Negroid. In 2001 a black ad agency hired to launch a campaign for a black college was found to have rejected student-actors with natural hair styles and dark skin.

And yet while "if you black, get back" is an indictment of self-hatred and colorism, it simultaneously acknowledges that the light-skinned fare better. Perhaps it's self-hating to "offset" dark skin with a luxurious weave, but it may also be merely calculating. One of the most intelligent, unselfconscious black TV sitcoms (Girlfriends) posited a situation wherein the ensemble's darkest woman rejected a very black, though in every way superior, suitor so that her children would not be Negroid. Vehemently, she explained that her own darkness had cost her friends, love, employment, and respect throughout her life, and she made no bones about having done everything in her power to offset it, including a weave. Her friends, two of them visibly biracial and one with a very long weave, accepted her justification, dropped their protests, and sympathized.

Some argue that black women's unrelenting attention to their appearance, especially their hair, speaks not to an infatuation with whites but to blacks' innate sense of style and innovation. They argue that it is in part a residual Africanism and tells you nothing about the self-image of the twenty-first-century black woman in a waist-length blond wig. The reminder that Africans often emulated animal beauty (e.g., by filing their teeth or elongating their necks) is a useful, calming reminder that admiration and emulation are transcendent human traits; Roman wives dyed their hair red when Irish slave girls began appearing as their husbands' concubines, yet it is unlikely that the free felt inferior to the owned. It is a sign of mature homage to give the rippling beauty of a mass of titian curls its due; only America's context of white norms as the starting point of every discussion obscures that fact.

No one who has seen the scholarship on the astonishing art of traditional African hairstyles and garments can fail to agree that blacks have come by their sartorial and cosmetic virtuosity honestly. These traits flourish most richly among the black folk, the submiddle class and non–Ivy League, the class most distant from white norms, just as natural hair styles flourish there the least. These blacks often see natural hair as repugnant, while wigs, extensions, mutable hair colors, and the like connote merely fashion. These things are openly spoken of. Black comediennes regularly do routines structured around the goings-on in the "Chinese shops" where they acquire their fake hair and in the ghetto hair salons where coloring, straightening, and lengthening procedures are undergone. If they were self-hating, they wouldn't speak of it.[28] It's the black bourgeois who get the unacknowledged nose jobs, the sudden hair, and the green eyes that no one ever mentions. And it is they who are most embarrassed by the purple "dukey braids" and Fu Manchu fingernails of the black postal worker or cafeteria lady. It is they who most believe white lies about black ugliness and white beauty, black stupidity and white genius. They are the ones who long to be loved by whites and want them to confess to their sins so that they can bestow a harsh forgiveness, the only kind of power these blacks can imagine themselves wielding. Whites must act in order to equalize the relationship, while blacks stand by for further concessions.

More than anything else—more than physiognomy, more than cultural traits, more than the class structure, more than residential segregation, more than the most virulent racism— it is the low self-esteem and backward-looking focus of these please-love-me blacks that retard their progress. The day they stop demanding redress from the powerful white majority and the "me next" immigrant class is the day blacks may claim full from-this-moment-on equality.

Let us be clear: whites, and the minorities who may have suffered but nonetheless outrank blacks, have no intention of accepting any more responsibility than they already have for America's history of black oppression or for the present effects of that oppression. They point to the macrolevel advancements— *Brown v. Board,* the 1964 Civil Rights Act, the Voting Rights Act, the movement dead, the trillions spent on urban renewal and welfare programs. They subtract from that sum the costs of black crime and any other black misbehavior (uncorrelated with the societal origins of those problems)—and announce themselves greatly satisfied with their own generosity. The past (the slavery and Jim Crow part, not the glorious heroism of America's founding part) ended for white people in 1980 with the election of Ronald Reagan. After one grudging generation of change, white people declared themselves to have had quite enough.

But Reagan had opposed even that much change. He'd opposed both the Civil Rights Act of 1964 and the Voting Rights Act of 1965 and was a founding member of the Republican Party's "southern strategy," to woo white Democratic voters rightward with winks and whispers ("law and order"), code words and coddling ("states' rights"). He owed his political fortune to the support of powerful, unreconstructed racists like Jesse Helms.

But the coup de grâce was the Great Communicator's first speech after the 1980 convention, in Philadelphia, Mississippi. Just sixteen years earlier the young civil rights workers James Chaney, Andrew Goodman, and Michael Schwerner had been murdered there by local Klansmen in one of the most heinous crimes of the civil rights movement. Reagan, however, failed even to acknowledge that the infamous murders had taken place, so contemptuous was he of black complaint and any hint of white capitulation. Instead, he spoke in racial semaphore: "I believe in states' rights and I believe in people doing as much as they can for themselves at the community level and at the private level."[29]

That was the end of the civil rights movement and the second abandonment of Reconstruction. It was the end of white acceptance of further responsibility to blacks, let alone to justice or to any need even to consider whether social structures and outcomes were just. On the killing fields of Philadelphia, Mississippi, symbol of centuries of unpunished white-on-black violence, symbol of white intention to retain its access to the black body, whites forgave themselves and moved on. Henceforth their actions would be, by definition, not racist. Was it white flight when they fled a neighborhood when blacks moved in? No, it was pragmatic, if regretful, concern for their family's safety, they said. Were the police guilty of brutality? No, it was just that blacks committed all the crimes—and with such violence, one might add. It's the drugs. Mortgage redlining? It can't be happening—capitalism is always and everywhere rational. Employment discrimination? That doesn't happen anymore, but if it did, it would be because blacks are just so unqualified; they have a hard time fitting in. They make the customers uncomfortable. I had one before, and he just didn't want to work.

It defies human nature for people to see themselves as evil, let alone responsible, and American whites and immigrants are no different. Just a few years after apartheid ended, white South Africans were decrying their "victimization" at the hands of the black majority, given that they'd had "nothing to do" with apartheid. This headline from 2002 says it all: SOUTH AFRICAN WHITES SAY DECK STACKED AGAINST THEM: MANY NON-BLACKS COMPLAIN THEY ARE UNFAIRLY PENALIZED BY AFFIRMATIVE ACTION.[30] In Bosnia the perpetrators of genocide saw themselves as the victims, vilified by an international media determined to abuse them. An American war journalist told of a Serb officer who showed her photos of a Muslim home. "Look at how they live!" he said in disgust, pointing out mean furniture and dirty windows. He made no mention of the family lying massacred among their pathetic possessions. An American visiting Japan noted:

> what is infuriating about the [Hiroshima] museum is the contextlessness of it. It posits a world that begins at 8 a.m. on Aug. 6, 1945, a world in which Japan is simply a victim, the A-bomb purely a war crime and America . . . simply a criminal state. . . . [I]n what history there is, there is the usual Japanese whitewash. Japan "recruited" Korean laborers to work in Hiroshima's war factories (yeah, recruited with the barrel of a gun!), Japan "was hurtled into war" by Pearl Harbor. "Was hurtled"? Didn't Japan do the hurtling?

More irritating is that American reasons for dropping the

bomb are totally ignored or distorted. In this entire vast museum . . . there are exactly three sentences devoted to why the bomb was used. These sentences are in a tiny typeface [hidden] behind another exhibit. . . . listed under a headline "Hurried Use" were.

1. to force Japan to surrender.
2. to win the war before [the] USSR entered it
3. to measure the effectiveness of the bomb.[31]

Nobody knows the trouble you've seen, even if your trouble is the difficulty of finding good servants. A Vietnamese or Colombian immigrant does not accept that the descendants of slaves have anything on him; he can distance himself from the American past and its effect on the American present while helping himself to the benefits made possible by that past. They see no contradiction between invoking the heroism of the frontiersmen while simultaneously disallowing evil coincident institutions to be associated with the present. They triumphantly deny having forebears who immigrated here before 1865, but they feel free to avail themselves of institutions and social structures that predate their family's arrival. What is the most often repeated lie in America? That we are "a nation of immigrants." Slaves were not immigrants, and conflating the two is just another attempt to disguise the past and mute blacks.

It's adopting George Washington but not George Wallace. The Fourteenth Amendment but not the Jim Crow Black Codes. The Homestead Acts that gave stolen land dripping with Indian blood to any immigrant fresh off the boat, but not the forty acres and a mule of which two centuries of slavery could not make blacks worthy. Reconstruction and the mollification of whites oppressed by having to give up slavery, but not lynchings. Not minstrel shows, not the serfdom of the black sharecropper, not the disenfranchisement of the taxed and draft-subject black polity, not the unfettered sexual access to black women's bodies justified by their inherent wantonness. Not the humiliation of an entire race of people whose labor America ruthlessly set out to steal and whose belief in itself America set out specifically to crush. Modern whites and even the freshest of immigrants live proudly with the glorious past of American achievement; they are blasé about the ugly, willfully amorphous past of American infamy. It's the present and the future in which they might be inconvenienced with which they cannot live.

No doubt, humans are selective in their outrage.

They are fascinated with their own sufferings, real or imagined, and simply bored with others'. Worse, they are annoyed, if those sufferings inconvenience them. This is just as true of blacks as of whites. There is no justice. A quick trip around the globe proves that, and it has ever been true. Evil reigns unchecked until . . . it is checked. The dead do not come back to life. Lash marks do not disappear. The victors write the history books and neuter their crimes with the mellifluous phrasing of epic verse. The world will never know what Africa might have been had its future not been both squandered and stolen. A sad little e-mail recently made the black rounds arguing that natural disasters follow the path that the slave ships took instead of accepting that the sun rises each day over the just and the unjust alike.[32] Adults realize and accept this. Adults don't get mad, they get even; living well is the best revenge.

The farther we come from the days of obvious oppression, the less tolerant are whites of calls for them to exhibit shame, guilt, or a sense of responsibility. Certainly, the less willing they are to concede the problematics associated with all the Great Society programs, the "failure" of which they claim now absolves America of the need for further investment in black uplift. They have made all the amends they ever intend to make. They have already given too much, really, considering their lack of personal involvement with slavery and Jim Crow. They see themselves as generous, given that no one is alive today who owned slaves and that the notion of white skin privilege is one at which to hoot. Jim Crow, as well, has been rehabilitated as a period of generalized white rudeness at worst and, at best, a defense of traditional values and states' rights, rather than as the means by which slavery, serfdom, second-class citizenship, and structural inequality were woven into the fabric of American life. Villains in mainstream civil rights movies (which are almost always about white people; blacks are mostly there to be murdered or to sing gospel) stand in as whipping boys for actual white people who get to ritualistically cleanse their consciences and glory in their own vicarious heroism, white heroism being the true point of these movies. Finding a white of the relevant age today who believed in Jim Crow or will admit to being part of the mob scenes in movement footage is like trying to find a seventy-year-old Frenchman who *wasn't* part of the Resistance or who *did* collaborate. It's surprisingly easy, however, to be regaled with tales of whites who defied racial norms in some personal, off-the-record way.

The reason whites deny the past and remain unmoved by its present effects is not because they are racist and selfish. Rather, they are racist and selfish because privilege is all but impossible to give up and is equally impossible to hoard without warping one's personality. Martin Luther King had to die because he kept reiterating this point: one cannot retain both privilege and morality.

The rich must argue that people are poor by choice rather than by policy. Whites must argue that blacks are criminal by nature rather than because of a systemic lack of opportunity (except to be prosecuted). Immigrants must argue that their suffering in their homeland frees them of responsibility for conditions in the land to which they've contributed nothing. Haves need to believe that they're better off because they are smarter and work harder. All one need do then is work backward from the maintenance of one's own privilege to explain away its effect on the have-nots. That, and relinquish another chunk of one's humanity, because power really does corrupt, even at the micro-level.

One reason blacks' complaints, however justified, are counterproductive is that they aim at the wrong target. It's not the racism per se, it's the overlapping but unacknowledgeable needs that result in racism. Those farther up the privilege pile need to simultaneously retain their perks while also retaining the right, along with their forebears, to feel blameless. Hence the rehabilitation of the Confederate flag. It's really not about southern whites flaunting their racism, the way high school boys weakly camouflage "fuck you's" amid flagrantly fake coughs. They, being human, can neither renounce their inheritance nor accept the responsibility for it. The only way out is to wave the magic wand and not have been born of evildoers. Hence the Confederacy must be fumigated and recapitulated as an antiseptic vessel of pure tradition. They have convinced themselves that it wasn't about slavery but about honor. They had to. More than feeling blameless, whites, like everyone else, want to feel heroic, generous, and superior—and most of all, entitled.

THE EMPTINESS OF MULTICULTURALISM AND AFROCENTRISM

Blacks who helped win the Revolution, the West, and America's wars may have been airbrushed from America's memory of itself, but so has Yuri Kochiyama. She is the Japanese American activist who held her dying comrade Malcolm X on the floor of the Audubon Ballroom; the memory that she has been excised from is black America's.

Probably only a scattered few blacks know (or would care to) of the shared African Asian legacy forged in the cane fields of the Caribbean—Cuba in particular—where slaves and coolies labored making sugar. In the nineteenth century Chinese were kidnapped or lured from their villages and introduced to the lash. Havana recorded the sale of 125,000 Chinese; no one knows how many forced laborers went undocumented. Less than 50 percent of them survived eight years in the hell that was the sugar plantations. (Most blacks have no idea of the difference between the North American slave experience and the much more vicious Caribbean one.)

Nor do most blacks know that it was not as slaves that Africans and Asians first met; contact, cooperation, and respect preceded the white man. In 1416, after sporadic previous encounters, African ambassadors made their peaceful way to China and bestowed gifts of exotic animals like giraffes, oxen, and zebras. In 1418 the Chinese Muslim admiral Cheng Ho and the Imperial Chinese fleet of 300 ships and 28,000 men returned both the favor and the ambassadors.[33]

Who knows now that Richard Wright was a master of haiku? That Ralph Ellison was a devotee of flamenco? That Malcolm X was half-Grenadan? That Frederick Douglass was half white, part Indian, and an ardent transracialist as well as a feminist and internationalist? That Katherine Dunham incorporated Asian dance forms and rituals into her performance art? That black volunteers fought fascism in the Spanish Civil War, even as the 1930s America they faced was staunchly segregated? That Howard University, founded in 1867, is named for white Civil War general Oliver Otis Howard? That Bayard Rustin, invaluable behind-the-scenes adviser to the civil rights movement, affected an English accent, recited English poetry over opponents he felled on the football field, and was homosexual? That when Carter G. Woodson established Negro History Week in 1926, he chose February because he felt that the three greatest Americans were born then: George Washington, Frederick Douglass, and Abraham Lincoln, in that order.[34]

Blacks may say they are "multicultural," but they tout only black history and culture. They may say "Afrocentric" but not until reduced to its thinnest vein, mere blackface. Kwanzaa, indeed. Fertility dolls, wall masks, kente cloth accessories—consumerism as politics. What about traveling to Africa? What about learning the classical Arabic in which Sudanic Africa's precolonial history is recorded? What about taking an interest in the continent, or at least in West Africa, the way American Jews do in Israel? Outside the academy wearing natural hair styles is as close as most blacks come to any Afrocentrism beyond the rhetorical. More, most blacks *separate themselves* out from their historic interconnectedness with Asia and North Africa—why?

To be facile, they don't care because they don't know and are complacent. Just as whites dismiss African culture because, if it were important, they'd know about it, blacks dismiss any aspect of their personality that isn't slavery- or Jim Crow–related. What's important is that which refers back to whites in a way that disfavors whites.

The more complicated explanation for their indifference is that "multiculturalism" and "Afrocentrism" are as much euphemisms when used by blacks as by whites. They mean: "a pox on Western culture; it is innately oppressive. I can't appreciate Shakespeare because then I would be a collaborator and no longer black. Blackness, the only thing I have the confidence to claim or know how to be, is my culture."

W.E.B. DuBois saw it differently: "I sit with Shakespeare and he winces not. Across the color line I move arm in arm with Balzac and Dumas, where smiling men and welcoming women glide in gilded halls. . . . I summon Aristotle and Aurelius and what soul I will, and they come all graciously with no scorn nor condescension."[35] DuBois was being a little too grateful, but his point is valid: knowledge and art don't discriminate, they give themselves to the world, just as the medicines derived from African knowledge work as effectively on a Montanan as on a Mauritanian. Also, the meanings of art and knowledge change over time and with greater access: Alexander Dumas, we know now, was black. Art is democratic; rejecting true multicultural-ism, given the world's mongrelization, may well mean rejecting yourself.

This debased Afrocentrism is really a form of resistance; a mudcloth handbag tells the world nothing about a black person that her skin already did not. The problem is that it can also be self-eliminative and isolationist. If blacks celebrated the vastness of their vision and experience, they'd have to share the world's regard, not to mention its pity, with others. Just like whites, they want the glory, even of their victimization, all to themselves. They are no more empathetic of others' problems than whites are of blacks'. They are bored, annoyed even, at the gall of the Chinese in trying to include themselves as victims in slavery's holy hell, at some Japanese girl deflecting attention from mar-tyred Malcolm. Like whites, blacks don't think there is very much to themselves, just the mess that whites have made of them. They do not exist in their own right—they exist as a living rebuke to America.

In the 1940s, noir writer Chester Himes made the same point. When his character Bob Jones is asked whether Bigger Thomas, the hero of Richard Wright's *Native Son,* is the appropriate symbol of Negro oppression, he responds, "Well, you couldn't pick a better person than Bigger Thomas to prove the point. But after you prove it, then what?"[36]

AFRICA-BASHING

Blacks are ambivalent, trending toward horrified, about Africa. American to the core, they have internalized Western contempt for it. Of Africa they are equally ignorant and essentialist; the link some claim to feel does not extend much beyond kente cloth mousepads and Hallmark Kwanzaa cards, especially since the demise of apartheid. Black comedians joke about going to get "one a them African bitches" (she would be "nekkid, riding on a zebra") to replace the avaricious American ones, the point being to acquire a woman untouched by civilization. Hopefully, his African bitch won't boil him in a pot of water and dance about it. In answer to a question that he thought was an insult to his intelligence, basketball star Magic Johnson once rejoined, "Where you think I'm from: Africa?" on the nation's leading chat show. Preparing for a trip to Zaire, Carl E. Officer, the black mayor of East St. Louis, Illinois, announced that he would carry his own blood supply in case of accident; he didn't want to be transfused with "monkey blood."[37] African immigrants stockpile appalling anecdotes about the ignorant racism they face from American blacks; they are asked whether they live in houses, or if tigers chase them. After filming a movie there, black actor Will Smith said:

> [South Africa] was the most beautiful place I've ever been in the world. And that pissed me off. I was angry that I was so miseducated. It was actually a shock to see fine women, and I don't know why. Because you can listen to black comedians

who haven't been to Africa talk about Africa, and you know, "bones in the nose" and all that type of stuff. There are parts of South Africa that [make you feel like] you're in Manhattan or Detroit or Philly.[38]

Perhaps. But when blacks read that nearly a thousand "witches" were slaughtered before the Ugandan military was able to stop it, they despise Africa, too. When they read that South Africa has one of the world's worst rape problems, in which African men gang-rape girls as young as five months old because they believe virgins cure AIDS, that half of all South African women will be raped with little recourse to justice, that white settlers are macheted, that females are sexually disfigured by their loved ones, and that the violent crime rate is ten times America's, they too think that Africa is a savage beast that cannot be civilized. They think Africa has bones through its heart. Knowing only a caricature, they prefer not to think of Africa at all, except indirectly through its dance, its art, its fabrics, and innumerable "libations" poured to amorphous "ancestors" before fashion shows and fraternity meetings.

A more thoughtful, explicit rejection of a psychological link to Africa, however, comes from a black journalist, Keith B. Richburg, who covered the genocide and civil wars there from 1991 to 1994. He witnessed such corruption, ignorance, and inhumanity that he became sickened by the African soul. So transformative was his time there, he wrote a book about it, describing how it enhanced his Americanness, forever ridding him of any ambivalence for his Western birthright.[39]

Awaiting safe passage past government-sponsored, murdering soldiers one night, Richburg had an epiphany:

Are these really my people? Am I truly an *African* American? . . . I am terrified of Africa. I don't want to be from this place. In my darkest heart here on this pitch black African night, I am quietly celebrating the passage of my ancestor who made it out. . . .

There are some photographs I have kept. . . . The first . . . shows a . . . Kenyan man . . . trussed up like a chicken, . . . surrounded by a jubilant mob. . . . The man's co-workers had . . . stripped [him], verified the presence of foreskin, and arranged for a ritualistic circumcision . . . on the spot. He was . . . rolled ceremoniously through Nairobi's streets. . . . [A] tribal chieftain . . . would perform this rite . . . with no anesthesia, probably using a dull, rusted, unclean blade. . . .

[Another photo] shows . . . a teenager, . . . held down by a mob, screaming with terror. One of his hands has been chopped off. An older man is . . . gleefully holding . . . a giant meat cleaver . . . smiling, preparing to drop down hard and chop off the other hand. [The] boy has been caught stealing. . . . This was in Nairobi, supposedly one of the most modern capitals of black Africa. And these scenes were happening within walking distance of my own home.

How could I possibly relate to these Africans, when we are separated by such a wide gulf of culture and background and emotion and sensitivity? . . . And what frightens me most of all is that these smiling people in the photographs look just like me.

Had my ancestor not made it out of here, I might have ended up there in that crowd, smiling gleefully, while a man with a cleaver cuts off the hands of a thief.[40]

Interesting that Richburg's debased alter ego would mill in the crowd like the nameless white vigilantes in movement footage who spit on praying black grandmothers, then go home to mow the lawn. He would be neither chopped nor chopper, circumcised nor circumcisor. He would be happily complicit embodying the black soul adrift in the nameless noir of the depravity that is Africa. His evil too would be banal. Whites look, when forced, at their animal selves in the jubilant photos commemorating lynchings, in movement footage, in rioting crowds at concerts or sports championships, in videos of policemen brutalizing unarmed black civilians and think, *That's not us. That's not me. That's an aberration. This is out of context— you don't understand.* They see people, not white people. Blacks look at Richburg's photos and think, *That's who we really are. That's all we are. This picture is self-explanatory. Why can't we be civilized, like white people?*

Repeatedly, Richburg speaks of not wanting to be from Africa in his "darkest"—not deepest—heart, of his ancestors having "made it out." They'd escaped, been rescued even. They were refugees, not kidnap victims.

However correct his assessment of Africa, it is clear that he sees slavery and Jim Crow as the price to pay for having the sub-human scourged from his soul, *à la* Zora Neale Hurston, who said, "Slavery is the price I paid for civilization, and the choice was not with me. It is a bully adventure and worth all that I have paid through my ancestors for it."[41] Easy for her to say. That Africa's present condition is only one of many different trajectories upon which it might have embarked does not occur to Richburg (or Hurston).[42] What if its colonizers had been mentors? What if they'd taught Africa about democracy and individual rights instead of how to perfect its slave trading? What if America had imposed indentured servitude rather than lifelong slavery and subhuman status on its captives? Might some of the slaves not have returned to Africa with modern skills and technology, with DNA and family members from throughout the world who would adopt rather than colonize Africa, and who would bring invigorating ideas about liberty? It doesn't occur to him because, like his countrymen, he thinks

Africa is tainted at its core and that only exorcism can cure it. To be sure, the question of Africa's stagnation is a fair and a vexing one; even DuBois wondered, "Why has civilization flourished in Europe, and flickered, flamed, and died in Africa?" Unlike Africa-bashers, though, he wants to find the answer rather than stand "meekly dumb before such questions." That's because he doesn't think the answer will turn out to be Africa's, and Africans', innate unworthiness. Rather, the mystery of Africa's lag may be solved by mere geography, as Sowell observes:

Where geography creates population "islands" on land . . . or peoples who find only isolated patches of agriculturally viable land, as in . . . sub-Saharan Africa—there have been conspicuous cultural lags behind others who were either in contact with more of their own people or with other cultures more accessible by rivers, harbors, or plains. . . .

The enormous importance of rivers and harbors to economic and cultural development is indicated by the fact that nearly all the world's great cities have developed on rivers or harbors. This reflects in part the vast differences in costs between transporting goods by water and transporting them by land. . . . [E]ven in the twentieth century, the cost of shipping an automobile from Djibouti to Addis Ababa (342 miles) has been estimated as being the same as the cost of shipping it from Detroit to Djibouti (7,386 miles). . . . These same high transportation costs shrink the cultural universe as well. . . .

Although Africa is more than twice the size of Europe, the African coastline is shorter than the European coastline, whose twists and turns produce harbors and inlets all around the continent, while the relatively smooth coastline of Africa offers far fewer places were ships can anchor in a harbor, sheltered from the rough waters of the open sea. Moreover,

there are entire nations in Africa . . . without a single navigable river. . . . [J]ust as rainfall patterns limit the navigability of
rivers . . . , so the many rapids and waterfalls of Africa limit
the distances over which rivers can be navigated, even when
they have sufficient water. Because many of Africa's rapids
and waterfalls occur not far inland, even large rivers may
provide no practicable access for large-scale commerce from
the sea. The Zaire River, for example, is 2,900 miles long and
has a volume of water second only to that of the Amazon, but
it has rapids and waterfalls near the sea, thus preventing
oceangoing ships from reaching one of the largest networks
of navigable rivers in the world.

Across Europe and Asia—and, later, the Western Hemisphere and Australia—man's dependence on waterways has
been demonstrated again and again in the sites of leading
cities, from London to Bombay and from Sydney to Rio de
Janeiro. These ports became not only economic centers but
also cultural centers and centers of progress in general, as
cities have led the progress of civilization. Africa's most
famous civilization likewise arose, thousands of years ago,
within a few miles on either side of its longest navigable river,
the Nile. The two largest cities on the continent today—Cairo
and Alexandria—are both on the Nile. However, a general
lack of navigable waterways to facilitate economic and cultural interchanges has in Africa been reflected in a general
dearth of large cities, on what remains the world's least
urbanized continent. . . .

Although Africans are less than 10 per cent of the human
race, their many languages are one-third of all the languages
in the world, one index of their cultural fragmentation. . . .
The great number of languages and dialects . . . constitute as
well a severe handicap in themselves, inhibiting effective economic or political consolidation of numerous separate peo-

ples. . . . For the peoples of sub-Saharan Africa, the most formidable barrier to cultural interchanges . . . was the Sahara
Desert itself, which is larger than the continental United
States. It was not until the second millennium of the Christian
era that the central rain forest of Africa and the land south of
it were much influenced by the civilizations which had arisen
in other parts of the world—and, until the sixteenth century,
the influence of these civilizations was conveyed only through
Islamic intermediaries.[43]

Africans were neither too dim nor too apathetic to protect
themselves. They simply lost the topographical lottery.

Graves illuminates another obvious point that racist explanations predicated on African inferiority miss:

The classical response to concerns that the problems of
African Americans resulted from the degraded conditions of
slavery was to compare their lot to that of their "free"
brethren in Africa. Modern IQ theorists routinely compare
Africans to African Americans to try to prove a generalized
deficit in African intellect. In the scheme of these theorists,
the degraded conditions of blacks in the United States match
the lack of social progress of blacks in Africa.

However, if we properly understand that the African slave
trade affected both those who were enslaved and those who
remained, we can see that this comparison is not relevant.
The reduction of African population due to slavery opened
the way for the colonization of Africa. Consider just how
many lives were lost to the slave trade. There are three estimates of the magnitude of the trans-Atlantic slave trade in
Africa from 1450 to 1870, ranging from about 11 million to
30–60 million to as high as 100 million people enslaved. In
addition, the sub-Saharan slave trade included at least 9 mil-

lion people who were part of the Muslim trade to the east. The loss of individuals of reproductive age slowed growth on the African continent. One estimate takes the 19 million persons (10 million to North America and 9 million to the Muslim trade) removed from Africa and assumes a per capita increase in population half that exhibited by the North American slaves to postulate that the population of Africa at the end of the period of the slave trade was 99,420,000 less than it would have been had the slave trade not existed.

This realization also affects our understanding of the origin of European economic supremacy, particularly when we examine how the European populations benefited from the slave trade. In 1600, Africa and Europe had populations estimated at 55 million and 100 million, respectively. Europe's and Asia's populations doubled between 1600 and 1850, whereas the African population grew by only 30 per cent. The loss of potential population also contributed to the stagnation of African economic growth and made the continent vulnerable to colonization by European powers (which further accelerated stagnation). The fact is that African labor fueled the economic growth of Europe and its North American colonies, economic growth that in turn allowed the European populations to increase in number and in fitness at the expense of sub-Saharan Africans. This is the rationale for the charge of genocide in conjunction with colonialism and the slave trade. Africanist scholars . . . have named the slave trade as the root of the present-day problems faced by African nations.[44]

Whatever role Africa's geography and birth rate played in its cultural fragmentation and economic difficulties, it is a much likelier explanation than the innate inferiority of its people. Also, given that they have been free of their colonial overlords for only a generation, we have little idea of what modern Africans are capable. Perhaps the West should beware what the next generation of Africans might have in store for them:

> The history of conquest constitutes much of the history of the human race. The conquerors of one era are often the conquered of another. Ancient Rome imposed its yoke from Britain to North Africa and the Middle East, yet Rome itself has also been conquered many times by foreigners, its treasures looted, its people tortured, its women raped, and the defenseless slaughtered. . . .
>
> Before ancient Britain was invaded and conquered by the Roman legions, not a single Briton had ever done anything to leave his name in the pages of history. . . . An estimated one thousand years passed before the material standard of living in Europe rose again to the level achieved under the Romans. As late as the early nineteenth century, no city in Europe had as dependable a water supply as many European cities had had in the days of the Roman Empire.[45]

There is no reason, save racism, to assume that Africa cannot rebound with as great a success as England's. Occam's razor, a guiding Western principle, evaporates when blacks are under study, even with blacks.[46]

In Africa, in the faces of the bestial crowds that, hideously, look just like them, American blacks who have internalized white contempt for the heart of blackness see the soothed savage in themselves, they see the near-beast that whites see when they look at Africans or at NBA players. They look into the primordial mirror of the Motherland and are terrified to see that the bars on their cages are loose. They fear that full moon (a white woman's purse hanging ripely on her arm, a big-screen TV in a store window just as a blackout begins) that must bring out the werewolf in them. Only America, with its jackbooted police and straitjacketing racism, can control the African beast within them. The West, with all its superiority, is the only silver bullet strong enough to control an animal like them. Says Richburg:

> [F]or black Americans, I think, the reaffirmation of some kind of lost African identity is rooted more in fantasy than reality. Why would we, as Americans, want to embrace a continent so riven by tribal, ethnic, and religions [sic] hatreds? And besides, how can we, sons and daughters of America's soil, reaffirm an identity that for us never existed in the first place?[47]

No modern Westerner ever lived in ancient Rome or Athens—and few could trace a family tree branch within five hundred miles of them—but they still identify with them. They choose to. An African identity too can be acquired or even nonchalantly inherited, like a house you knew nothing of that you inherited from a dead great-uncle you never met. How else did Islam and Christianity spread throughout the world? Pantheists, Zoroastrians, or Jews one day, killed or converted the next.

There are Catholics in the American Southwest who light candles over their tamales on Friday but don't know why. Called Crypto Jews, their ancestors were forced to convert during the Inquisition. Some practiced in secret, but knowledge of their Judaism, let alone its substance, drained away over the generations. Eventually the last elder died before thinking the time was right to mention that they were "really" Jews. The modern black may be equally Crypto West African, especially given the segregation that functioned as existential amber to preserve culture. If Baraka and Murray are right, many more Africanisms than blacks are aware of reside within them still, from language to comportment to musical forms. If you know nothing of Africa's past or present, how do you know you aren't like an African?

Modern blacks, though, are so crypto that Africa embarrasses them; it could not do this if there was no relationship. What should embarrass them is the crass calculation in this line of rejection: were Africa modern and bustling, blacks would identify with it, perhaps reject America for it, but since it's often backward, better to deny it three times before the cock crows. One wonders what would happen if Africa awarded shares in diamond mines to any black who could prove lineage to the region.

Blacks assume a kinship with Africa until it makes them look bad, at which point they feel greatly indebted to those who "altered the base of their lineage and shifted it from its base in Africa to its new homeland in America." This is not to say that forced, unsanitary, unmedicated circumcision isn't wrong. But the formulation of the objection is also wrong—Africa's problems are not the result of innate black depravity, any more than black America's are.

After much soul-searching, Richburg finds after all "that black skin is not enough to bind him to Africa and that he is an American first, foremost, and singularly. . . . Thank God I am an American." Slavery was the tough but still-bargain price that blacks paid to avoid being African.

An unembarrassed African American realizes that, whether Africa is tainted at its core, whether it is more bad than good or vice versa, is irrelevant. He must still make his way in a world that does not wish him well; it has its selfish uses for him but otherwise acknowledges no sense of connection. He cannot help understanding that while America punished him for his blackness, that blackness didn't stop Africa from pimping him, then throwing him away. Shared blackness didn't make Africa come rescue its discarded ones once the horror was obvious or even no longer profitable. Disowned and abused by all who should have called them sons, blacks are free; they don't have to take Africa personally. They can choose to, but they don't have to. They have no debts to repay. Like the parent who abandoned a child who grows up to be rich and famous, it's too late now for Africa to expect a Mother's Day gift, though blacks may choose to offer one. The African American is adrift with his fellow orphans, but he is blameless. Unencumbered by responsibility except to himself as a moral, rational human being, he's earned the right to name his place in the world. He was prevented from exercising free will before but is now free to make a conscious choice—Africa, America, or any destination marked in his DNA, because you play in the bloodline, you pay.

Blacks are the oldest civilization, yet, they are to believe, the least worthy. They are to believe that white culture is culture. They've had millennia to earn their place in the world and have yet to do so. They never will. They should cease troubling the waters. Blacks themselves do not know what to believe and are easily swayed by either camp. Shrouded by time, misled by racial nostalgists, and lied to by fabricating Afrocentrists, blacks know virtually nothing about the truth of their origins. Of what they do know, it's either all good or all bad. Woodson understood the importance of addressing this deep-seated black confusion about African identity. He is worth listening to at length:

The Negro is as human as the other members of the family of mankind. The Negro, like others, has been up at times; and at times he has been down. With the domestication of animals, the discovery of iron, the development of stringed instruments, an advancement in fine art, and the inauguration of trial by jury to his credit, the Negro stands just as high as others in contributing to the progress of the world.

The oppressor, however, raises his voice to the contrary. He teaches the Negro that he has no worth-while past, that his race has done nothing significant since the beginning of time, and that there is no evidence that he will ever achieve anything great. The education of the Negro then must be carefully directed lest the race may waste time trying to do the impossible. Lead the Negro to believe this and thus control his thinking. If you can thereby determine what he will think, you will not need to worry about what he will do. You will not have to tell him to go to the back door. He will go without being told; and if there is no back door he will have one cut for his special benefit.

If you teach the Negro that he has accomplished as much good as any other race he will aspire to equality and justice without regard to race. Such an effort would upset the program of the oppressor in Africa and America. Play up before the Negro, then, his crimes and shortcomings. Let him learn to admire the Hebrew, the Greek, the Latin and the Teuton. Lead the Negro to detest the man of African blood—to hate himself. The oppressor then may conquer, exploit, oppress and even annihilate the Negro by segregation without fear or trembling. With the truth hidden there will be little expression of thought to the contrary.[48]

Africa may not have been heaven, but neither was it hell. All that's known for sure is that it is a place blacks did not leave voluntarily. As they try to decide how to feel about Africa, they should consider a few things. First, that the aspirations of American-born blacks—enfranchisement, individual liberty, opportunity—are American, not African. The enslaved or Jim Crowed black strove for a freedom he could not have experienced or even conceived of in Africa. Second, that no matter how bad conditions have been and continue to be for them here,

Africans nonetheless sent their own sons and daughters to the West to live and be educated, even as pogroms raged against their cousins. Finally, blacks should consider the words of two stowaway Guinean boys found dead in the cargo hold of an airplane in Brussels:

> We beseech you on behalf . . . [of] the love of God, who has granted you all the experience, wealth, and power to ably construct and organize your continent. We call upon your graciousness and solidarity to help us in Africa. Our problems are many: war, sickness, hunger, lack of education, and children's rights. We want to study, and we ask that you help us to become like you. . . .
>
> [I]f you find that we have sacrificed our lives, it is because we suffer too much in Africa. . . .
>
> Be mindful of us in Africa. There is no one else for us to turn to.[49]

They plead for their entire continent, not just for themselves; perhaps Africa has more than paid for what it did to its children. Perhaps blacks can find in their hearts the mercy that was not shown to them. They are certainly not required to, but perhaps they should consider it.

THE BABY WITH THE BATHWATER:
BLACK FUTILITY AND KNOW-NOTHINGNESS

Perhaps the most breathtaking paragraph that a blasé bourgeois black will ever happen upon is this one from a memoir by Tom Jones, CEO of Citigroup Assets Management. Jones writes of taking part in a black student revolt at Cornell in 1965 that had taken over the student union building:

[A] white fraternity busted in [to throw] us out . . . I recall thinking that if . . . my ancestors had been willing to draw the line against how much torture they accepted, our entire history would have been different. In short, you simply can't be enslaved unless you cooperate to a significant extent. You can't be oppressed unless you cooperate. Why? Because you always have another choice: fight and die.[50]

A picture of Jones calmly hoisting a rifle on the steps of the student union swept the nation. All this for a black studies program!

Jones, having faced the only Gethsemane available to him, has earned the right to say aloud that which animates much of blacks' sense of humiliation and intense need to keep up what is to them the group's threadbare appearance. Blacks have so far chosen not to be angry with their slave-trading ancestors, or with their far more numerous Arab slave masters,[51] but they are furious with their forebears who allowed themselves to be enslaved. If they could hear themselves thinking, if they weren't so embarrassed, they'd feel a bittersweet wistfulness, like black Republican Alan Keyes, who wept over slave histories as a child:

I always wondered, why didn't people resist to the point of fighting and dying, . . . Why would human beings let themselves be oppressed, when they could have said, "give me liberty or give me death," and gone out in a blaze of resistance?[52]

But those suffering from civic fraud syndrome are too afraid to confront either themselves or their past. They're afraid they'll agree with whites about how pitiful they are and always have been. They must bellow at whites so they can't hear themselves thinking, *Why didn't you throw yourselves over the side of those ships? Why weren't you too rebellious to make good slaves? Why didn't you talk back, come to the defense of a slave child being beaten, and die nobly? Why didn't you run away so often, Massa was forced to beat you to death? Why didn't you fight a slave breaker for twenty-four hours straight like Frederick Douglass and then escape North to lead the revolution? How could you have been so weak as to chop someone else's cotton, have his babies, and go on living? How could you choose to live as slaves? Did you just punk out? Did we? Would I have?*

But of course these impossible thoughts must be denied, and the focus must remain on white evil because there is no way out of a psychological morass to which one cannot admit. So this unresolved trauma and chronic insecurity have left the modern African American chagrined, perpetually off balance, adrift, ever tensed for the taunt implicit in white intransigence: *Your mama wore slave shackles! Your daddy rode in the back of the bus like a good boy!* In a reversal of the way some Jews blamed themselves for having survived the Holocaust, blacks blame their ancestors for having survived America. Children believe that running away will "show" their parents; blacks believe that the mass suicide of blacks would have "shown" whites. If they could think these thoughts out loud, if they could invoke Bloody Mary and spit in her eye, they could get over it. But they are too afraid. As with white denial, attitude is all—anger at whites is much less confusing. Rendered slap-happy by history, they wander aimlessly through the civic landscape. Tom Jones's experience continues to be illuminating:

The university granted us the money to get an Afro-American studies program going. That wasn't enough for some of the most militant black students, who charged that Cornell was institutionally incapable of [responsiveness] to the educational needs of African Americans. . . . So they went down to Greensboro, N.C., and tried to start something called Malcolm X University. It never came to fruition. . . .

I felt that if we could achieve [certain] things then Cornell would provide a wonderful educational experience for African Americans. *I wasn't about rejecting the university;* I wanted to reform the university. In the end, there was a very ugly confrontation with some of the black student leaders who felt that I wasn't militant enough. That deeply affected me. Once I left Cornell, I never again joined a movement. . . .

One of the reasons the split occurred . . . was that I've always been of a mind that you have to forgive. You have to accommodate. You have to move on. Otherwise, you become . . . a "prisoner of history." And if there's one thing I was determined I would not be, it was that.[53]

"People are trapped in history," Baldwin noted, "and history is trapped in them."[54] Standing in for his ancestors, Jones confronted the white man determined to die rather than yield and thereby achieved catharsis. When his moment of truth came, he stood his ground. Self-conscious blacks, insufficiently avenged by the anticlimax of winning a mere black studies program, guilty at not having paid the ultimate price either, remained unmollified—they could not torture America as it had tortured them. They demanded the hiring of black faculty, the renaming of buildings. What they actually wanted was beyond the white man's power to bestow; their past remained the ignominious one of a slave's, their mothers unrestored to virginity, their fathers still impotent to protect their families, their bloodlines still awash with rogue DNA. Forcing your firm to honor Martin Luther King Day—not enough. Campaigning for Jesse Jackson—

not enough. Growing 'locks—not enough. Traumatized and overcompensating, lost blacks who suffer this way simply go on being black—he who struggles against white oppression—long after the oppression ended. They are ghosts endlessly haunting the scene of the worst thing that ever happened to them instead of checking out the afterlife. They're right; America hasn't done enough to rectify the past. But it can't. There is only the future. Novelist Octavia Butler made this point brilliantly in *Kindred*. The protagonist, dragged back through time to safeguard her slave ancestor, comes to realize she's really there to protect her slaveowner ancestor: if he dies, she'll never be born. Should she have let him die? Should she have murdered him? Even a Psychology 101 student could have a field day with those blacks who answer in the affirmative.

Prisoners of history are precisely what they are, doomed to spend eternity reliving their degradation, driven to reject that which is now prepared to be reformed. No matter what Cornell University did in response to their revolt, the "revolutionary" students weren't going to be satisfied because what they really wanted was to go on being oppressed so they'd have something special to do, so whites would keep looking at them. This drive animates much of the current push for reparations, even though blacks don't really want money. They don't even really want an apology. They want membership. DuBois understood this intuitively when he lauded the Yankee schoolmarms who flocked south to teach the freedmen:

> This was the gift of New England to the freed Negro: not alms, but a friend; not cash, but character. It was not and is not money these seething millions want, but love and sympathy, the pulse of hearts beating with red blood;—a gift which today only their own kindred and race can bring to the masses . . . the contact of living souls.[55]

Since they can't admit that what they really want is a sense of connection with whites, they can only speak of money. Knee-jerk defiance and loop-tape denunciations are all that remains of a once-viable, once-necessary politics of blackness. Pre-1980s, blacks had no option but to count the black jellybeans on TV, on juries, in statehouses, in patrol cars, in boardrooms, and in prestigious schools. They needed to have internal debates about individual conduct. It was justifiable, even heroic, to squelch one's preferences and do what the leaders proclaimed was best for the group. But now that they are safe, blacks cannot go on being "black"; they must ascend to the autonomy of full citizens, to the maplessness of full humanity. The safety once found in having a common enemy is no longer necessary, because blacks can trust America. That time has passed, if only because it must.

NARROW MEN: THE BLACK POLITBURO

"For Bigger's tragedy is not that he is cold or black or
hungry, not even that he is American, black; but that
he has accepted a theology that denies him life, that he
admits the possibility of his being sub-human and feels
constrained, therefore, to battle for his humanity according
to those brutal criteria bequeathed him at his birth. But
our humanity is our burden, our life; we need not battle
for it; we need only to do what is infinitely more difficult—
that is, accept it. The failure of the protest novel lies
in its rejection of life, the human being, the denial of
his beauty, dread, power, in its insistence that it is
his categorization alone which is real and which
cannot be transcended."

—JAMES BALDWIN, "EVERYBODY'S PROTEST NOVEL"[56]

How does a politics of blackness sustain itself when two blacks face off against each other in elections? When a black person has a white parent, white stepsiblings, or white in-laws? When both the policeman and the person he shot in the back are black? When a black woman clutches her purse at the sight of a black man? When black security guards tail black shoppers? When busy black doctors don't spend time trying to convince blacks to try new treatment options because they'll probably say no? When a black man prefers blondes? When blacks bypass rap or R&B for classical, salsa, rock, or zydeco? How does such a politics handle the fact that:

- A black woman heads a chapter of the National Association for the Advancement of White People.
- Mormon Brigham Young University, with a less-than-one-percent black student body and an antiblack religious history, elected its first black student body president. He said, "We don't want to split the campus up into the special interest or minority groups. We want to view the campus as a whole, unify the BYU campus. I don't plan on butting heads with the administration."[57]
- A black woman is studying to become the first black woman rabbi (outside the Ethiopian Jewish community). "Judaism resonates," she says, "not just as religion but as a culture, an ethnic group."[58]
- A white man won the Gordon Parks screenplay award for a movie that pays tribute to his African American godfather. When he turned up at the awards banquet, mayhem ensued. The filmmaker was forced to return the ten-thousand-dollar prize, which was then given to a (really? visually? biologically?) black filmmaker.
- A black man learned that his great-great-grandfather was a slave who had been forced to work for the Confeder-

ate infantry. He, with two brothers, joined the Sons of Confederate Veterans.

- An Evanston, Illinois, antigang public service announcement featured an Olympics of hate crimes that depicted a white skinhead, a robed Klansman, and a black gangster receiving Olympic medals. It asked which thug killed more blacks each year. When the answer was revealed to be the gangster, black locals demanded the spots be canceled.

Freedom means that people choose to do things they never did before because they couldn't. How does a movement-based political agenda sustain itself in the face of the success that it itself has wrought?

It doesn't. It becomes farce.

It defends O. J. Simpson, even though he was guilty and had distanced himself as far as possible from his blackness. It never considered that an evenhanded consideration of the evidence and equanimity at a just outcome might both shame the devil and set a standard for excellence. No, blacks had to "win"— that is, deprive whites of their preference. It defends Marion Barry, a corrupt crack-head mayoring a black city with a crack problem. Why? Because whites didn't like it. It believes Tawana Brawley, long past the point when any child gives up on Santa Claus. Why? Because she accused whites of hideous acts, the kind of thing they "would do." It prioritizes affirmative action above all other goals, even though the black masses derive little benefit from it. Why? Because it disguises the elite black interest as the general black interest. And also, whites don't like it.

The O.J.- and Barry-defenders are no different from the Founding Father worshipers. Anything "black," however odious, must be defended or denied, and anything "white" attacked or dismissed. George Washington's slave-mongering matters, but O. J. Simpson's wife-beating doesn't. David Duke's racism signifies, but not the Nation of Islam's. Racial profiling of blacks is wrong, but feel free to throw Arab Americans up against the wall. Tawana Brawley's inconsistencies mean nothing, those of a testifying cop, everything. Why? Because whites got away with gang-raping and torturing nigger gals for centuries—big deal, they finally had to pay for one. They've snickered publicly about railroading and murdering blacks since Reconstruction— see how they like O. J. getting away with murdering one of them.

It's Kabuki. It's a stylized acting out of unresolved trauma and revenge fantasies. It's neurotic. It's pointless. It's counter-productive. It's demeaning. It keeps blacks from looking in the mirror or finding better uses of their civic time.

These reenactments by proxy of race-based injustice are as close as blacks can come to doing to whites what was done to them. If only blacks wanted to be better than whites! If only they would flamboyantly sidestep the bait and rise above America's petty racializations! But they seem only to demand inclusion in the power to perpetrate injustice; they want some-one else to be the niggers; they want whites to be history's bitch this time.

This attitude goes far in reaffirming that only transracialism— an acceptance of the fact that exteriors tell you little about a person and nothing about how people should be treated—can save America from miring itself ever more deeply in injustice. Poor man's justice—simply being able to stick it to someone else—is no justice at all. Payback lessens both the payor and the payee.

Just like unreconstructed whites who routinely rely on anti-intellectualisms and denial to fend off black critiques, blacks simply disregard any facts or pragmatic considerations that would impede their long march toward that final showdown with racism, after which whites will beg black forgiveness and welcome them to the family. With so much less property and power to protect, black know-nothingness need take only a few forms.

THE SILENT TREATMENT, THE WITCH HUNT, AND THE PILLORY

The much-venerated monthly *Ebony* publishes an annual list of the "100 Most Influential Black Americans." Though declaring itself neutral as to the individuals or any of their associated ideologies, no black conservatives make the list, though many are influential. The gatekeepers who compile the list exclude them from black America's approval, let alone its awareness, because they are not liberal Democrats and because they proffer internal critiques. When leading black politico-scholars are similarly surveyed, the entrenched black political class is routinely rewarded with the stamp of approval, however odious its politics is to rank-and-file blacks. Politically nonconforming blacks, however influential, are chastised, implicitly threatened, and exiled through such mechanisms.

One wonders at the list-compilers' definition of "leadership."[59] Does it take into account the frequency of effecting outcomes that benefit nonelite blacks? Does it encompass congruence with the attitudes of the black majority? Or those in a position, however indirect, to open doors for other blacks or shatter stereotypes? Or those with new, effective ideas for uplift, or well-executed old ones? Or those, however involved or uninvolved in racial politics, who set a standard of moral, entrepreneurial, scientific, artistic, professional, or civic excellence? Or does it simply refer to the degree to which a "leader" positions himself as a "race person" and politically harasses whites? The latter must be true, given the prevalence of the inept, the corrupt, the amoral, the unrepresentative, and the un-American who comprise the usual contingent of the officially approved. But community surveys paint quite a different picture of the mind of the black masses. One has to wonder: how much less contemptuous of them are blacks' intracommunal overlords than their extracommunal ones?

The civil rights bourgeoisie's unrelenting refusal to tolerate divergence from an orthodoxy often at odds with community values is its most clearly enunciated posture of immature intransigence as well as the clearest articulation of its antidemocratic tendencies. It refuses to engage in constructive engagement with dissenters, however reasonable or potentially helpful they may be, and instead deems them apostate and exiles them in disgrace.

An article circulated on an academic-activist leftist listserv discusses the black girlfriend of a white cop who tortured a black man: its title was "White Police Penetrating, Probing, and Playing in the Black Man's Ass: The Sadistic Sodomizing of Abner Louima." The girlfriend is described as having "embrace[d] white privilege signified by the white phallus."[60]

If only they were satiric! Blacks are libeled and lied to in black bourgeoisie–controlled cultural channels as they are in white ones.

Pragmatic leaders would at least consider détente with well-placed ex-communicants like Supreme Court Justice Clarence Thomas, but instead the black political class makes clear that any who undertake such discussions will share Thomas's fate. They can't see that ostracizing and vilifying Thomas leaves him nothing to lose by marching ever farther from the fold with his pronouncements. Had he a relationship with his community as a contentious but respected elder, how could it fail to moderate his political behavior? Where loving members of a tolerant community would show mercy and at least agree to disagree with a brother painted into a corner by history, the black political class revels in his disgrace. It polices his humiliation, not because it improves things for blacks, but because it keeps them in line.

Emerge, which billed itself Black America's newsmagazine (and is now defunct), ran a cover that caricaturized Thomas as a lawn jockey with a Jemima-handkerchief on his head; inside, he was shown shining the court's leading white conservative's shoes. An anonymous donor offered $150,000 to reopen Savannah's black library on condition that it be renamed in honor of Thomas. Outraged liberal activists geared for battle because "a predominantly black community" ought not be forced to patronize a library named for such as he. These "leaders" preferred that black Savannah have no library rather than one named for a black Republican.

They who define themselves in opposition to the eternal, conscious evil of any who dare disagree would rather be feared than successful, would rather be kowtowed to than just. As W.E.B. DuBois noted in speaking of Booker T. Washington and his accommodationist phalanx, "It is as though Nature must needs make men narrow in order to give them force."

This class, DuBois would say, is "spiritually descended from Toussaint the Savior, through Gabriel, Vesey, and Turner, and they represent the attitude of revolt and revenge; they hate . . . and distrust the white race generally. . . ." Those nineteenth-century warriors, though, would have traded their swords for plowshares long ago: they wanted to win the war for their freedom, not wage it forever.

The Black Politburo never misses an opportunity, however trivial, to conduct a thorough witch hunt of those blacks who persist in thinking for themselves. Even the most black-identified, Democrat-registered, affirmative-action-supporting black just surfing the Net and living his life is confronted daily with the knowledge that his "leaders" are tyrants:

- On Tom Joyner's extremely influential nationwide black radio show, R&B singer Brian McKnight found himself being grilled for having performed at the 2000 Republican National Convention. The powerful DJ vowed to lead a boycott against the singer's albums. "I'm an entertainer, and it had nothing to do with politics," McKnight heretically said. Also, the DJ "tried to make [my not voting] seem like I thought I was too good to vote. That was not it at all. Part of having the right to vote is having the right not to vote when you can't find a candidate that reflects your views."[61]

- Entertainer and movement stalwart Harry Belafonte is "worried" about young black megastar Will Smith because of his lack of overt activism.

- Prominent scholar Henry Louis "Skip" Gates, a perennial target due to his mainstream views, routinely has his "black card" pulled, as on this academic-activist listserv:

  If he were truly in awe of Black folk like he is pretending to be, he would have married one. . . . Also, my travel partner called to tell me [he] was reading a script by [a scholar]. [This scholar] is good . . . but she's not Black. Sheesh!

- Popular black actress Gabrielle Union grew up in a small white town and had a multicultural clique of friends but longed for black companionship. After enduring her high school classmates' ignorance (like dismissing her athleticism as natural to blacks), she made for the University of Nebraska, in part because of its large black student

population. Once there she was immediately deemed not
black enough. Hazed for having too many white friends,
she transferred after one semester. Malcolm X's daugh-
ter had much the same experience.

Initially, one wonders what accounts for the hysteria of the
civil rights bourgeoisie. Then one notices its selectivity—it is
merciless with those who are either powerless or who oppose
their agenda, but gives a Gallic shrug at the transgressions of
those who are powerful and in a position to help elite blacks—
and the question is answered. Power has made them as cynical
and callous as whites.

Yet Carter Woodson could calmly note that blacks "have
been up at times, and down at times." Albert Murray observed
that however disadvantaged blacks might be, they still

respond to beauty, style, and elegance—even as their wonderful ancestors found delight in the magnolias and honeysuck-
les, the crepe myrtles and cape jasmines, the terrain, the
fabulous thickets, woodland streams, and verdant hillsides,
the gourd vines and trellis work near the cabins, the graceful
lines of plantation mansions and even the deep richness of the
soil they tilled during the darkest and most oppressive days of
slavery.[62]

Why believe that either a slave or a slum dweller couldn't
"enjoy a spring rainscape unless he also has the right to vote"?[63]
DuBois could note that blacks had "emerged from slavery,—not
the worst slavery in the world, not a slavery that made all life
unbearable, rather a slavery that had here and there something
of kindliness, fidelity, and happiness." Although they faced the
lynch rope every time they made a public utterance, they were
still able to maintain their perspective, let alone their maturity.

Today's leaders think that when they don't get the biggest office at their foundation-funded bully pulpit it is another Selma.

If only as a matter of self-defense, the hip-hop generation is poised to rout its moribund elders. It must, because those elders are out of ideas. Worse, they insult their intelligence, an outrage blacks resist no less when perpetrated by their fellows than when perpetrated by whites.

Martin Luther King led the Montgomery bus boycott at the age of twenty-five, but few under the age of fifty-five have been allowed to ascend to a position of power in the black leadership, and even fewer from outside movement and Democratic Party paths. This is the Movement Generation's most know-nothing, most shortsighted, and most potentially disastrous power grab. Its refusal to identify, nurture, and entrust power to the next generation will boomerang on the entire community; the young-sters have noticed, they resent it, and they're more vocal about it all the time.

"Our black leaders are not leading us," said Derrick Blas-singame, age fourteen, as he announced the formation of Black Youth Coalition Against Civil Injustice after the Cincinnati riots of 2001.

NO MASSES, NO MOVEMENT: BLACK BOOMERS SHOUT REPARATIONS IN THE COURT—BUT GO SILENT IN THE 'HOOD warns another recent headline.

WE HAVE NO LEADERS TO SAVE OUR BLACK MEN.

BLACK LEADERS OWE HIP HOP AN APOLOGY.

WHO SHALL LEAD THE BLACK RACE?[64]

Who indeed.

"For years," young writer Jeff Chang notes,

intergenerational conflict has underscored the relationship between the civil rights generation and the hip-hop generation. Baby boomers of color wholeheartedly supported many of the repressive anti-gang and anti-crime laws that led to the widespread racial profiling and jailing of youths of color. Although C. Delores Tucker denounced rap misogyny, many hip-hop feminists felt her 1995 crusade against gangsta rap was a generational attack.[65]

"We often see our parents themselves . . . as the enemy within," writes Bakari Kitwana, author of *The Hip Hop Generation: Young Blacks and the Crisis in African American Culture.*[66]

Détente is long overdue with both dissenters and the next generation.

Young blacks (those born after 1964) see America differently than those born before. They should; it is a different place. Movement blacks still flamboyantly grieve for Forty Acres and a Mule. Young rapper Nelly flamboyantly lusts for Forty Acres and a Pool. One looks backward, the other to the future.

Taking freedom for granted and long used to seeing black faces on TV, in boardrooms, and in the halls of Congress, young blacks have a different political agenda. To be sure, there is considerable agreement among the different age cohorts, especially compared with black-white opinions, but the divergences cannot be forever obscured. In particular, blacks born after the Civil and Voting Rights Acts diverge from their elders' politics. They more strongly support school vouchers, they distrust federal government action more, and they favor devolution more often. They support partial privatization of Social Security and are entrepreneurial and pro-business. They view voting more negatively than do older black Americans, especially those who were born when blacks could not vote. Most interestingly, about one third of them declare themselves political Independents; older blacks are overwhelmingly Democrats. Young blacks seem to trust America not to reinstitute the Black Codes while they're on the StairMaster. They seem to be . . . Republicans, quite possibly from disgust.

The hip-hop millionaires in particular have been politically active for some time and almost entirely outside the traditional corridors of black power. The first people to spend a night at the White House after President Bill Clinton's election were Baby Face and Tracey Edmonds, both Los Angeles–based entertainment entrepreneurs; Edmonds is now spearheading an Africa-focused AIDS program with the former president. This agenda-setting Hollywood power couple has little relationship with the Democrats. Millionaire entrepreneurs like Russell Simmons and Master P, and hip-hop intellectuals like Chuck D and Davey D as well, are exerting powerful, politicized, and well-financed leadership among their peers, all with little recourse to, or much respect for, the civil rights establishment. Already the first young, avowedly hip-hop politicians are running for local office in New Jersey and New York. How will a politics of blackness handle their open critique of the movement blacks they seek to unseat?

BLACK CINDERELLA

"When my father left, my mother did what women have done
for years: She found within herself a warrior spirit that helped
her grow. Why [did she call herself] 'Black Cinderella'?:
No prince is going to come for me. I have to buy my own
shoes and walk to leave footprints for you children."
—COLIN CHANNER[67]

"[W]e as a community have to acknowledge our own
culpability. DaBrat, Foxy [Brown], and [L'il] Kim are what

has been happening to young Black women while the
brothers (and some sistas) were busy rescuing
The Endangered Black Man."
—JOAN MORGAN[68]

The premier magazine for black women ran a feature with the
title "All By Myself: What We Can Learn from Loneliness." It
pictured a gorgeous young black woman drinking alone and
looking pensive. Black ministers build dynasties in part by ministering to the millions of lonely black women; they croon to
them, pimp daddy style, that Jesus is their boyfriend. Books
with titles like *Loving Me: A Sisterfriend's Guide to Being Single and Happy* fill black shelves; they expend entire chapters
exhorting black women to pass on convicts and physical abusers.
One called *The Single Life: Being Your Best for God As He Pre-
pares His Best for You* soothes black women with the thought
that being single can be "a celebration rather than a burden."
The Prisoner's Wife is a how-to for all the black women with
lovers in the penitentiary, many of whom they committed to
after their incarceration.

Conjugal visits or Jesus as your babydaddy—this is the black
woman's choice.

When infant mortality, homicides, unemployment, education
level, and incarcerations are taken into account, there are five
black men for every ten black women. Black women outper-
form black men in every social indicator, from employment to
college graduation rates. Blacks lead the nation in marriages
that end in divorce (two-thirds) and in the number of men who
intend never to marry. Less than one-third of black women are
married. The black-white marriage rate is composed primarily
of black men marrying out. Blacks are the perennial loss leaders.
As scholar Orlando Patterson puts it, blacks are the most unpartnered and alienated people in the world.[69]

Black women who aren't, or weren't, alone are disproportionately serving life sentences for killing the black men who
brutalized them. Across all socioeconomic categories, black
women are 35 percent more likely to be battered than whites.[70]
Husbands, boyfriends, and former lovers injure black women
aged 15–44 more than anything or anyone else, accidents and
muggings combined;[71] black girls are more likely to be victims
of crime than black boys.[72] Most African American female characters in the top-selling video games are victims of violence, the
consequences of which are rarely shown; most video victims
simply pull up their thigh-high dominatrix boots and strut away
unfazed. Black women can take it. They have to. They are three
times more likely to have had intercourse by thirteen, often with
a much older man. Unsurprisingly, but without much comment,
black girls' crime and delinquency rates are skyrocketing. They
are least likely of any group to exercise or take physical education classes; half are obese. No one cares enough to see that they
take care of themselves, which paves the road to an endemic disregard of their own health.

The average black video features a light-skinned, light-eyed,
long-haired or Latina woman, nearly naked and reduced to the
basest pelvic-thrusting vulgarity. The average rap lyric is an ode
to misogyny, objectification, and antifemale violence. Female
artists return the favor with songs excoriating black men. Black
women are heartbroken and depressed and alone, and they
think black men hate them. Some are beginning to think they
hate black men.

There are four archetypes of black female tragedy: the invisible woman, cowering in fear in her own home or behind bars
for killing her black abuser; the woman sworn to a man on
long-term lockdown; and the woman raising mismatched children with long-lost fathers (the most common). The fourth is
the spinster.

National Security Adviser Condoleezza Rice epitomizes the loveless, overaccomplished black woman home alone with her bulging resume. Her diction is so articulated as to appear painful. Her hair is as stiffly straight as the religious application of petrochemicals can make it. Her suits are severe. No one wants her for anything except her mind. Like other overachieving black women, she's no doubt stood in lonely equality with her white male peers and heard them lament the lack of women with whom to dally. To white men, she's not a woman. To black men, she's not a fuckable woman; even the vaunted black penis cannot bridge the chasm between them. One reads this headline—IS CONDOLEEZZA RICE SET TO BECOME THE US'S FIRST BLACK AND FEMALE VICE-PRESIDENT?—and thinks: *Run, Condi! Run! Not for office. For your life.* Her having thrived is somehow an affront, or perhaps simply a turn-off, to the black man. What black masculinity does to white men, black female competence does to black men.

Why? Perhaps black women *are* harridans, as men so often claim. Indeed, one may wonder whether black women's bluster is cause or effect. This is the most pressing unresolved trauma from slavery and continuing racism: rejection of the black woman, who is forced to love everyone and therefore no one, she whose nurturing means everything and nothing, she who is never allowed to say no, whether due to the lash or to her inexhaustible pity. If she can't say no, at least she can complain; when black men do that, though, it's called petitioning for redress of grievance, not bitching. "*White Southerners,*" Albert Murray notes in speaking of black men's traditionally low rates of stable fatherhood and employment, "*were not the only people who benefited from the magnanimity of the black mammy.*"[73]

Black women have been sad, manless, and exploited for half a millennium. Thomas Sowell relates the sad fate of the typical female African slave—the ones in Islamic lands:

In the Ottoman Empire, there was a hierarchy of slave prices, reflecting the varying demands and supplies. Because slaves were so often used for domestic purposes, rather than for heavy labor, in the Ottomon Empire, far more women than men were taken as slaves from Africa—so much so as to leave sexually unbalanced societies in parts of East Africa. African women were more likely to be used as housekeepers, while European women, and especially Circassian women, were more likely to be concubines. Slave prices reflected these conditions: Males were generally sold for less than females and African females for less than Circassian females.

The dimensions of treatment are many and all slaves were not treated alike, even in a given society. African women in the Islamic lands were less likely to be freed than European women and had little to look forward to, except drudgery as long as they lived, without even a family life of their own. More African women than men were enslaved in the Islamic world, just the opposite of the situation among Africans taken in bondage to the slave societies of the Western Hemisphere, and these women were typically restricted from having sexual contact with men. The net result was that relatively few black children were born in the Middle East—and few of those born survived to adulthood. Thus, despite the fact that even more vast millions of slaves were taken from Africa to the Islamic countries of the Middle East and North Africa over the centuries than to the Western Hemisphere, there is no such black population surviving in these Islamic nations today as the 60 million people of African ancestry living in the Western Hemisphere.[74]

Maybe this is why American black women reproduce in ways seemingly irrational; it guarantees them someone to love in a world that regards them as workhorses whose preferences are irrelevant. Black women's degradation as the embodiment of the complicated horror of slavery resonated for DuBois, who described two tortured survivor-symbols that staggered away from the moment of emancipation. Slavery, of course, was a man,

> a gray-haired gentleman, whose fathers had quit themselves like men, whose sons lay in nameless graves; who bowed to the evil of slavery because its abolition threatened untold ill to all; who stood at last, in the evening of life, a blighted, ruined form, with hate in his eyes.[75]

The freed slave could only be symbolized as a woman, violated and despised for it. She was

> a form hovering dark and mother-like, her awful face black with the mists of centuries, [who] had aforetime quailed at that white master's command, had bent in love over the cradles of his sons and daughters, and closed in death the sunken eyes of his wife,—aye, too, at his behest had laid herself low to his lust, and borne a tawny man-child to the world, only to see her dark boy's limbs scattered to the winds by midnight marauds riding after "damned Niggers." These were the saddest sights of that woeful day; and no man clasped the hands of these two passing figures of the present-past; but, hating, they went to their long home, and, hating, their children's children live today.

Black women are afterthoughts; few men clasp their hands even now. It is easier for black women educators to helm white colleges and universities than black ones, though they are overrepresented in those ranks. Black women fill their churches— 75 percent of membership rolls—but only five percent are deemed worthy to lead them. Black men's problems serve as a proxy for black *people's* problems. Their oppression justifies their oppressing black women—everybody's got to have a nigger to beat.

A telling example appeared in national news anchorman Dan Rather's remembrance of John F. Kennedy Jr.:

> [He] went to the prison cell where [rapist] Mike Tyson . . . was held, and he quietly, in his own way, kept up that bond. And as a result, he could walk in any African-American community in America, not only in complete safety, but with honor.[76]

Aside from the assumption that those black animals would ordinarily kill a white on sight, aside from the fact that his simply being a Kennedy would itself have been his ghetto pass, would JFK Jr.'s championing of a black man provide him safe passage through the neighborhood of the black woman Mike Tyson raped? Why is the rapist, rather than his victim, the symbol of injustice? Why was supporting accused sexual harasser Clarence Thomas, but not supporting his black accuser, part of the politics of (conservative) blackness? Why do blacks ostracize Jesse Jackson's mistress but not Jackson?

"Black men" and "black people" are synonyms; black women are doubly invisible. They are made the modern equivalent of the happy slaves and the contentedly Jim Crowed whom whites fought so hard to protect from "civil rightsers" in movement days. When black women complain about being the unloved, disrespected workhorses of the community, outside agitators (white feminists) are blamed for having filled their heads with traitorous nonsense. When their privilege is at stake, black men are just as know-nothing and narcissistic as whites—everything is about them. Black women's complaints are not to be considered in their own right; the subject must be changed; their demands must be constructed as just another conspiracy to keep

the black man down. That would make black women—what?
Insane? Suicidal? Or just plain stupid?

As the racist threat fades, black female acquiescence to this
patriarchy is crumbling and is producing an ambivalence that
is becoming difficult to ignore. Diarist Carole Stewart McDonnell put it this way:

> Black male pain just isn't romantic. A Black man in pain on
> television usually has some tangible or political problem. I've
> always hated politics. . . . When I met Luke, my husband, I
> knew I was in love. . . . I was no longer a mirror of anyone
> else's dynamics.[77]

Tentatively, black women are beginning to free themselves.
They are marrying out of the community rather than being
either alone or disrespected. They are offering public critiques
of black sexism. Their TV dramas and magazines take increasing cognizance of intracommunal gender disparities; *Essence,*
the premier women's magazine, ran a year-long series called
"The War Against Black Girls" that thoroughly dissects the
daunting reality facing them. It begs the question, though, of
who it is that is waging war on them ("society" isn't putting so
many of them in the hospital) and why.

As for blacks generally, the first step to freedom for black
women is to sing the song of themselves and acquire self-
respect. Demands for acknowledgment of black female reality
bounce from one black woman's computer to the next:

ONLY A BLACK WOMAN . . .
Can take a week of leftover scraps and make a gourmet meal.
Can cuss a man out, make him feel like shit, then make love
to him and make him feel like a king.

Can raise a doctor, an Olympic athlete, and a straight A
   student in a "dysfunctional, underprivileged, underclass"
   ghetto.
Can heat a whole house in the winter without help from the
   gas company.
Can put a black man and his nonwhite date on pins and nee-
   dles just by walking into the room.
Can live below the poverty level yet set fashion trends.
Can fight two struggles every day and make it look easy.

Black women must be exhausted, yet still they take time to
scratch out defiant, hysterical exhortations like these, the e-mail
equivalent of "Kilroy was here," the pixellated version of scratch-
ings on a jail cell wall. *Notice me, please. Love me. Please. Help
me.* With epistles such as these, black women enunciate their
pain and demand respect; they move beyond the bluster.

The next step is to abandon Superwoman status. The flamboyantly dressed comedienne Sommore commented in the 2002
Queens of Comedy video, with what looked like humble sin-
cerity:

I don't understand all these sisters talking about how they
can raise a bunch of kids alone. I can't raise no kids alone—I
want a husband. I may dress like a Power Ranger, but a sister
needs some help.

Poet Laini Mataka put it this way:

THE STRONG BLACK WOMAN IS DEAD
On August 15, 1999, at 11:55 pm, while struggling with the
reality of being a human instead of a myth, the strong black

woman passed away, without the slightest bit of hoopla. Medical sources say that she died of natural causes, but those who knew and used her know she died from: being silent when she should have been screaming, mulling when she should have been raging, being sick and not wanting anyone to know because her pain might inconvenience them. An overdose of other people clinging on to her when she didn't even have energy for herself.

She died from loving men who didn't love themselves and could only offer her a crippled reflection. She died from raising children alone and for not doing a complete job. She died from the lies her grandmother told her mother and her mother told her about life, men and racism. She died from being sexually abused as a child and having to take that truth everywhere she went every day of her life, exchanging the humiliation for guilt and back again. She died from being battered by someone who claimed to love her and because she allowed the battering to go on to show she luuuuvvvvvddddd him too.

She died from asphyxiation, coughing up blood from secrets she kept trying to burn away instead of allowing herself the kind of nervous breakdown she was entitled to, but only white girls could afford. She died from being responsible, because she was the last rung on the ladder and there was no one under her she could dump on.

The strong black woman is dead. She died from the multiple births of children she never really wanted but was forced to have by the strangling morality of those around her. She died from being a mother at 15 and a grandmother at 30 and an ancestor at 45. She died from being dragged down and sat upon by unevolved women posing as her sisters. She died from pretending the life she was living was a Kodak moment instead of a 20th century, post-slavery nightmare!!!!!!!!!!! She died from tolerating Mr. Pitiful, just to have a man around the house. She died from lack of orgasms because she never learned what made her body happy and no one took the time to teach her and sometimes, when she found arms that were tender, she died because they belonged to the same gender.

She died from sacrificing herself for everybody and everything when what she really wanted to do was be a singer, a dancer, or some magnificent other. She died from lies of omission because she didn't want to bring the black man down. She died from race memories of being snatched and snatched and raped and snatched and sold and snatched and bred and snatched and whipped and snatched and worked to death.

She died from tributes from her counterparts who should have been matching her efforts instead of showering her with dead words and empty songs. She died from myths that would not allow her to show weakness without being chastised by the lazy and the hazy. She died from hiding her real feelings until they became monstrously hard and bitter enough to invade her womb and breasts like angry tumors. She died from always lifting something, from heavy boxes to refrigerators.

The strong black woman is dead. She died from the punishments received from being honest about life, racism and men. She died from being called a bitch for being verbal, a dyke for being assertive and a whore for picking her own lovers. She died from never being enough of what men wanted, or being too much for the men she wanted. She died from being too black and died again for not being black enuff. She died from castration every time somebody thought of her as only a woman, or treated her like less than a man.

She died from being misinformed about her mind, her body and the extent of her royal capabilities. She died from knees pressed too close together because respect was never part of the foreplay that was being shoved at her. She died from loneliness in birthing rooms and aloneness in abortion centers. She died of shock in court rooms where she sat, alone, watching her children being legally lynched. She died in bathrooms with her veins busting open with self-hatred and neglect.

She died in her mind fighting life, racism, and men, while her body was carted away and stashed in a human warehouse for the spiritually mutilated. And sometimes when she refused to die, when she just refused to give in, she was killed by the lethal images of blond hair, blue eyes, and flat butts, rejected to death by the O. J.s, the Quinceys, and the Poitiers.

Sometimes, she was stomped to death by racism and sexism, executed by hi-tech ignorance while she carried the family in her belly, the community on her head, and the race on her back!!! The strong, silent, shit-talking black woman is dead!!!

Or is she still alive and kicking???

The black community does not yet know what to make of its ever-less-quiescent daughters with their ever-growing complaints. On the one hand, it tells them to remain quiet in the temple. To applause, comedienne Adelle Givens scolds them for using the common dismissal "I can do bad all by myself" with "Sisters, you keep saying that, you might just miss your man." E-mails with subject lines like "God, Send me a Man!" arrive in in-boxes with regularity. In it, the unnamed single black Everywoman prays for companionship; at the end, God himself appears to scold her for passing on the gold-toothed bus driver, the ex-con, and the unemployed (some versions include a scorned white man):

You pushed them aside with looks that could kill.
You couldn't even manage a smile.
And if you continue to treat people that way
You are certain to be alone for awhile.

Bitch. You're alone because you deserve to be.

On the other hand, the *Sister, I'm Sorry* video—in which black men stand as proxies for all the husbands, fathers, brothers, and sons who've hurt their women and apologize—swept the black nation. At least, the female part of it. (Widely distributed and written about, it aired on the Oprah Winfrey show, among others, in 1998.)

As with racism, when black women are willing to face the consequences of their defiance, a change will have to come.

If black men tyrannize black women, black women tyrannize their children.[78] Aloof, rather ruthless mothers are a staple of ghetto memoirs. One memoirist's mother "developed a toughness that at times made her seem emotionless, but her determination and consistency stabilized our lives. I never saw life break her down."[79] What would have happened to him if it had? Still, anyone who wasn't suffering from post-traumatic stress disorder could feel the rage and terror in this:

YOU HAVE A BLACK MOTHER IF . . .

1. You've been called from upstairs to go downstairs to get the remote, *TV Guide,* change the channel, or get her something to drink when she was close enough to do it herself.

2. She's ever asked if you wanted something to eat . . . and then said, "Well, come on over here and make it then."

3. She told you you better stop crying after she finished beating you.

4. You've ever been slapped so hard that you did a 360 and fell on the ground.

5. You've ever been beat with an extension cord, hanger, or switch.

6. You've ever been told to pick your own switch, and it didn't matter how small the switch was that you picked— it still hurt.

7. You told her you was thirsty, and she tells you to swallow your spit.

8. You've ever been beat on the way home in the car and then got beat at home, too.

9. You get in trouble and she won't let you explain yourself.

10. She told you, "You wanna cry? I'll give you something to cry about."

11. The white people in the main office of your school (including the principal) are scared of her.

12. You were scared to go home with a bad report card.

13. You've never been grounded . . . just beat.

14. You've ever been smacked in front of your friends and family.

15. Whenever you asked her to buy you something, she said no without even looking at what it was.

16. She told you you would get an allowance for doing chores but never paid, saying it was only what you were supposed to do.

17. You've been beat for something she knew your sibling did, but you were older or you were just in the vicinity or the offending sibling simply couldn't be found.

18. The phrase "I'm going to tell your mother" was the worst thing you could ever hear.

19. The phrase "I'm going to tell my mother" was the worst thing other people wanted to hear.

20. The house looked like it'd been hit by a tornado because you tried to run away from her when she was chasing you with a belt.

21. She had to pray to God to keep from killing you while you stood waiting for punishment ("Oh Lord! Please don't let me kill this ungrateful child").

22. You've ever been snatched, not grabbed, by your clothes because you'd done something wrong.

23. You've ever thought about running away from home, but didn't because you knew that if your mother found you, you would be dead.

What does it say about a group that could find that funny? Is it any wonder that such children grow up to perpetuate the cycles that hamstrung their parents, that they grow up to be the most unpartnered, alienated people on the planet?

TURMOIL, AMBIVALENCE, INSECURITY, SORROW: EXISTENTIAL CRISIS

"When I discover who I am, I'll be free."
—RALPH ELLISON

"If I am not who you say I am, then you
are not who you think you are."
—JAMES BALDWIN

No doubt, black heads are nodding righteously at these words. This is because they focus their analysis only on the second half of Baldwin's formulation. But what of the first—what is blacks' true identity? Heretofore the mere denial of white accusation has taken the place of self-definition. But who are blacks, apart from their oppression? At the turn of the century DuBois offered *The Souls of Black Folk* to illuminate "the strange meaning of being black here at the dawning of the twentieth century." America, he wrote,

> yields [the Negro] no true self-consciousness, but only lets him see himself through the revelation of the other world. It is a peculiar sensation, this double-consciousness, this sense of always looking at one's self through the eyes of others, of measuring one's soul by the tape of a world that looks on in amused contempt and pity. One ever feels his twoness,—an American, a Negro; two souls, two thoughts, two unreconciled strivings; two warring ideals in one dark body, whose dogged strength alone keeps it from being torn asunder.
>
> The history of the American Negro is the history of this strife,—this longing to attain self-conscious manhood, to merge his double self into a better and truer self. In this merging he wishes neither of the other selves to be lost. He would not Africanize America, for America has too much to teach the world and Africa. He would not bleach his Negro soul in a flood of white Americanism, for he knows that Negro blood has a message for the world. He simply wishes to make it possible for a man to be both a Negro and an American, without being cursed and spit upon by his fellows, without having the doors of Opportunity closed roughly in his face.[80]

Mercifully, even that great mind could not have foreseen that a hundred years later, after blacks were free, the strange meaning of blackness would still be obscure. On a usually unselfconscious sitcom *(Girlfriends)* four upscale black professional women get into a fight jostling for entry to an exclusive nightclub. The episode's main point centered on whether one should help one's friends in a fight even if one disapproves of fighting. An important subsidiary consideration, however, was whether blacks should fight in front of whites.

If blacks stop operating according to whites' playbook, how will they know who they are or how to act or even what they like? If they're not criminal, lazy, immoral, or dumb, then what *are* they? We know the negatives—what we don't know are the affirmatives of the black personality. Once articulated, of course, the ridiculousness of the question becomes apparent. The affirmatives of the black personality are the same as whites'—limitless, unpredictable, uncategorizeable, mutable—otherwise racism is sensible, let alone justified. Yet blacks only gingerly tap at the glass jar encasing their souls. There isn't a realm into which this insecurity does not ooze:

> I always considered myself a little too militant for golf. . . . [G]olf was definitely something I chalked up in the white man's column. . . . I recently spent a few hours whaling away at a little dimpled ball with a crooked stick. And I had a great time doing it. And the next chance I get, I'm going to do it again. And I'm not afraid to say it out loud. Please don't talk about me too bad.[81]

Bonani Jones jests, but not much. Why must he apologize for liking golf? He feels a whiff of contempt for whites and their supposedly pampered, supposedly pointless lives, but he also feels social dislocation. This man is confronting the timidity of the formerly oppressed to claim his world. He is exhilarated by his own daring, by his broadening horizons, and by the dawning understanding that the peripherals needn't fundamentally alter his self-perception. If golf can't make him feel like a sell-out, perhaps the white woman clutching her purse can't make him feel like a second-class citizen.

It is in facing *themselves,* rather than in constantly beseeching whites for reassurance, that blacks will find true freedom. The question of street brawling ought to be a moral one—should one ever resort to it?—not a political one. When blacks dare to locate their decision-making and sense of self-worth in transcendent values like morality, maturity, and strength of character, they'll find that their decisions are often the politically desired ones. No, the *Girlfriends* shouldn't have fought in front of white folks, because they shouldn't have fought at all, except to protect themselves or others. Fighting is wrong, whatever whites witness. When blacks learn to look past whites, when they focus on actualizing as individuals, they'll find that the solutions to these conundrums are obvious, albeit difficult. Focusing on black responsibility for upstanding behavior cannot fail to uplift the black community.

Without a politics of blackness, what is the algorithm by which blacks decide who's on their side and who isn't, what they're for and what they're against?

Black Issues in Higher Education magazine ran a full-page article on the ascension of a black conservative, Gerald Reynolds, to head the Office of Civil Rights in the Department of Education. It was mostly straightforward reportage, except for the photograph. Rather than showing the man about whom the article was written—the black conservative who'd won—it showed the black paleoliberal Wade Henderson, who'd led the opposition to his candidacy, with a similarly themed caption. The photo was a Freudian slip, making clear whose side the journal was on; more significantly, it was schizophrenic. How did the magazine know with whom to commiserate when blacks were on both sides? The article should have been entitled: "We

Lost, Right?"[82] The conservative is the multiple personality that blacks can't let themselves in on, even though he redecorates the house every time he's in control.

In addition to blacks' DuBoisian double consciousness, there are also two black ids. One seeks to transcend race, while the other seeks to make blacks powerful qua blacks so as to defeat whites. These ids struggle to either merge and expand or fully separate into lesser entities. James Baldwin knew that "freedom is not something that anybody can be given. Freedom is something people take, and people are as free as they want to be." Decades later, we know he meant a notion that was much more radical than freedom from whites. But how do blacks find themselves when, for centuries, they've had to subjugate their will, their personal preferences, and even their thought processes to the group's survival? This subjugation has resulted in contradictions and complexities that can only surprise those with a vested interest in blindness, like white conservative Eric Cohen, who made this observation:

> The black America that dominates our national dialogue, it seems, has two cultures but one politics. One culture was represented at Mount Paran Baptist Church. . . . It is the culture of [its pastor] Rev. Lawson, deeply religious, largely female, pro-life, pro-school prayer, and pro-abstinence. The other culture is self-destructive, largely male, plagued by violence, drugs, rage, death, misogyny, and illegitimacy.[83]

So focused was this author on dividing and conquering, on doling out his all-important white approval in precise dollops and his holy white condemnation in dripping gobs, that something both crucial and obvious got past him. The credit-to-their-race group is the parents, siblings, children, lovers, cousins, and neighbors of the second. That twain often meets. Those two groups understand each other, and each knows how the other ticks. They are intimately aware of and affected by each other; they are bound together. They share cereal boxes.

Both know that police brutality is just as corrosive of the black community as drug use, and that the vast numbers of the uninsured poor are as corrosive as illegitimacy. The church ladies want the members of that "other black culture" to straighten up and get religion, but they know that if they did, they'd just get to join them in menial labor, chronic job insecurity, and life on the bottom rung. The church ladies know that the "other culture" doesn't have to self-destruct. But they also know the forces that drive them to it and how hard they are to rise above. They see the black underclass as clearly as they see the white over-class. And they agree with their shiftless, jobless, drug-addicted grandchildren about white racism. That's why there's one often-counterintuitive politics speaking for a necessarily contradictory personality.

SLUMMING

This question of identity haunts post-movement blacks, as it must if they are to evolve and thrive. *The Pact,* a memoir written by three inner-city black men who recovered from bad choices to become dentists, illustrates this turmoil. When the time came for them to pose for a promotional photo for the rap group they formed in college, they had an unacknowledged existential crisis:

> To look like real rappers, we had to appear tough, not like the college boys we had become. We scouted the campus for the perfect photo background. The green grass and stately trees surrounding Seton Hall just wouldn't do. Finally, we

found the perfect spot: the upper deck of the student parking
lot. The bare look of the concrete at night and the three of
us in our baggy jeans, badboy expressions, and hats flipped
backward looked just about right.[84]

They had to dress up like the ghosts of their former selves, so
uncomfortable were they with the gentle, hardworking, self-
denying, and guilt-ridden collegians they'd nearly killed themselves to become. Bobby Vicious, the newsman on Tom Joyner's
extremely influential, nationally broadcast *Morning Show* radio
program, exhibits a similar schizophrenia. In his hourly updates
he delivers mainstream information with the news profession's
traditional inflections and pronunciations, though it's obvious
that he is black. But when it's time to sign-off, he gets ghetto:
"De news wi' the flava for mah peeps."

However confused, this impulse is also constructive. Like the
delighted brother who learned to love golf, blacks are playing
with all sorts of existential fires to see if they'll get burned. The
defunct early-1990s comedy sketch TV show *In Living Color*
offered a lighthearted, unselfconscious look at black life. It featured, for instance, the hilarious pseudo-intellectual convict who
spends his time on lockdown reading things he doesn't understand and spouting oh-so-serious nonsense. And the stereotypi-
cal Jamaican American family in which every member of the
large, jovial mob, from grandparents to toddlers, had "tree jobs,
mon," and worked around the clock.

Matured, black TV comedies today seem introspective, un-
leavened with affection. They critique more than they affirm.
On the satiric comedy show *Mad TV* there is a recurring character whose very name is intracommunal commentary: Bunifa
Latifa Halifa Sharifa Jackson. She is coarse, vulgar, ignorant,
dishonest, sneaky, racist, promiscuous, and loud; she dresses
like a whore and trades sex for anything she wants. She yells

"racism" often, both opportunistically and in the sincere belief that all obstacles to her desires are race-based. You can only laugh at, never with, her. She is painful to watch. Another recurring skit features two women with a talk show who snap excruciatingly on their white guests; they would seem to be a cakewalk-style commentary on white overreaching (and further proof that the black folk are not in awe of whites), except for their crudeness and grotesque obesity. *Mad TV* also skewers the buffoonish, minstrel-show representations of black life found in black-produced sitcoms, music, and movies. *Saturday Night Live,* another satiric sketch comedy show, has recurring skits about the laziness, poor work ethic, venom, and general spiritlessness of postal workers, (pre-9/11) airport screeners, and municipal employees, played as "ghetto" blacks. No doubt all were created by the minority actors who portray them. This is cinema verité of the soul.

Many black-produced movies, including those produced by black actresses, portray even highly educated, highly accomplished black women as vulgar, oversexed sassy mamas who "keep it real" with the frequent use of words like *dick* and *pussy.* They have corner offices two years out of law school and single-handedly negotiate billion-dollar deals while doing the Electric Slide in a nightclub—Bunifa goes to B-school. These representations are concocted by working-class performers for an appreciative working-class audience. The characters and situations created by popular black novelists are often just as crude, uninformed, and instrumentalized. As for black standup comics, they are enough to make the bourgeoisie commit *seppuku*—all bowel-movement, bad-credit, oral-sex, infidelity, jail, and fat jokes. Racism is only rarely mentioned. The difference between the movies, novels, and stand-up comedy and the sketch comedy representations lies in intention, acculturation, and class mentality; the former mean to critique, the latter to celebrate. They do not see their folk culture as pathological, undesirable, or deviant. They know the difference between a movie glorifying gold-toothed drug dealers and one glorifying gold-toothed MBAs. They do not aspire to white behavioral norms, their differences from which they well understand; any medium-grade black comic can tell you everything you need to know about whites. These blacks like themselves just the way they are and wish only for greater access to their nation's material wealth.

The explosion in black comedy is almost entirely a working-class phenomenon, the hallmarks of which are unselfconsciousness ("What's all this talk about white folks needing to find themselves? I know who I am. I'm black. I know that because I got bad credit."), innate conservatism ("They need more black judges, 'cause we don't be going for all that crazy nonsense, like multiple personalities. Black judge say, 'Multiple personalities? Too bad, fifty years, 'cause one of y'all could have called the police.' "), and a near total lack of interest in politics. Among forty-five performers on one season of Def Comedy Jam, there were only three references to anything outside black daily life; if racism is still such a struggle for blacks, why aren't they talking about it? Instead, they talk about what black people do to each other—love, sex, money, work, family. Every group observes and satirizes that which affects them most, and blacks are observing and satirizing themselves, not whites. Or at least, not much beyond whites' inability to dance or lighten up. They know the ceiling is low for them, and they know why. They're simply not rendered neurotic by it because they have so little contact with their overlords.

Proceeding from a middle-class awareness entails its own problematics. A befuddled self-consciousness permeates modern black magazines; they haven't quite figured out how to be assimilated, successful, and black. On the one hand, *Code* (the now-defunct *GQ* aspirant) specialized in witty, irreverent pieces on upscale black life and critiqued both hip-hop excesses and movement sacred cows. It was obsessed with celebrities, luxury cars, high-priced gadgets, and exclusive resorts. Its editorial stance assumed black success and the freedom to focus on the frivolous, like three-hundred-dollar vintage wines and hand-tailored suits. For Martin Luther King Day 2000, along with rhapsodies to the great man, *Code* also featured one blasphemous writer's hilarious attempt to force his firm to honor the holiday; militance notwithstanding, he was equally interested in having more days off.

But *Code* also published a "Pimp Daddy" issue. One feature advertised www.pimpdaddy.com: "Whether you are sending a shout-out to your favorite lady or need to set a rival straight about your turf, there's a card for you." You could submit a free-style design, and if yours was selected for inclusion by the webmaster, you'd get a free one-year pimpdaddy.com e-mail address. Hi mom. How many black women would subscribe to imaho.com?

In two separate articles in the same issue, *Savoy* magazine (the black *Vanity Fair* aspirant) approvingly described two black actors (Will Smith and Mathew St. Patrick) as, respectively, combining "the thug and the intellectual" and blending "gentleman and thug."[85] Yet the previous issue had told the tale of a biracial teenager raised with her suburban white family who threw herself into her "blackness" by seeking out its violent, drug-ridden substrata. She was raped and murdered by a black man who was apparently all thug. The article was an indictment of equating blackness with pathology, yet the two actors' thuggishness is cause for compliments.

Granted, the "pimp daddy" and "gentleman thug" phenomena are black camp, but should they be? In speaking of her megastar husband, Mrs. Will Smith's full comment to *Savoy* was, "The thug and the intellectual—I had to have both. I need that guy who can take me to the Ice Cube concert and then to the White House." One doubts that she truly means her husband is a violence-prone criminal. One suspects, rather, that she fears that the rarefied company they now keep will make them seem to be "acting white" (à la the newly minted gentlemen of *The Pact*).

Successful blacks are embarrassed. They are dislocated socially (both "thugs" and Mrs. Thug had humble beginnings), and they worry that their full bellies will make them not only oblivious to injustice but perpetrators of it as well. Just like rich white people. Worst of all, they fear that other blacks will think them Uncle Toms. Smith's alleged "thuggishness" insulates them both; she'd have to be "down," a " 'round the way sister," to want a thug, no?

Thug, then, is "thug," a code word. It's "Joe sent me" at the speakeasy door. "Thug," like Bobby Vicious's sudden blackspeak, is a cheerful middle finger to the dominant culture. It connotes two things: a virility outstripping that possessed by white men and a fervent identification with one's blackness, if only rhetorically. To a "thug," a "real" black man, the White House is a frill, the 'hood a necessity, even if he visits the former much more often than the latter. Especially if he does. It is insufficient merely to exist inside black skin while being the upstanding husband, father, and artist that Smith appears to be—his blackness must nonetheless be demonstrated. One must like Ice Cube, especially if, as here, one has a small golf course on one's servant-strewn property. Living on a golf course with servants is not "black," regardless of how hard one worked, while black, to acquire them.

This belabored blackness is also smug, black-male-supremacist contempt—it's a penis-measuring contest with white men who are by definition neurotic, boring, and unmanly. Whites may own the world, but they look damned gawky shuffling about their holdings, while a black man is cool. He pimp-walks, however oppressed he may be.

When it suits their purposes, blacks work hard to perpetuate the stereotype of themselves as well endowed, sexually ferocious, and dangerous. Being human, they are as intellectually opportunistic as whites. More to our purposes, the image of black sexual prowess also gives the lie to the notion that the black masses are self-hating; they are anything but. One need only hear black women go to town on the white women they work for and with; blacks may envy whites their power, but never their perceived neuroses and lack of élan.

From blacks, the notion of "acting white" is an existential inquiry. From whites, it is more narcissism and contempt, as when they lament the schoolyard harassment that high-performing blacks supposedly endure. It is a sly way of complimenting themselves while highlighting the unworthiness and barbarity of the average black.

Whites surely must grasp the difference between wanting to be successful and wanting to be white. To them, of course, anything good is white, so to work hard in school is to reject blackness and aspire to whiteness. Yet the high-performing black youngster faces no more harassment than the fat kid, the skinny kid, the kid with the braces, the rich kid, or the Jehovah's Witness kid who can't say the Pledge of Allegiance. Poor white kids beat up the smart ones, too. When whites are involved, behavior is readily boiled down to its human motivations—love, greed, weakness, shame, bravery. But when blacks are under the microscope, the ground shifts. Occam's razor is dulled, useless.

A low performer, especially a child, who harasses a high performer does not realize that what he really means is "I'd give anything to win all the prizes like you do, but I don't know how."[86] All he can manage is "You think you white." The source of what black self-hatred actually exists, especially in the class-room, is a subconscious belief in white superiority. No black soldier or athlete who excels is accused of acting white, because blacks don't feel inferior in this regard; an egotistical para-trooper or athlete would be described as having "the big head." Since whites make blacks feel badly about themselves academi-cally, whiteness is ascribed to blacks who make other blacks feel badly in this way. It is much easier to refuse to try geometry or college on bogus political grounds than to try and fail or even to admit to fear.[87] Fear is uncool and blacks are cool, no matter what. DuBois knew that underachieving blacks thought:

> we cannot write, our voting is vain; what need of education, since we must always cook and serve? And the Nation echoed and enforced this self-criticism, saying: Be content to be ser-vants, and nothing more; what need of higher culture for half-men?[88]

A preteen can look around his crumbling school with tattered texts, and more special-ed classes than regular ones, and know what his nation thinks him capable of: the military, the delivery truck, the unemployment line, jail. He'd have to be white to believe he had a future. He'd have to be free, as students who take risks, like AP courses, are. The low performers don't need to be told it's cool to be smart—they need to be shown that they're valuable enough for society to invest in. Blacks believed in education until they were taught it was a chimera. The newly freed slaves devoted themselves to education to such an extent that, as E. Franklin Frazier noted:

> At no time or place in America has there been exemplified so pathetic a faith in education as the lever of racial progress. Grown men studied their alphabets in the fields, holding the

"blue-back" speller with one hand while they guided the plow with the other. Mothers tramped scores of miles to towns where they could place their children in school. Pine torches illumined the dirt-floored cabins where men, women, and children studied until far into the night. No mass movement has been more in the American tradition than the urge which drove Negroes toward education soon after the Civil War.[89]

The urge which drove Negroes away from education was whites'; it took Jim Crow to turn blacks against hope.[90]

The charge of acting white is both a declaration of defeat and a neurotic compliment; it is a dismal measure of some blacks' internalized oppression and of some whites' racism that so many could truly believe that blacks prefer underachievement. Furthermore, blacks' claims of rejection on these grounds are usually generated inside their own heads; what better way to hide one's cowardice in social situations than by assuming one's exclusion? Or they are often much enhanced; what better way to boast without appearing to?

All grown up, the existential inquiry involved in "acting white" has mainly to do with lifestyle choices. Does one date interracially? Travel to Africa or to Europe? Eat sushi? Use standard English or "thuggish" Ebonics? And above all, where does one live?

Recent sitcoms have tackled this last, quintessential post-movement quandary, usually through nouveaux riches blacks transplanted to the suburbs. Consciously acting out the uneven drama that is black uplift, the male protagonist is often a high school drop-out or working man turned successful entrepreneur while the female is a college grad. Before the show descends into sitcom clichés, its quest is to hold on to its blackness.

But why not just live near other black people if proximity to whites is so destabilizing? And why, exactly, does proximity to whites destabilize the black identity? Given their only 13 percent presence in the population, increased integration can only presage increased destabilization—perhaps blacks should reconsider their abhorrence of segregation. Why is the orderly quiet of suburbia something of which to be contemptuous? Do blacks really prefer sirens and gunshots, as they so often joke on screen and in interviews? A preference for the same neighborhood as whites hints at other shared sensibilities; is what's really bothering them the discovery that whites are not so very different from themselves? More than a generation ago Albert Murray observed that:

> in spite of their common destiny and deeper interests, the people of the United States are being misled by misinformation to insist on exaggerating their ethnic differences. The problem is not the existence of ethnic differences, as is so often assumed, but the intrusion of such differences into areas where they do not belong. Ethnic differences are the very essence of cultural diversity and national creativity.[91]

Why else would so many whites struggle to master chopsticks or the merengue? He continues:

> American culture, even in its most rigidly segregated precincts, is patently and irrevocably composite. It is, regardless of all the hysterical protestations of those who would have it otherwise, incontestably mulatto. Indeed, for all their traditional antagonisms and obvious differences, the so-called black and so-called white people of the United States resemble nobody else in the world so much as they resemble each other.[92]

Successful blacks seem to be protesting just a little too much, fishing for approval and forgiveness for the briar patch they've flung themselves into. They feel guilty at having abandoned, fled even, their brethren, and they highlight at every turn how different they are from their new neighbors; *they* go to Ice Cube concerts. Or they would if it didn't conflict with PTA meetings. They are "thugs," the authentic version of which would have precluded the very progress that is now making them uncomfortable. They are thugs who captain the neighborhood watch, garden obsessively, and hold weekly cook-outs. Without a one-size-fits-all blackness, they're off balance. Blackness is collapsing under the weight of its contradictions, just as overt racism did.

This accounts for the emergence of "black camps" wherein affluent black parents pay to have their children spend time in the 'hood and mingle with "thug" children. Such parents worry that their children are "missing out on reality and becoming generic." One girl was sent to such a camp because she preferred classical music and didn't know the music and games that her elders had played as children. African American vernacular and cultural references often went over her head.

Notice that all the angst and dislocation, the flaunted blackness, comes from the parents. Note the essentializations: "reality" for blacks is poverty and danger, blacks don't listen to classical music, blacks sling slang, blacks are poor, blacks must seek out other blacks, however inorganically. Note the contempt for whites—"becoming generic."

Racial tourism of this type can be understood only as identity training-wheels, as existential breadcrumb trails leading back to a stabilizing point of origin that is no more home to these campers than the space and computer camps they also no doubt attend. Like the proverbial Ice Cube concert, it inoculates the camper—and especially his parents, who chose to leave the proximity of blacks—against having their "black cards" pulled. When the black office secretary bemoans another shooting in her neighborhood, the alum of Camp WannameetaNegro can chime in, nonchalantly dropping the place names and street corners of his "old stomping grounds," without mentioning the circumstances of his knowledge, and raise himself in the estimation of both his black and white co-workers. Fraud syndrome, slumming, and insecurity. But blacks will outgrow it—how many actually move back to the 'hood?

DECLARATIONS OF INDEPENDENCE

At least among the young, an existential revolution is unquestionably under way. The first blush of hip-hop generation artistic freedom gave America the ultimately loyal *In Living Color,* affectionate honesty and interest bestowed where it had never been before. But in the new millennium young blacks are analyzing themselves and their world and finding that racism, including blacks', is ridiculous and doesn't bear up under scrutiny. Freed from understanding how bad discrimination truly was, they know that the only battle left is emotional and intellectual—they thumb their noses at racialism. They are breaking ranks, loosening the straitjacket, taking their blackness out for a spin, and holding it up to the light.

Outside the artistic realms as well, everyday blacks are finding new ways to demand full freedom and petition even the *black* powers-that-be for redress of their grievances. One young woman, Yolanda Adams, published her declaration of independence (redacted here) in *Essence,* the premier magazine for black women:

I DON'T WANT TO BE BLACK ANYMORE
I am one of many who find it easier to work and live outside my community. Without regret, I am more comfortable socializing with Whites than with Blacks. . . . As a community, [we

are extremely color conscious]. . . . Though [I am dark], I have never been Black enough to satisfy some. . . . I was often taunted for being "proper" or "acting White" because of how I dressed and spoke. . . . Our communities have become havens for drug abuse and lawlessness; they are economic wastelands. I think of Ethiopians who perished in the middle of the desert, and I wonder why they didn't just move near water. This is how I see our community. So I moved to a place where I can thrive, where I can take a walk without fearing I might get cut down by an errant bullet, where I feel comfortable going to sleep at night.

Living is not about being Black, and being Black is not all there is to living. I have never taken an oath of allegiance to the Black community. And I never will. . . . And I am not saying I want to be White. I simply want to be neither. . . . For better or worse, I have decided I don't want to be Black anymore.[93]

In demanding her freedom, Adams notes two phenomena that make it impossible for her to continue to be "black," both the Politburo and the nihilistic criminal. She knows both are caused by racism, but she still won't excuse them because that would force her to choose blackness—opposition to whites at all costs—over her personal integrity. Since that is her only identity choice, the only allowed mode of blackness, she voted with her feet and abandoned her post in an immoral war.

Another wrote to a popular black infotainment website:

I'd like to know why you decided to include the Rahway prison riot as an important moment in Black History for November 24th. I hope it has nothing to do with the incredibly large number of Blacks in the prison system, a statistic that I'm not proud of. Please tell me more. Why was this a big day in my history?[94]

The website's knee-jerkedly defiant answer: "This event happened and it involved black people." The problem is not that there can be no justification for memorializing prison riots as important to black history; the problem is that those who deemed the event important couldn't supply that justification. That writer probably believes both that the criminal justice system is racist *and* that racism doesn't justify crime. Are old-school blacks who control media outlets capable of similarly nuanced analysis?

Just like the newby golfer, the legion of young blacks bound for boardrooms have the leisure and the freedom to contemplate black existence. Surprisingly, that train of thought often leads to other blacks' effect on that existence, not to whites. Many seem to agree with comedian Chris Rock's infamous disquisition on the difference between "black people" (whom he loves) and "niggers" (whom he hates).

Much to the consternation of the Black Politburo, the democratizing influence of the Internet and general media proliferation have enabled the mass airing of intracommunal grievances. During the days of the Great Migration, black northern newspapers brimmed with scoldings aimed at the "cornbread and cabbage" Negroes who embarrassed them with their cornpone ways and their tendency to shout.

Judging by e-mails that make the black rounds, not much has changed.

YOU KNOW YOU'RE GHETTO CORPORATE IF . . .

1. You don't officially start the workday until Tom Joyner goes off the air. You can't function when the batteries die in your desk radio.
2. You use the company's postage machine to stamp your

letters to your mate in the penitentiary *or* the only time your man picks you up from work is on payday.

3. You paint your nails at your desk. They are so long you can barely type. You wear aqua, red, and neon green suits with shoes and stockings to match. You change your shoes as soon as you get to work with those dingy-ass house shoes under your desk.

4. On your many personal calls you laugh so loud, co-workers from across the room come to ask you what's so funny.

5. You talk about how much money you make.

6. You tell off your supervisor and co-workers on a regular basis and wonder why you haven't been promoted.

7. You get chicken, ribs, or fish and French fries every day at lunch. Before someone uses your telephone, they have to wipe the chicken grease off the handset.

8. Your version of a conference call is when you call your friends and plan what you are doing for the weekend. You come to work on Friday dressed for Happy Hour.

9. You cuss creditors out for calling you at work. Friends and family members call you at work to cuss you out because you screened them out at home.

10. Your kids call your job and say "Let me speak to my mama." You bring your kids to work, and they run all over the office. To beat [internal monitoring systems], you have developed codes for personal calls with your friends and family (e.g., let the phone ring two times and call me back). When your friends leave you messages, they leave names like Pookie, Shay Shay, Boo, Tootie. . . .

11. Your change your hairstyle from French roll to freeze curls to roller sets every other week—not to mention

the rainbow assortment of dyes. Someone automatically knows that it was you that brushed their hair in the bathroom sink by the gel flakes you left.

12. You've handed out more business cards at clubs than Career Fairs. . . .

13. Your e-mail inbox receives more jokes and personal e-mails than business e-mails.

The Internet revolution has made it possible to know what blacks say when they talk to themselves. While these offerings express some affection, pathos, and even admiration for the "niggers," they also show as much annoyance and condescension. Internally, better-off blacks express little romance for the ghetto poor or the working class, especially those who remain impervious to black-middle-class volunteer efforts and scoldings. They also show little sense of allegiance: no one thinks *they* are a nigger, but they think niggers abound. In the anonymity of the Web, blacks flip through the family photo album and laugh at the absurdities of black life as well as at white stereotypes. They also laugh at certain kinds of black people; they distance themselves from the "niggers" and wonder how they should feel about them. They wonder why ghetto blacks don't emulate their bourgeois manners so as to move ahead. They suspect that ghetto blacks are holding back worthy blacks like themselves. They smell, as Baraka noted, the smell of the dry rot of the middle-class Negro mind: "the idea that, somehow, Negroes must *deserve* equality."[95]

THE TOP TWELVE BLACK STAGE PLAYS

12. Who Drank All the Kool Ed? (A Mystery)

11. I Ain't Seen Daddy Since the 70's

10. Momma, I'm Pregnant (AGAIN!)
9. Momma, Our Check Ain't Come! (A Tragedy)
8. Baby Don't Quit That Job, The Test Was Blue!!
7. Now I See the Light! Even Though They Cut Off My Lectric
6. The Five Different Baby Daddy Blues
5. Sha Nay-Nay's Revenge (A Touching Musical)
4. How to Succeed in Sleeping with Your Best Girlfriend's Baby's Father Without Even Trying (A Ghetto Comedy—laugh until you cry)
3. The WIC All-Star Revue
2. LAWD, I Hate My Babies' Mommas! (Starring Jesse Jackson, Shawn Kemp, and Bobby Brown)

Drum roll, please . . . and the number one Black Stage Play of '99 is . . .

1. Oh Lawd, Momma Dun Bu'nt up the Chicken!

GHETTO RESUME
Resume of Roasalie Anastasia Shanekia "Pookie" Jones

ADDRESS: 2036 South Side Skreet, Compton, CA 11122
PHONE: Cut off right now but will be back on by the 15th.
OBJECTIVE: To one day fulfill my dream of being a Soul Train dancer, and you know just gittin my life togetha and stuff. I also hope to one day to hope to be the best cosmo-tologecalist (you know what I mean, beauty specialist) in my 'hood.
SKILLS: I do hurh and nails in my kitchen, and I use my glit-ter and weave bonding glue for arts and crafts and stuff. I do braids in any texture or color: synthetic or real human

hurh. Black, blonde, brown, dark brown, dark black, gold blonde, dark gold blonde, red, maroon, blue and rainbo colors.

EDUCATION:

- The 'Get Yours" Home Correspondence Course, Inc.
- Big Mama's House of Hair 'N Nails 'N Fried Chicken 'N Stuff.
- (• Graduated with honors for the most extensions don in a year)

WORK EXPERIENCE:

- Big Daddy's Motel Motor Lodge Bar & Grill Pool Hall & Bait'n Tackle Shop (Jan. 10, 1998–Jan. 30, 1998)
  Reason for leaving: Big Daddy kept hittin on me.
- My Baby's Daddy Day Care Center Car Wash & Shoe Repair (Nov. 2, 1998–Nov. 10, 1998)
  Reason for Leaving: They tried to work a sistuh ta deaf and I got thangs ta do!
- The Golden Tooth Dental & Jewelery Emporium (Mar. 1, 1998–Nov. 1, 1998)
  I loved this job cuz they gaveded me a free toof ary monf and now I can spell my baby daddy name but they done up and fired me cuz I let one of my homeboys sniff that laughing gas. He just smelt it, he don't do drugs no mo.
- Kim Fung Toi's Hous of Rice & Skrimps and Stuff (you don't even wanna know)
- Jimmy's Jheri Curls & Motor Lube (Nov. 6, 1997–Nov. 7, 1997)
  Reason for Leaving: Hospitalized for spine injury when I slipped on overflow of activator.
- The Ike Turner Hoe Slap Recovery Center
  (They have lovely accommodations; yes, I worked there & was a patient too.)
  Reason for leaving: Center closed down cuz Tina Turner

done refused Ike's request to give us a benefit concert and donate the money to Ike. Ike say Tina done got beside herself since she a big star and arythang. He say he remember her when she was Anna Mae Bullock from Nutbush.

YOU KNOW IT'S A GHETTO SALON WHEN . . .

1. All the stylists wear house slippers.
2. Four people are booked for the same one o'clock appointment.
3. Your stylist calls *you* at her salon talkin' bout "I overslept but I'm on my way."
4. The Asian man from the carryout comes to personally take food orders.
5. A crack-head comes in every few minutes trying to sell deodorant or batteries. Street vendors revolving-door through to peddle everything from baby clothes to Gucci shades to FUBU gear to Rolexes.
6. You have to divide your tips 'bout four different ways cuz one permed you, one shampooed you, one wrapped you, and your stylist finished you up.
7. Every trip takes HOURS.
8. The tape man is there selling tapes for five dollars.
9. Your stylist has to finish her wing dinner before she can start on your hair. *Or* Your beautician says she'll wash out your perm as soon as she's finished lunch.
10. They send Boo-Boo's baby girl to the ninety-nine-cent store for your ten-dollar "deep conditioner."
11. Your ears are ringing because "Back Dat Thang Up" is blaring on the radio, and she's singing along.
12. Her boyfriend and his boys come by, and you pray she's finished before there's a drive-by.

13. A playpen, portable crib, or stroller, complete with child, is a permanent fixture.
14. You have to supply any of your own hair care products *and/or* the beautician must go to the beauty supply store to buy supplies after you explain what you want done.
15. Conditioner is extra.
16. You want your real hair styled, and no one knows how.
17. There's a permanent "out of order" sign on the bathroom door.
18. You can't see your finished hairdo because the stylist has plastered all the mirrors with pictures of herself and her friends, mostly wearing something scandalous.
19. There's a receptionist station—but no receptionist.

ONLY BLACK COUPLES

- Are engaged for five years or more.
- Never bother with divorce but just separate for twenty years or more.
- Are late to church, work, and everything else *except* when the club is free before eleven.
- Refer to diabetes as "sugar."
- Are strapped with a posse at their own weddings, in case an ex shows up.
- Show up at weddings, graduations, etc., with a new designer outfit on, fresh nails and hair, but no gift—and then eat like pigs and take food home.
- Spend twenty dollars' worth of gas paying bills instead of mailing them (because they are late!).
- Consider "clubbing" a monthly expense.
- Leave unpaid bills instead of an insurance policy when they die or are too sick to work.

- Borrow money for a wedding and live in an apartment.
- Have mothers who use curse words and religion all in one sentence (e.g., "Lord, give me strength because I'm about to knock the shit out of this child!").
- Swear that the Korean lady at the flea market gives them (and only them) the best deals.
- Spend the settlement money on everything *but* getting the car fixed.

YOU KNOW YOU'VE BEEN TO
A GHETTO WEDDING IF . . .

- You were afraid to leave your car unattended.
- The programs hadn't arrived yet.
- The usher didn't know which side was the bride's and which the groom's and moreover thought it was a stupid question.
- The only AC was a hand-held fan from the local funeral home.
- The wedding started a half-hour after the time on the invitation.
- The groom was late.
- The bridesmaids' gowns didn't match.
- A groomsman had his tux leg rolled up.
- You smelled marijuana as the wedding party went down the aisle.
- A member of the wedding party was carrying a cell phone.
- A member of the wedding party took a cell phone call during the ceremony.
- No one in the church had set his beeper to "vibrate."
- Including the preacher—who answered his beep on his cell during the ceremony.

- You couldn't hear the vows over the crying babies, one of whom was having his nasty diaper changed right in front of you.
- The singer didn't know the words to the song—and her music was coming from a boombox.
- The parents of either bride or groom were under thirty.
- The bride and bridesmaids had miraculously grown their hair fourteen inches in one week.
- A member of the wedding party was wearing shades.
- There were more than forty people in the wedding party.
- The mother of either the bride or the groom had her shoes off during the ceremony.
- The happy couple already had more than six kids between them.
- Any Al Green song was played during the ceremony.
- The strippers from the bachelor/bachelorette party were in the audience.

THE GHETTO RECEPTION

- The couple had to stop at the Food Giant for beer on the way to the hall.
- Many of the guests were armed.
- The announcer mispronounced all the names of the wedding party.
- The "Lectit Slide" lasted for fifteen minutes, during which none of the bridesmaids were still wearing shoes.
- The lady serving the punch advised you to keep your cup.
- You saw groomsmen making trips to 7-Eleven and KFC to restock the buffet.
- At least one fight broke out.
- All slow dances looked like a *Dirty Dancing* competition.
- The man offering the toast didn't know the bride's name.

- They were toasted with malt liquor.
- The DJ had an entourage of more than eight people.
- The photographer, a bridesmaid's co-worker from the post office, got drunk, joined the party, and stopped taking pictures an hour into the reception.

YOU MIGHT BE A BLACKNECK IF . . .

- Your neck does the snake when you're in a heated discussion.
- Your initial credit was established at a rent-a-center or check-o-matic.
- Your credit is no longer accepted at the rent-a-center or check-o-matic.
- An extension cord or Hot Wheel track was your worst enemy.
- Your curfew was ever determined by a street light.
- A horse's mane and your hair have the same texture.
- A "track meet" describes an appointment with your hair dresser.
- You carry a cell phone with no service.
- Everything you eat requires a touch of hot sauce.
- Your steering wheel is wrapped in fake fur.
- Now and Later candy and a dill pickle are/were considered delicacies.
- There's a big wooden spoon and fork on your kitchen wall.
- The Cool Whip container is now your cereal bowl.
- You ever went an extended period with your cornrows or braids needing to be redone.
- You got in for free and still complained.
- You ever had roach clips hanging from your rearview mirror.
- You ever used a hot comb or bought a blowout kit.
- You ever bought tennis shoes at the grocery store.

- The screen door has no screen.
- You ever went outside with a Jheri curl bag on your head or curlers in your hair while wearing house shoes.
- "One nation under a groove" was your national anthem.

Then you might be a blackneck! (Or you might be from the ghetto. There are many riffs on this theme.)

BLACK FOLKS IN HEAVEN

Gabriel came to the Lord and said, "I have to talk to you. I know we have affirmative action and we are supposed to have twenty thousand black folk in heaven, but they are causing so many problems. They have torn down the Pearly Gates, swinging on them. They stole my horn and got barbecue sauce all over their robes, ham hock, spare ribs, and pig feet bones all over the streets of gold. Some are walking around with only one wing. Watermelon seeds are all over the clouds. Some refuse to wear their halos—they don't fit right over their naturals and Jheri curls."

The Lord said, "We need to check with someone who has more experience dealing with them. Let's call the devil."

The devil took a long time answering. When he did, he had to put them on hold several times, each time for longer and longer. Finally he said, "Lord, I am sorry, but I can't talk to you right now. These black folks down here have put out the fire and installed air conditioning!"

BLACK FOLKS AND COMMUNITY SERVICE

One day a florist goes for a haircut. When he tries to pay, the barber says, "No thanks. I'm doing a community service." The florist thanks him and leaves. The next morning, when the barber arrives at his shop, there is a thank-you card and a dozen roses.

The next day a cop goes for a haircut. "Free of charge," says the barber. "I'm doing this as a community service." The cop also leaves a thank-you card and a dozen doughnuts for the barber to discover the next morning.

A brother goes for a haircut. His, too, is rendered gratis as a community service. The next morning, what does the barber find when he arrives to open his shop? A dozen brothers waiting for a free haircut.

LEROY THE GOLD-TOOTHED REINDEER
(sung to the tune of the Christmas carol)

Leroy the gold-toothed reindeer
Had a very nappy fro
And if you ever saw him
He was at the liquor sto'

All of Leroy's "homeboys"
Use to playa hate his game
But they can't mess with Leroy
'Cause he got a big ole thang

Then one smoggy Christmas day
Santa came to say
"Leroy, have you seen my sleigh?
I know you had it the other day"

So Leroy broke out runnin'
And Santa pulled out his "nine"

And Santa shot poor Leroy
Dead in his black behind

TWELB DEYS OF CRIMMUS

On de fert dey of Crimmus ma boo dun give ta me
A 78 Cutlass Supreme

On de secont dey of Crimmus ma boo dun give ta me
Too gold teets an a 78 Cutlass Supreme

On de therd dey of Crimmus ma boo dun give ta me
Tree hot wings, too gold teets, and a 78 Cutlass Supreme

On de fort dey of Crimmus ma boo dun give ta me
Fo pig feets, tree hot wings, too gold teets, and a 78
    Cutlass Supreme

On de fit dey of Crimmus ma boo dun give ta me
Five bags of WEED!!!!!! Fo pig feets, tree hot wings,
    too gold teets, and a 78 Cutlass Supreme

On de scixt dey of Crimmus ma boo dun give ta me
A scix pak of forties, five bags of WEED!!!!!! Fo pig feets,
    tree hot wings, too gold teets, and a 78 Cutlass Supreme

On de sebint dey of Crimmus ma boo dun give ta me
Sebin hommies chillin', a scix pak of forties, five bags of
    WEED!!!!!! Fo pig feets, tree hot wings, too gold teets,
    and a 78 Cutlass Supreme

On de ate dey of Crimmus ma boo dun give ta me
Ate pimps a pimpin', sebin hommies chillin', a scix pak of

forties, *five bags of WEED!!!!!! Fo pig feets, tree hot*
wings, too gold teets, and a 78 Cutlass Supreme

On de nite dey of Crimmus ma boo dun give ta me
Nyne playa haters, ate pimps a pimpin', sebin hommies
chillin', a scix pak of forties, five bags of WEED!!!!!!
Fo pig feets, tree hot wings, too gold teets, and a
78 Cutlass Supreme

On de tint dey of Crimmus ma boo dun give ta me
Tin freaks a freakin', nyne playa haters, ate pimps a
pimpin', sebin hommies chillin', a scix pak of forties,
five bags of WEED!!!!!! Fo pig feets, tree hot wings,
too gold teets, and a 78 Cutlass Supreme

On de levint dey of Crimmus ma boo dun give ta me
Levin jacked-up hoopties, tin freaks a freakin', nyne playa
haters, ate pimps a pimpin', sebin hommies chillin', a
scix pak of forties, five bags of WEED!!!!!! Fo pig feets,
tree hot wings, too gold teets, and a 78 Cutlass Supreme

On de twelt dey of Crimmus ma boo dun give ta me
Twelb gubmint cheez, levin jacked-up hoopties, tin freaks a
freakin', nyne playa haters, ate pimps a pimpin', sebin
hommies chillin', a scix pak of forties, five bags of
WEED!!!!!! Fo pig feets, tree hot wings, too gold teets,
and a 78 Cutlass Supreme

THE BOURGIE BLACK'S BLUES

These e-mails could be presented to a grand jury as indictments.
No Klansman could have written a more virulent screed. While

they are often affectionate, the venom (or frustration, depending on how much you like blacks) they contain is unmistakable. Black America's love-hate relationship with itself has yet to be resolved; articulating the grievances is a necessary first step. Certainly, few who thought this description applied to them forwarded such e-mails, and there is little doubt that black people wrote them.

Criminals and "ghetto" blacks are only one source of black existential angst. Blacks who have to put up with the loud talk and neck-swiveling of the GS-5 administrative assistant don't have their own offices. Truly professional blacks have only bathroom, hallway, and office party contact with the black office worker in neon green pantyhose, unless they choose otherwise. For the most part their struggle is with themselves and what they are in the processing of becoming. They're trying golf and liking it. They're dating interracially and finding only run-of-the-mill relationship issues. As they repay their student loans and peruse their tax bills, Republicans are beginning to make a creeping sort of sense to them. They feel alone and wonder if they're sell-outs. They wonder if they can trust America. More, they wonder if becoming fully American—successful and free—is all it's cracked up to be. Does the white guy in the suit really have it all?

YOU'RE A CORPORATE NEGRO IF . . .

1. You know all the company mailroom workers, janitors, cafeteria workers, and security guards.
2. You think anyone without an office job is ghetto.
3. You keep getting e-mails about being a "Child of the 1980s," a "fancy Negro," or "You Know You Ghetto When . . ."
4. You answer your phone in standard English until you

hear that it's a personal call—at which point you switch to Ebonics. You wait till the white people leave the elevator to start talking slang with a fellow Corporate Negro.

5. You suddenly want to use your middle initial on everything *Or* You start using your first initial and middle name on everything (e.g., "S. Renee Johnson") because you don't want your co-workers to know your real first name is "Shaniquithia" [or "Moet Alize" or "Quintella" or . . .].

6. You work on your unemployed friends' résumés at work. You work on your relatives' court cases/garnishments/restraining orders/bail bonds at work.

7. You have ever had to leave work at two P.M. to find a Western Union because a relative was going to be evicted/repo'd/jailed/unable to get their car out of the shop and they'd be fired if they missed work one more time—unless they got money by close of business. They had weeks to deal with this drama but waited till you'd have no choice. They bought a big-screen TV the day before. On credit.

8. You're sure that *you're* not a Corporate Negro but that all your black friends are. You live for any after-work office party where you'll be surrounded by other Corporate Negroes. You think being a Buppie is a good thing. You consider casual day a privilege.

9. When O. J. was acquitted, you tried to front like you thought he was guilty to your co-workers.

10. You have no *real* friends at work.

11. You feel burdened when invited by your white counterparts to hang out with them after work. You feel left out when uninvited.

12. Your way of fighting "the cause" is forwarding militant, indignant e-mails to all the black people you know.

13. You've got a copy of *The Source* or *Vibe* magazine stashed somewhere in your desk.
14. You received this e-mail and/or plan to forward it to other Corporate Negroes.
15. You actually believed your supervisors the first time they told you that they were interested in diversity hiring and wanted your input.

The first version of "Corporate Negro" had ten entries. Later versions got longer, to the point that ten were edited out to arrive at this list. Each of the many iterations received has had jubilant messages attached, indicating which line the sender originated. A middle-class-born, Harvard-trained lawyer added the last one.

Mention of that copy of *Vibe* or *The Source* stashed in a drawer resonates poignantly for mainstreamed young blacks. While few would claim to be "thugs," many feel the pull of an articulated black identity as they navigate the white-dominated mainstream. While not exactly strangers in a strange land (or Douglass's "strangers and sojourners"), they are nonwhites in a decidedly white land.

At office parties the entire company watches expectantly as they take the dance floor, assuming they will get down like *Soul Train* dancers; drunken white co-workers corner them and perform wall-eyed versions of the Robot in which they are supposed to join; they learn to run for the exit the moment the inebriated "New York, New York" chorus line begins; the men will be automatically signed up for any office sports except hockey or golf; the women will be automatically signed up to help plan Black History Month and any minority outreach function; they face heated, out-of-the-blue demands to explain why any black anywhere did anything; every year they will have to resist the urge to actually answer the oft-repeated, furious "question" as to "when White History Month" is. Low-level black employees expect them to be their Martin Luther King, but if they offer advice on office protocol, they are told off for being bourgie. When they mention their hometown or alma mater, they will be asked if they know Raheem Smith, however large the hometown or alma mater. They will be fixed up with that one other black person whom a white co-worker knows, without regard for compatibility. They will have to fend off many requests to explain "what is it that those rappers are saying, Bob-ster?" They will have to remain calm while their names, however short, are mangled into goofy nicknames like Bob-ster. They will be invited only to "black" social events, like museum exhibits on Africa or the Dance Theater of Harlem. Never, ever, not in a million years may they seem "uncooperative," "not team players," "oversensitive," or God forbid, "angry." Not even when plans are afoot to invite a Confederate reenactor to the annual picnic. Not even when, for the hundredth time, the two Tremikas who work six floors apart are confused while the eight Susans in Word Processing never are. Everyone else's stupidity and ignorance become their problem.

"The black man came from Africa, not Howard University," Amiri Baraka notes,[96] and the mainstreamed black is made to know this every day on the job, every Saturday night when she holds the purses while the white girls dance. Being the Lone Ranger is both tiring and alienating. White people never have to explain themselves; they can be hippies, bikers, nerds, apolitical. But successful blacks are always surprising whites by what they are not—good dancers, athletic, political, interested in explaining how extension braids work. That stashed copy of *Vibe* is a refuge—it's a safe place to be black if only for a few minutes. One woman put it this (redacted) way:

I find that hip-hop speaks more strongly to me as I grow older and more successful at separating what I think from what I say, and distancing who I am from where I happen to be. As I shore up the many discretions of adult life, it becomes even more bracing to hear someone else tell it like it is. . . .

"The Man's claws are digging in my back," Big Pun sings, "I'm trying to hit him back." . . . A day full of corporate [and bourgeois] pieties almost requires rap as a purgative.

Hip-hop has a particular resonance for those of us whose great social achievement is a careful cultivation of middle-class propriety. That someone could sing of housing projects, foster homes, and welfare cheese—how cowards admire courage! If hip-hop has given a platform to those who have negotiated how to stay on top and remain from the underground, the music is, for people like me, one of the few ties to a past we can't express in polite company.[97]

The bourgeois respectability that blacks have long sought turns out to be a snug fit as the confinements of race give way to the confinements of class. Following the contested 2000 presidential election, a rap lifted from artist DMX struck a chord among professional blacks and made the e-mail rounds protractedly. It read:

THE NATIONAL AFRICAN AMERICAN WORKPLACE ANTHEM

1. Stand up at your desk . . .
2. Throw both of your hands in the air . . .
3. Recite the Anthem:

Y'all gon make me lose my mind, up in here up in here.
Y'all gon make me do some time, up in here, up in here.

Y'all gon make me ack a fool, up in here, up in here.
Y'all gon make me lose my cool, up in here, up in here.

4. Calmly return to your seat and patiently thumb through
   the classified section as you wait for security to escort
   your crazy behind to the parking lot.

However angry blacks were about those elections and the
sordid underbelly of race politics they revealed, there was no
black revolution or even disruption of daily life. Blacks wrote
their congressman, switched their voter registration from Independent back to Democrat, watched the news, and forwarded
that e-mail instead, between staff meetings and carpools. Reading and circulating such protests, like hoarding those back issues
of *Honey*, takes the place of acting them out. It validates the
mainstreamed black's sense of isolation and absurdity and keeps
her from snickering aloud while the racist CEO, who vigorously
mentors her, speaks. Successful though she is, she is still outside,
because when and where she enters, her race enters with her,
whether she likes it or not. Amiri Baraka:

[T]he middle-class spirit could not take root among most
Negroes because they sensed the final fantasy involved. . . .
The poor Negro always remembered himself as an ex-slave
and used this as the basis of any dealing with the mainstream
of American society. The middle-class black man bases his
whole existence on the hopeless hypothesis that no one is
supposed to remember that for almost three centuries there
was slavery in America, that the white man was the master
and the black man the slave.[98]

In the 1960s when the progress under way made clear just
how bad things really were for blacks, intellectuals and artists

like Amiri Baraka "went crazy" for them, spewing venom and threatening mayhem. In response to a white woman who asked if there was any way whites could help, Baraka once replied, "You can help by dying. You are a cancer. You can help the world's people with your death." The absence of much black-on-white movement violence makes clear that blacks were too civilized to consciously want whites dead, but having someone say they did was immensely cathartic. In the 1960s Baraka and his ilk were a purgative that blacks sorely needed, as rap is today. He animated that enraged and vengeful corner of the black subconscious, the one directly across from the corner that is wistful and lovelorn. What one writer disapprovingly described as "his inexhaustible and unmatched passion for berating Whitey" caused many a black head to nod in agreement. Such ranters filled the role that modern members of the Black Politburo do today—they keep whites guessing. As Jesse Jackson says, you can't tell a man who's hurting how to holler. Especially if you did the hurting. Clandestine copies of protest materials, a Mumia mousepad, and a month or two in sudden cornrows is how the young black professional hollers.

Now, though, the problem is less anger than anomie. They may still fear the police somewhat, but they also fear identifying with the police. Most of all, they fear having nothing worthwhile to live for—once you've gotten the office to observe Black History Month, what's next? Nothing but SEC filings and more depositions between you and next February. Oppression made the simple fact of buying a home or mastering the violin a courageous act of defiance, but now—where's the romance? Where's the agenda? Who, or what, do they organize around? If the answers aren't printed in *Vibe,* one wonders what will become of members of the new black middle class. Will they become generic? Or will they forge a new identity for themselves?

SELF-SUSTAINING SORROW:
WHO DECIDES WHEN THE PAST IS OVER?

To escape the gravitational pull of the past, blacks will find it useful to look at their existential woes in a global context. Everyone's searching, everyone's trying to reconcile modernity with history and trying to figure out who to be, a decision that is often quite arbitrary. It's not just blacks; the whole world is confused. It knows too much.

A HEMINGS FAMILY TURNS FROM BLACK, TO WHITE, TO BLACK.[99]

FEUD FROM A.D. 431 ENGULFS US CENSUS. Both Assyrian and Chaldean Americans claim descent from the original civilizations of Mesopotamia and are suing over the decision to lump them as Assyrian/Chaldean/Syriac.[100]

AMERICAN INDIANS ON THE RISE. Their numbers more than doubled in a decade; here's why it's cool to be Indian.[101]

[As Jews are faced with a 52 percent intermarriage rate] NEW STUDIES WRESTLE WITH "WHO'S A JEW." A Jew who practices Judaism? A born Jew who professes no religion? A born Jew who converts out?[102]

REFORM SAYS NO TO ORDAINING INTERMARRIEDS.[103]

CHINESE JEWS? . . . " 'Moshe' is a descendant of Jewish traders who had arrived in Kaifeng during the eleventh century. . . . Early on, they took Chinese [spouses] and Chinese names. They passed their ancestral heritage from father to son, rather than matrilineally. . . . [B]y the early 1800s, the last rabbi had passed away, along with the few remaining readers of Hebrew, and the local synagogue began to fall into disrepair. . . . Moshe believes that 'we Jews wear hats,' . . . and '. . . We Jews don't eat meat.' Ironically, because he [reported] that he does not eat pork, his official papers list him as a 'Hui,' or Chinese Muslim ["Jew" not being an option.] 'I don't mind what . . . they write on my papers. My father and grandfather were Jewish. My ancestors were Jewish. I want to go to Israel, learn Hebrew, and come back and teach my son and other people about our Jewish ancestors.' "[104]

MANY CRYPTO JEWS DISCOVERING WHO THEY ARE AND GOING BACK TO THEIR ROOTS. Five percent of Hispanics in the American Southwest may be Crypto Jews, people whose ancestors were forced to convert during the Spanish Inquisition but who practiced underground Judaism. Generations later all that was left, if anything, were fragments of rituals without explanation. One woman "discovered" she was Jewish after a "moving" Passover Service prompted her to look through an archive of Sephardic Jews who were persecuted in Western Europe during the Inquisition. Finding her last name there, she converted from active Catholicism to Judaism and attends a conservative synagogue. She transferred her sons from Catholic school to Hebrew academy and started a support group for Crypto Jews because "I was not who I was told I was."[105]

A lot happens in two millennia.

The Chinese Jews and the Crypto Jews provide the most useful examples for assessing blacks' modern attempts to make sense of who they are. Moshe's enemy was inertia, simply the deterioration of memory and custom over time, as a tradition failed to thrive so far from its roots. Aware of the romance of his exoticness but with little living substance, he was adrift, not oppressed. His was a sidelined, not stolen, history. As the writer put it, "whether Moshe is in fact Jewish is less interesting than why he so much wants to be." Reduced to minstrelsy, Moshe, the Jewish "thug," would have been better off having never known his scrap of history.

Unlike the withering away of Chinese Jewry, much of what has happened racially and ethnically around the world was affirmatively awful and rarely avenged, the most difficult kind of history to transcend. Yet, savage though their ancestors' treatment was, are the Crypto Jews really Jews? More troublesome than a decision to be Jewish because of a name in a ledger is the supposed transmission of a religious identity across centuries through some sort of spiritual vibration. What of the centuries of Catholicism—when did those conversions stop being coerced and become heritage? Who's to say that all those Jews would have remained Jewish through those centuries? People "pass," convert, or lapse with regularity. Might not those children kidnapped overnight from one religion to the next grow up to reject a coerced Judaism because they are "really" Catholic?

One suspects that both Moshe and the more attenuated Crypto Jews are really just lost souls looking for a cause or a way to feel important. They are like the heroine of the movie *Plenty* who thrives as a World War II Resistance member but is lost when peace comes. She spends the rest of a pointless, meandering existence searching for the meaning she can find only in opposition to injustice. It never occurs to her to cast down her bucket where she is and fully invest in the life she's actually living.

Blacks' enslaved ancestors were also forced to convert to Christianity. Does that make Colin Powell *really* an animist, or Aretha Franklin really a Muslim? Perhaps they should embrace polygamy. Reclaiming some researched native tradition—coldly triangulated by probable dates, probable trade routes, and scribbled scraps of names on ancient ledgers—would be a chic affectation, like kente cloth placemats. That would be trying to be who blacks were instead of who they are, multigenerational Americans with a proud tradition.

This romance of a lost narrative of victimization superimposed on mundane reality provides a psychic framework that can either ennoble and motivate or embitter and imprison. For blacks, this narrative of loss has been too recent and too relevant to resist. For centuries their freedom, their families, their traditions, their religions, their knowledge was obliterated as a matter of policy—for no other group was this true. Blacks lost everything, knowledge especially. As Amiri Baraka put it, "The context of the Africans' life had changed, but the American-born slaves never knew what the change had been."[106] This haunts them and causes them to favor gospel songs with lines like:

> Truth forever on the scaffold
> Wrong forever on the throne

and believe it. You can't be a true American and believe that, yet you can't be a black reader of the New York Times and believe otherwise. Embedding the hyperbolized truth in their irresistible music is the primary way that blacks have managed to make America hear their voice, that voice of exile, alienation, and reproach. But their sadness is everywhere.

One slave memoirist met another fugitive at church in New York. They became instant friends. Shortly thereafter one of the friends died. When her brother escaped and joined the survivor in New York, he informed her that her dead friend had in actuality been their sister. They'd been separated so early in their lives that they hadn't known each other's faces, just each other's hearts. Blacks have had centuries to ponder what, besides their freedom, has been taken from them.

Much of what animates blacks' discontent is really sorrow.

Anger fortifies, but sorrow saps the will; if you live on a tight-rope, better to be fortified than sapped. Nameless, formless, and unquantifiable, sadness permeates the atmosphere of they who invented the blues. Knowing that they lack even the knowledge of what was taken from them, blacks are like old ladies crying over a house aflame. Or they would be, if they could allow themselves to feel their pain instead of their rage; that's why the house is still on fire. Like veterans who experience car backfires as gunshots, they can't leave the war, and their particular kind of defeat, behind, though they know they must.

Wisps of black despair suffuse American culture and are readily discernible through their threadbare militance. Stephen Foster, author of "My Old Kentucky Home," saw it clearly. It is unfortunate that that "darky"-strewn song has become bowd-lerized and verboten, because Foster was up to something very different than apologizing for slavery and Jim Crow's counter-revolution. He was commiserating:

> The head must bow and the back will have to bend,
> Wherever the darkey may go:
> A few more days, and the trouble all will end
> In the field where the sugar-canes grow.
> A few more days for to tote the weary load,
> No matter 'twill never be light,
> A few more days till we totter on the road,
> Then my old Kentucky Home, good-night![107]

No blind black man making a guitar cry in a Delta juke joint painted black hopelessness more poignantly than "No matter 'twill never be light." "Kentucky Home" had to be suppressed because it was understood as a victory song, the musical equiva-lent of a Roman legion feasting while forcing the vanquished to set fire to their own homes. But viewed without a belief in white supremacy, black sorrow, the true message of the song, is obvious.

Now blues and hip-hop music, which take so seriously their every impulse, provide black grief's clearest articulation, but it saturates society. The brother of a man slain by a police officer said, "There's no rhyme or reason for this. My brother was a dentist."[108] Black members of which social class and profession are cops allowed to wrongfully kill? What he really wanted to do was wail, "*What else do we have to do! What more can we do to make ourselves palatable to you people! Why can't you tell the niggers from the blacks? Why do you hate us so much?*" Baraka sees that cry as another aspect of the slave mentality and as stemming from an acceptance "of the superiority of the white man, or at least the proposition that the Negro, somehow, must completely lose himself within the culture and social order of the ex-master."[109] A citizen, a free man might well still have lost a brother to a rogue cop but he would have insisted instead, "*My brother was innocent and did nothing to suggest otherwise.*"

DuBois knew that the unaskable question animating white contempt of blacks was "How does it feel to be a problem?" Too smart to play the master's game, he "answered seldom a word," focusing instead on self- and group improvement. He worked toward a day when he could answer as only a free person could: "How does it feel to be irrelevant?" Instead, in a statement announcing the 2001 State of the Black World Conference, the supposedly militant spokesman sputtered wistfully, "[P]eople of African descent, who gave birth to humankind, the givers of life and civilization, are now disdainfully viewed as impoverished beggars, wards of charity and Western welfare." That man wants to cry. That man feels like a problem. Claud Brown, author of *Manchild in the Promised Land,* being unschooled and unself-conscious, was all too aware of black sadness:

The Georgians came as soon as they were able to pick train fare off the peach trees. They came from South Carolina where the cotton stalks were bare. . . . [But] there was a tremendous difference in the way of life we lived up North. There were too many people full of hate and bitterness crowded into a dirty stinky, uncared-for-closet-size section of a great city. . . . The children of these disillusioned colored pioneers inherited the total lot of their parents—the disappointments, the anger. To add to their misery, they had little hope of deliverance. For where does one run to when he's already in the promised land?[110]

Blacks are sad because they want to be loved and they are not, they want to belong and they do not. They are sad because they know that, at any moment, their white friends can suddenly remember that they are white:

We both ordered navy beans and something else, and they put [his white best friend's] on the counter, but they had put my beans in a sack they wanted me to take out. . . . [He looked at the sack, shocked, and then looked back at his friend to see his reaction.] I remember him sitting there eating those beans like nothing was going on, like he forgot who I was. So I began to realize that your so-called white friends, whenever it comes to a point of choice, might just let you down. . . . And I can still see his gray eyes today. It's like I want to cry even today. I'm sixty years old, and I almost want to cry today because he just kept eating those beans. But what was even more humiliating was that I accepted that sack and took it back to school to eat secretly. I was so embarrassed about complying, conforming. I think from that day on, I took peanut butter and jelly.[111]

Your white friends can suddenly point out that they like you "because you're not like those other blacks" or suddenly opine that "some people just don't want to work" as a news story about an employment discrimination lawsuit airs. They can remain impassive while a friend of theirs says "nigger." They can react with disgust when you try to fix them up with a black friend. Your white friends can sucker-punch you and make you lose your footing. They can make you doubt things. Eldridge Cleaver said in the 1960s that "every brother on a rooftop can quote [Franz] Fanon" and his justifications of political violence on behalf of the oppressed. Why then did so few put him into practice?

"Nobody loves me but my mama," B. B. King wailed, "and she may be jiving, too."[112] Adept at camouflaging their emotions, especially from themselves, blacks often employ humor to mask their longing. In his 1964 memoir *Nigger*, comedian Dick Gregory joked:

Last time I was down South I walked into this restaurant, and this white waitress came up to me and said: "We don't serve colored people here." I said: "That's all right, I don't eat colored people. Bring me a whole fried chicken." About that time these three cousins come in, you know the ones I mean, Klu Kluck and Klan, and they say: "Boy, we're givin' you fair warnin'. Anything you do to that chicken, we're gonna do to you." About then the waitress brought me my chicken. . . . So I put down my knife and fork, and I picked up that chicken, and I kissed it.[113]

He jests, but not much.

Yet blacks have no monopoly on suffering, and it would ease theirs to put it into a global perspective. The briefest perusal of headlines, book titles, or conference announcements makes clear that ours is an age of grievance for which the bills have come due.

> *California May Force Schools to Drop Indian Mascots*
> *Justice and the African Seminoles*
> *Dutch Colonialists Clamor for Scholarly Affirmative Action*
> *WWII Vets, ex-POWs Rally for Japan to Apologize for Enslavement*
> *Victim of Virginia's Old Sterilization Law Says Amends Can't End Pain Over Loss*
> *Museum Helps Jewish Family Regain Relic Nazis Stole*
> *[Ethiopian] Treasures to be Returned [From Britain]*
> *The Stolen Generation: 100,000 [Australian] Aboriginal Children Forcibly Adopted by Whites*
> *Litigating the Legacy of Slavery*
> *Return of German Relics [from Russia] Is Urged*
> *Germany to Compensate Slave Laborers*
> *"Colonial Compensation" Call Fuels Concern*
> *Tokyo School Board Approves "Flawed" History Book*
> *Slavery's Legacy Seen in the Ivory Tower and Elsewhere*
> *Native Groups Mourn on Thanksgiving Day*
> *Hitler's Forgotten Victims [German Blacks]*
> *EU Nations Left in the Spotlight Over Slavery Apologies*
> *Canadian Town Tried to Bury Its Founding by Black Pioneers*

If everyone's a victim, isn't everyone also a victimizer? There doesn't seem to be anyone on the planet without an at least somewhat legitimate tale of group-based woe. But that also suggests that all the tales are at least somewhat attenuated, as with blacks; their hands may have been shackled, but they've also been bloodstained.

Journalist Tananarive Due describes what she sees as legitimate black grievances against the Cuban community in her native Miami:

> In 1991, soon after Los Angeles riots incited by a videotaped police beating of a black man named Rodney King, Miami was the only city in the United States to snub Nelson Mandela when he made his tour after being released from a South African prison. While Mr. Mandela was being honored with parades in the streets of Atlanta, and addressing Yankee Stadium in New York, Cuban-American leadership in Miami signed a document denouncing Mr. Mandela because he had refused to distance himself from Fidel Castro, who had been supportive of the anti-apartheid movement. That leadership included Xavier Suarez, the mayor of the city of Miami.[114]

No doubt a Cuban or Cuban-American memorializing her role in the fight against Cuban Communism will render this historical moment with different emphasis. Who's right and who's wrong? It all depends on where you begin or end the timeline.

Because blacks do not stand outside of either Western or American history, they cannot stand outside its crimes, alleged or proven. When Iranians took the American Embassy hostage in 1979, they released the blacks.[115] They knew that blacks were neither valuable nor somehow quite guilty of America's crimes. But came September 11, and the anti-American terrorists were equally happy with the black dead as with the white. That's progress, albeit ironic. Blacks can no longer have it both ways—vested when it suits them, homegrown outsiders when that offers more perks. American history simultaneously robes and strangles them. Both their progress and their demands create the conditions for their retroactive condemnation.

For instance, some blacks demand respect for unacknowledged black contributions to America's military might—but only as a one-way ratchet. Blacks exalt the Buffalo Soldiers but choose to know little of their role in helping to exterminate Native Americans so their land could be stolen; will they be any more forthcoming than whites if confronted by Apache and Comanche protesters? They demand acknowledgment of Teddy Roosevelt's black Rough Riders but never consider what the invaded Cubans thought of them. The Jim Crow that the Rough Riders endured when not invading other countries is unlikely to have engendered much sympathy for them among those they battled. Blacks have long been overrepresented in America's military yet rarely acknowledge their lusty contribution to what other nations consider to be American imperialism and neo-colonialism. One doubts that they incorporate these inconvenient realities into the Black History they justifiably want incorporated into America's curricula. More likely they too will air-brush the "problematics," offering up a one-sided dish of black heroism and self-sacrifice with never a hint of counternarrative.

The decoding of the human genome highlights another way in which blacks participate in the suppression of their own fully articulated identities. Easily a third of blacks carry European DNA, yet the excited discourse that has sprung up around these discoveries is only of tracing black bloodlines back to specific areas of Africa. What about Scotland? Why are Norway and Portugal off limits? Their penises weren't.[116]

One is unsurprised to find the white discourse unable to digest blacks' European connection (again, which is the slander: ownership of, rape of, or love of niggers?), but the black? How well trained and obedient is the American black! He curbs himself, like a good puppy, and stays on the existential paper. Regardless, the fact remains that, like Octavia Butler's *Kindred,* the American black would not be who he is without his European DNA. He could not be. He might be something better, he might be something worse; he just would not be who he is. Like it or don't, be happy, sad, angry, or blasé about it, but blacks must accept the fact that without whites' "contribution," many of them would not exist. Truly the perfect crime. What's remarkable about this state of affairs is how psychologically verboten the obvious is to blacks, even as they flaunt the melanin, hair, eyes, noses, and coordination that prove the point.

Like Senator McCain, who had to struggle with the obvious about his family's slave-owning past, blacks have yet to digest the truth about their family tree. Odd, given how oft-invoked is the systemic rape of black women, but then, that discussion isn't really about rape—it's merely a way to flagellate whites. Blacks flock to genealogy sites and trudge through illegible courthouse ledgers, but—again, mining those thinnest veins of Afrocentrism and multiculturalism—they continue to construct identities that omit all the whites they discovered except as oddities. Why? Malcolm could admit that his hatred of the whites in him was an artifice that he could, and did, shrug off. Blacks should follow his example and shrug off their ambivalence for their white forebears; insofar as they have any interest at all in their genealogy, they must accept the black with the white.

Assuming the worst about the whites in your line is as arbitrary as assuming the best about the blacks—your slave ancestor might have been the informer that gave away every slave revolt, he might have been the one who told where runaways were hiding, he might have been a rapist, a thief, or an idiot.[117] To have been a slave is not to have been a saint, just as not every black's great-grandmother was raped. Some were whores, some wouldn't have anything to do with a dirty nigger. Says Sowell:

[L]aws requiring slaveholders to maintain tighter control of their slaves were passed in cities across the South—and were ineffective in these cities, because both the slaveholders and the slaves had incentives to behave otherwise, and policing numerous urban residences was not feasible for city governments. The net result, as Frederick Douglass put it, was that the urban slave "was almost a free citizen. . . . Perhaps the most striking indication of the erosion of racial lines in urban settings was the much higher proportion of mulatto babies born to black women in antebellum Southern cities, as compared to black women on plantations. An estimated 1 to 2 percent of babies born to plantation slave women were fathered by white men, compared to nearly half in the cities. Southern cities of that era had a chronic surplus of white men over white women and a chronic surplus of black women over black men. Similar sexual imbalances have led to mixed offspring in many other times and societies, so the antebellum South was not exceptional in this. If most of the slave women who gave birth to racially mixed babies were simply raped by their owners, then such babies would undoubtedly have been more common on the plantations, where white control was greatest, rather than in the cities, where it was more lax.[118]

Even if you are the result of rape, you are still at least the sum of your DNA; why not visit County Cork on the way back from Côte d'Ivoire? Irish identity belongs to any black with Irish DNA as surely, and no more arbitrarily, than does West African. If a blood test makes you feel entitled to wear the mudcloth of a particular region of West Africa, there's nothing to keep that same test from making you feel entitled to wear a kilt. Nothing but that last plantation.

GONE NATIVE:

The Uncle Tom Imperative

Every Black History Month blacks tell America about Onesimus. The property of Cotton Mather, in 1721 he saved Boston from a smallpox epidemic. Having already lost three children to the incurable disease, Mather was beside himself with fear as the epidemic grew. Onesimus took pity on his master's suffering and told Mather of an inoculation he'd gotten as a child in Africa wherein pus from the infected was introduced into an open cut made on the uninfected. After producing a mild form of the disease, it conferred immunity. Within a year the epidemic was under control.

This event flies in the face of the white belief that Africa had no knowledge and that whites alone made America great. But more important, it flies in the face of blacks' supposed feelings of noncitizenship. Either Onesimus revered whites, or he felt invested in both his humanity and his community, however his community felt about him. So why do blacks celebrate such an Uncle Tom? Shouldn't he have let all the white folks die and shared his knowledge only with the blacks? More, shouldn't the blacks have infected all the whites and exulted in their agonizing deaths? How dare Onesimus take pity on a slaveowner? *His* owner? How could he not live a life of clandestine resistance, sabotage, and protest? How dare he contribute to the nation that enslaved him?

Another way the two black ids war so as to produce civic schizophrenia involves their choice of what to be proud of. Black History Month is when blacks most loudly announce to America who they think they are and what's important about themselves, announcements that are always revealing in their contradictions. Challenging the notion that blacks have contributed nothing either to the world or to America, exhaustive surveys of the history of black inventions and technological accomplishments claim that even slaves were "active in making improvements to the technology of their time." Like Ned, the slave who invented a cotton-picking device. Slaves were so inventive, we're told, that a debate raged over whether the slave or his owner should receive a patent. These surveys never include a discussion of the desirability of Ned and his inventive ilk contributing to the nation, the world, that oppressed them.[1] Blacks celebrate a slave who helped keep cotton king!

Another sell-out was Julian Abele, one of the first black architects (though few could tell) and one of the most renowned. He "turned out designs for 650 buildings, most of them places where blacks were admitted only as servants or manual laborers. The greatest moment—and greatest irony—of Abele's career came when he was asked to design an entire campus for Duke University, then the premier, whites-only university in the segregated South." And that Tom did it; he designed a university he never visited because he knew he'd have to enter through servants' entrances, if at all.[2] He built a beautiful place for whites to learn how to keep themselves in power, yet blacks celebrate this man who considered himself to be of "no ethnic group, who didn't like racial tags and lived an aracial existence."

Benjamin O. Davis graduated from the U.S. Military Academy

at West Point in 1936, the fourth black ever to do so. Like Cadet Henry O. Flipper, he was shunned for four years, assigned neither a dorm roommate nor tentmates in the field. He ate four years of meals in silence. Given command of the African American squadron in the Army Air Corps when President Franklin D. Roosevelt created it in 1940, he eventually led the renowned Tuskegee Airmen. He forbade his men to protest segregation, though they were being attacked when they went off base in uniform; he made them focus on their own exemplary behavior and on winning the war for the country that abused them.

Oddly, these Black History Month articles are not written to excoriate these collaborators, but to praise them.

Their childish lies of "never at any time feeling like an American" notwithstanding, blacks know in their hearts that to deny themselves the human's innate desire for achievement and self-expression is to deny black humanity and citizenship every bit as thoroughly as Simon Legree ever managed to. This drive to achieve, to communicate, to live a moral, useful life regardless of its mundane circumstances, this is the Uncle Tom Imperative. Blacks would have been entitled to equality in its absence, but they would not have deserved it. They would truly have been of less innate worth than whites.

To be called an Uncle Tom is an honor. Like our foundational black thinkers, Uncle Tom is often invoked but rarely read. He is not who the Politburo says he is. He was a moral, religious man of dignity and duty who accepted his lot as a slave because he had no choice yet by his behavior transcended it. He was an ancestor of whom to be proud; how has it been overlooked that he chose torture and death rather than inform on two sexually abused female runaways? To follow the Politburo's anti-intellectual, perverse construction to its logical conclusion, blacks should have cultivated no manners, created no art, pursued no knowledge, expended only the minimum energy at their tasks, and avoided any kindness or heroism that could not be confined to the black community. They should have actually *been* sub-human. But was Uncle Tom really supposed to let a little girl drown because she was white and in his line of ownership? Should he have been a slothful servant when his service was his only way of expressing himself? One is reminded of the elderly Jewish gentleman upon whom the Japanese performed cruel medical experiments during World War II. Before being immersed naked in frigid waters each day, he would greet his captors politely and comport himself with dignity. Why be a barbarian just because those around you are? *Especially* if they are? One-simus, Ned, and Uncle Tom weren't responsible for slavery, just for their responses to it. Abele, Davis, and the Tuskegee Airmen weren't responsible for Jim Crow, just for their own morality. All of them lived lives that each day disproved the lies that whites erected to justify their oppression. Uncle Tom wouldn't have had to die had he been willing to participate in his own degradation by acting like an animal.

Fortunately, blacks' ancestors held their heads high and achieved against all the odds. It was that sterling foundation that eventually shamed America into the civil rights movement; blacks would still be serfs had they lowered themselves to whites' level and met oppression with underachievement. That's why whites invested such effort into denying and obscuring black ac-complishment. With their perseverance and accomplishments, those generations established a trust fund for their children's grandchildren. It was their way of holding hands across genera-tions, leaving their heirs the only legacy available to them—excellence. They did not accept that truth would forever be on the scaffold, wrong forever on the throne. They sacrificed so that when freedom came, their grandchildren would not inherit a dry and dirty bowl of black history, empty but for slavery and Jim Crow. Instead, those grandchildren inherit centuries of hu-

manitarian, artistic, and technological achievement. They inherit
a long record of military excellence. They inherit Duke University, a black school. The truth will out, and it really will set you
free: in the 1980s Duke, which integrated in 1961, finally hung
Abele's portrait in its administration building. The great archi-
tect never got to experience his creation, but those for whom he
left it in trust—knowledge-seekers of all races and nationalities—
do. Thank God he was an Uncle Tom.

INTERNAL REVOLUTION:
THE JUNETEENTH OF THE BLACK SOUL

"I insist that the question of the future is how best to keep
these millions from brooding over the wrongs of the past
and the difficulties of the present, so that all their energies
may be bent toward a cheerful striving and cooperation
with their white neighbors toward a larger, juster,
and fuller future. . . .
[T]he future . . . depends on the ability of the representatives
of these opposing views to see and appreciate and sympathize
with each other's position—for the Negro to realize more
deeply than he does at present the need of uplifting the masses
of his people, for the white people to realize more vividly than
they have yet done the deadening and disastrous effect of a
color-prejudice that classes Phillis Wheatley [a freed African
slave who became America's first published black poet]
and Sam Hose [a murderer lynched by whites in 1899]
in the same despised class. It is not enough for the Negroes
to declare that color-prejudice is the sole cause of their
social condition, nor for [whites] to reply that their
social condition is the main cause of prejudice."
—W.E.B. DUBOIS[3]

"How much better would it have been to march
a million black men into the ghetto?"
—OVERHEARD AT THE MILLION MAN MARCH

Black people must take the reins of their uplift in their own hands. If they continue waiting for the perfection of the white heart, one can only hope that that change never comes. A white change of heart would be a gift, something that can be yanked away again. White largesse is nothing to take pride in, because freedom and citizenship are things that whites have no right to dispense, nor blacks to accept. Freedom cannot be delivered, nor self-respect served to the downtrodden. They must be claimed. Not long ago freedom was claimed at the end of a lynch rope or beneath the boot heel of the Ku Klux Klan. Today to claim the outstanding balance of their freedom, blacks need only believe in themselves, believe that this is their country too—and then act like it.

Blacks must look inside themselves and decide that they're tired of being the designated losers, tired of coming in last in every race, tired of fratricide, tired of making their peace with criminality and hopelessness, tired of fractured families, tired of watching the newly arrived outdo them, tired of underachievement, tired of soulless consumerism, tired of trying to make others love them, tired of being afraid to try. They must decide that they're ready to love themselves. They must face their fear of failure and commit themselves to themselves. They must stop dreading, stop caring, what white people think, if only because no one should set higher standards for blacks than blacks. After all, whites manage to live with black disapproval. They even manage to interpret that disapproval as proof of black depravity. Can blacks not manage a much less complicated, though watchful, pity for such deluded creatures?

Writing at the turn of the century from Jim Crow train compartments, DuBois was human enough to empathize with whites and their load of shame: "The present generation of [whites] are not responsible for the past, and they should not be blindly hated or blamed for it."[4] Even though he would doubtless agree that they yet bear considerable watching, he could still describe whites as "an essentially honest-hearted and generous people." Are his great-grandchildren capable of at least some of this magnanimity? The answer had better be yes because until they can forgive, empathize with, and assume the best about whites, blacks will never be truly free. A 1960s activist in deep south Tallahassee, Florida, Rev. C. K. Steele, was so tormented by racist white terrorists for his activism that his wife had a nervous breakdown. Still, Steele had no malice in his heart. When he received threatening phone calls, "instead of hanging up, Steele would often preach to the callers over the phone, telling them about nonviolence, redemptive love, and the life of Christ, even inviting them to call back after he finished his meal."[5] Without forgiveness and love for their white family, blacks remain handcuffed to their bitterness like a criminal to a wary U.S. Marshal. It's not as if either can contemplate much else. Such blacks will remain narrow men.

Blacks must recommit themselves to Martin Luther King's philosophy and tactic of nonviolence, but they must update it for use in this internal revolution. What is needed today is an ethic of psychological nonviolence existing in tandem with one of psychological separatism. They must transcend the ragtag remainders of racism by refusing to be demoralized by them.

"Never let anyone pull you so low as to make you hate him," Dr. King warned repeatedly. Hating and badgering whites can only further embitter blacks and distract them from the daunting work ahead. Blacks have to make a pragmatic peace with the societal pull-and-tug of interest group politics, however nastily played, and rise above racism. By all means, they must play to win. They must document racism. Block racism. Create art about racism. Outmaneuver racism. But they must not give in to melodramatic hyperbole, and, most of all they must not enshrine its eradication as their raison d'être. One needn't be a conspiracy theorist to wonder whether much of white racism isn't meant as a distraction from blacks' attempting real societal upheaval. What if all black people really felt like citizens? If they really were determined to achieve the ultimate score-settler—success? Carter G. Woodson would certainly counsel dispassion and calculation:

> In this [Negro history book] there is no animus, nothing to engender race hate. . . . No advantage can be gained by merely inflaming the Negro's mind against his traducers. In a manner they deserve to be congratulated for taking care of their own interests so well. The Negro needs to become angry with himself because he has not handled his own affairs so wisely.[6]

Having lost the proper circumstances for mass marches, rallies, and the like, blacks have lost the vehicle those events provided for personal and group uplift through self-help. Those heady days sent a jolt of pride, nobility, and self-determination through blacks that, for want of proper leadership, has today wasted itself in self-destruction, underachievement, anti-intellectualism, and bellicose finger-pointing.

Blacks must monitor white people, so as to safeguard their piece of the pie, but they otherwise should ignore them politically. Black self-worth simply cannot hinge on other people's behavior: So what if people eyeball them suspiciously? So what if rent-a-cops follow them around? So what if a random white woman clutches her purse when they pass? Is it not obvious that much of this behavior persists merely because it's effective, because it feeds whites' need to be central to everything? All blacks can control is their behavior, not other people's narcissistic and inglorious needs. If you know who you are, why does it matter so much that a powerless stranger has you all wrong? It can matter only if you agree that that person is superior to you in some way, a niggling doubt that too many leaders and too many neighbors have done everything to lodge in the black psyche. Warned Woodson:

> When you hear a man talking, then, always inquire as to what he is doing or what he has done for humanity. Oratory and resolutions do not avail much. If they did, the Negro race would be in a paradise on earth. . . . [U]nder leadership we have come into the ghetto; by service within the ranks we may work our way out of it.[7]

DuBois felt the same:

> In failing thus to state plainly and unequivocally the legitimate demands of their people, even at the cost of opposing an honored leader [Booker T. Washington], the thinking classes of American Negroes would shirk a heavy responsibility,—a responsibility to themselves, a responsibility to the struggling masses, a responsibility to the darker races of men whose future depends so largely on this American experiment, but especially a responsibility to this nation,—this common Fatherland.[8]

And here we arrive at the heart of the conundrum, the highdive that blacks have so long trembled to leap from that dimly lit crossroads where a civic direction must be affirmatively chosen. Should they go forward, toward a conscious and comfortable citizenship? Or should they go backward, away from their long-empty though custom-built chair at the American table? One marvels that this is a difficult question when it is the Constitution and the ideals of American freedom that blacks most frequently invoke, most esteem, and have vied for centuries to see honored. Why all the agitation about democracy, rights, and freedom, those most American of demands, if they are not seeking to complete their identities as Americans? Why demand an invitation to a party you refuse to attend?

In 1961 Ralph Ellison saw through this stubborn self-elimination:

> [T]he skins of those thin-legged little girls who faced the mob in Little Rock marked them as Negro, but the spirit which directed their feet is the old universal urge toward freedom. For better or worse, whatever there is of value in Negro life is an American heritage, and as such it must be preserved.[9]

Twenty years earlier Chester Himes's symbolic epiphany on the black behalf was both more succinct and more emotional: "That was the hell of it: the white folks had drummed more into me than they'd been able to scare out."[10] Blacks have America to blame for slavery and an aftermath of oppression but also to thank for letting slip the secrets of liberty and equality. After a generation or two of confusion, blacks can finally see that it is America they have been determined to perfect. Not white people, because white people are not America. Their hearts and minds are their own for which to answer.

Blacks, inner city or suburban, urban or rural, successful or struggling—all hunger for leadership that leads up and out, not back to white people. Leadership that doesn't tell them to aim downward for the lowest common denominator but that links arms to elevate, with loving sternness, those blacks lagging behind. Leadership that believes in the unlimited capacity of black talent, not the unlimited capacity of white evil. Blacks need leaders looking to the limitless future, not to the hunched-over past; leaders who are excited and hopeful, not bitter and defeated. Blacks need leaders who do not have all their hopes and dreams tied to the continued existence of white racism, the continued existence of black underachievement. They should run down the roster of those who speak for them and ask themselves at each face: "Would she know what to do with herself if white racism ended tomorrow? How invested in continued black failure has he become? What sort of a program would this group promulgate if they were not allowed to mention white people, ever?"

For too much of the black leadership, the answers are "no," "fully," and "don't understand the question."

That is unacceptable. Blacks deserve better. Blacks want to do better, and blacks can do better. They simply need to be reminded of what is possible rather than what is impossible. They need to focus on what they want rather than on what whites must do. All of this begins at home—in the individual black heart, in the individual black home, then in each black community. No group, however powerful, can withstand the force of a black nation committed to excellence, committed to its nation, but most of all, committed to itself.

NOTES

INTRODUCTION

1. For our purposes, *blacks* are those Americans descended from Africans who were brought here involuntarily as slaves. This definition would include free blacks, even those who owned slaves. Immigrants of African descent, even if descended from South American or Caribbean slaves, are not included in this definition. *The End of Blackness* is specific to the American experience of slavery and its aftermath.

2. Albert Murray, *The Omni-Americans: Black Experience and American Culture* (New York: Da Capo Press, 1970), 6–7.

3. Quoted in William Jelani Cobb, "Heavy Lifting as We Climb," Africana.com, February 1, 2001. Carter G. Woodson, *The Mis-Education of the Negro* (1933; rpt. Trenton, N.J.: Africa World Press, 1998).

4. Ibid., 100.

5. E. Franklin Frazier, *Black Bourgeoisie* (New York: Free Press, 1957), 98.

6. Nicholas Lemann, *The Promised Land: The Great Black Migration and How It Changed America* (New York: Vintage Books, 1992), 160.

7. Murray, *Omni-Americans*, 7.

8. Frazier, *Black Bourgeoisie*, 124.

9. Ralph Ellison, "Shadow and Act," in *The Collected Essays of Ralph Ellison*, ed. John F. Callahan (New York: Modern Library, 1995), 56–59.

10. Woodson, *Mis-Education*, 117.

11. The author will rarely invoke races other than white and black herein because this book is intended as critique, motivation, and direction for blacks on a practical level. The ways they are affected by and interact with Native, Asian, and Hispanic Americans, and the ways those groups interact with whites, are not at issue here.

12. Quoted in Woodson, *Mis-Education,* 110.

13. One reason for that ambivalence is that the Founding Fathers seem so dumb. *Harvard Magazine* recently described Benjamin Franklin thus: "The breathtaking range of Franklin's accomplishments—starting Philadelphia's first hospital, lending library, and college (now the University of Pennsylvania); inventing the efficient Franklin stove, a simplified clock, the lightning rod, and a musical instrument, the glass harmonica; launching a postal service, becoming a wealthy printer and bestselling author; writing the first great book of American literature, his *Autobiography;* plumbing the secrets of electricity, discovering and charting the Gulf Stream; and securing the decisive support of the French in the Revolutionary War, to name a few—reflect the fact that he apparently did not rest between tasks. His voracious curiosity about the world drove his mind to ceaseless activity." *Harvard Magazine,* November–December 2002, 23. But the same genius thought blacks were only slightly superior to animals. Where was the "voracious curiosity" about one of the most burning questions of his day—the true differences between blacks and whites?

14. Woodson, *Mis-Education,* 110.

15. Ralph Ellison, "That Same Pain," in *Collected Essays,* 70.

16. LeRoi Jones [Amiri Baraka], *Blues People: Negro Music in White America* (New York: William Morrow, 1963), 17.

17. DuBois, *Souls of Black Folk,* 139.

18. James Baldwin, Autobiographical Notes, *Notes of a Native Son* (New York: The Library of America, 1998), 7–8.

19. Earl Shorris, *Riches for the Poor: The Clemente Course in the Humanities* (New York: W. W. Norton, 2000), 125.

20. Murray, *Omni-Americans,* 210.

21. Woodson, *Mis-Education,* 154.

22. Erik Tarloff, "Erasure," Book Club, Slate.com, October 1, 2001.
23. Quoted in Murray, *Omni-Americans*, 15.

Prologue
BLACKNESS BEFORE THE DAWN

1. Joseph L. Graves Jr., *The Emperor's New Clothes: Biological Theories of Race at the Millennium* (New Brunswick, N.J.: Rutgers University Press, 2001), 25–26.

2. Thomas Jefferson, *Autobiography*, in *Writings* (New York: Library of America, 1984), 44.

3. Mark Twain, *Huckleberry Finn* (New York: Harper & Brothers, 1884), 306–307.

4. Quoted in Roger Wilkins, *Jefferson's Pillow: The Founding Fathers and the Dilemma of Black Patriotism* (Boston: Beacon Press, 2001), 87.

5. K. Anthony Appiah and Amy Gutman, *Color Conscious: The Political Morality of Race* (Princeton, N.J.: Princeton University Press, 1996), 38.

6. Thomas Sowell, *Race and Culture: A World View* (New York: Basic Books, 1994), 193–95.

7. This was largely due to its geography; see Part 11, pages 157–159.

8. Numbers 12:1.

9. Graves, *Emperor's New Clothes*, 25–26.

10. Wilkins, *Jefferson's Pillow*, 88.

11. "Touring the South during the 1850s, Frederick Law Olmsted asserted that on every large or moderate plantation he visited masters complained about runaways. Even in sections of the deep South where blacks had 'no prospect of finding shelter within hundreds of miles, or of long avoiding recapture and severe punishment, many slaves had a habit of frequently making efforts to escape temporarily from their ordinary condition of subjection.'" John Hope Franklin and Loren Schweninger, *Runaway Slaves: Rebels on the Plantation* (New York: Oxford University Press, 1999), 281. Attempts to run away were so common

that southern whites described the desire as "a disease—a mono-mania, to which the Negro race is peculiarly subject." "Through-out the South," Olmsted concluded, "slaves are accustomed to run away" (282). Moreover, as Franklin and Schweninger observe: "In 1860, there were about 385,000 slave owners in the South, among whom about 46,000 were planters. Even if only half of all planters experienced a single runaway in a year, and if only 10 or 15 percent of other slaveholders faced the same problem (both extremely conservative estimates) the number of runaways annually would exceed 50,000. Add to this the number of slaves who . . . continually ran away, and it becomes clear that Olmsted's impressionistic observation was far more accurate than the 'scientific' data provided in the United States Census." Although the Underground Railroad did exist, " 'Much of the material relating to it belongs in the realm of folklore rather than history.' It was not . . . a well-organized transportation system offering multitudes of slaves safe passage to the 'Promised Land of freedom.' Indeed, most runaways remained in the South, few were aided by abolitionists or anyone else, and many fled with a sense of terrible urgency" (xiv). You wouldn't know it from America's mythology of the white rescue of slaves, but blacks freed themselves.

12. Wilkins, *Jefferson's Pillow,* 89.

13. Jefferson, *Autobiography,* 44.

14. Ibid.

15. Thomas Jefferson, *Notes on The State of Virginia* (1781–82), in *Writings,* 264. Not only do xenophobia and racism blind even the most brilliant among the dominant group, they also render them deaf. According to Bob Herbert, "In his book *Deep Blues* [musician] Robert Palmer described a visit he made in 1979 to the Mississippi Delta home of Joe Rice Dockery, who had inherited . . . the remnants of a plantation on which an astonishing number of great blues musicians had lived and played. Mr. Dockery had grown up on the plantation but had never heard the music. 'None of us gave much thought to this blues thing until a few years ago,' he said. 'In other words, we never heard these people sing. We were never the type of plantation owners who invited

their help to come in and sing for parties. I wish we had realized that these people were so important.' " Bob Herbert, "Keeping the Blues Alive," *New York Times,* January 20, 2003, A19.

16. Ibid., 264–69.

17. Appiah and Gutman, *Color Conscious,* 47.

18. Ibid., 49.

19. Wilkins, *Jefferson's Pillow,* 88.

20. Appiah and Gutman, *Color Conscious,* 54.

21. Ibid., 56.

22. Nina Bernstein, "Love in Black and White," *New York Times,* January 26, 2003, sect. 7, p. 9.

23. A. Leon Higginbotham Jr., *In the Matter of Color: Race and the American Legal Process: The Colonial Period* (New York: Oxford University Press, 1978), 313.

24. Quoted in Charles Johnson and Patricia Smith, *Africans in America: America's Journey through Slavery* (New York: Harcourt Brace & Co., 1998), 329.

25. Graves, *Emperor's New Clothes,* 82.

26. Ibid., 75.

27. Nicholas Lemann, *The Promised Land: The Great Black Migration and How It Changed America* (New York: Vintage Books, 1992), 17–19.

28. Winson Hudson and Constance Curry, *Mississippi Harmony: Memoirs of a Freedom Fighter* (New York: Palgrave Macmillan, 2002), 21–23. Black women are still often seen as sexually available and unladylike. This excerpt appeared in a February 9, 1995, *Wall Street Journal* editorial called "White Male Rage Sweeps America" by Herbert Stein: "The existence of all these unmarried [black] mothers indicates a degree of sexual freedom on the part of the black male that the white male does not have" (A14). In 2000 Ford Motor Company vice-president Ron Goldsberry joked, from the podium, that a black female journalist could come to his room after the dinner to get the keys to the car she'd won in the National Association of Black Journalists' annual conference's raffle. He promised that she'd "have a good time." Askia Muhammad, "To Ford Exec: Black Journalists= Tramps," www.blackjournalism.com, December 12, 2000.

29. James Allen, ed., *Without Sanctuary: Lynching Photography in America* (Santa Fe, N.M.: Twin Palms, 2000), 12.

30. See, for example, the Associated Press's December 2001 three-part series: "Torn From the Land." The AP—in an investigation that included interviews with more than 1,000 people and the examination of tens of thousands of public records—documented 107 land-takings in 13 Southern and border states.

> In those cases alone, 406 black landowners lost more than 24,000 acres of farm and timberland plus 85 smaller properties, including stores and city lots. Today, virtually all of this property, valued at tens of millions of dollars, is owned by whites or corporations.
>
> Properties taken from blacks were often small—a forty-acre farm, a modest house. But the losses were devastating to families struggling to overcome the legacy of slavery. "When they steal your land, they steal your future," said Stephanie Hagans, forty, of Atlanta, who has been researching how her great-grandmother, Ablow Weddington Stewart, lost thirty-five acres in Matthews, N.C. A white lawyer foreclosed on Stewart in 1942 after he refused to allow her to finish paying off a $540 debt, witnesses told the Associated Press, December 1, 2001.

31. Associated Press, "Sterilization Program Targeted Blacks," republished on MSNBC.com, January 9, 2003.

32. Robert L. Blakely and Judith M. Harrington, eds., *Bones in the Basement: Postmortem Racism in Nineteenth-Century Medical Training* (Washington, D.C.: Smithsonian Institution Press, 1997), chap. 1.

33. From 1932 to 1972, 399 poor black sharecroppers in Macon County, Alabama were denied treatment for syphilis and deceived by physicians of the United States Public Health Service. As part of the Tuskegee Syphilis Study, designed to document the natural history of the disease, these men were told that they were being treated for "bad blood." In fact, government officials went to extreme

lengths to insure that they received no therapy from any source. As reported by the *New York Times* on 26 July, 1972, the Tuskegee Syphilis Study was revealed as "the longest nontherapeutic experiment on human beings in medical history."

Abstract of the Syphilis Study Legacy Committee Final Report of May 20, 1996. See hsc.virginia.edu/hs-library/historical/apology/report.html.

34. Appiah and Gutman, *Color Conscious,* 83.
35. Graves, *Emperor's New Clothes,* 2.
36. Lemann, *Promised Land,* 6.

One
TAKING THE WORDS OUT OF BLACK MOUTHS

1. Tananarive Due and Patricia Stephens Due, *Freedom in the Family: A Mother-Daughter Memoir of the Fight for Civil Rights* (New York: Ballantine Books, 2003), 69.
2. Ibid., 158.
3. Richard Wright, *Black Boy* (Englewood Cliffs, N.J.: Prentice Hall, 1998), 202.
4. Carter G. Woodson, *The Mis-Education of the Negro* (1933; rpt. Trenton, N.J.: Africa World Press, 1998), xiii.
5. W.E.B. DuBois, *The Souls of Black Folk* (1903; rpt. New York: Signet, 1995), 157.
6. The Justice Policy Institute concluded that state corrections spending grew at six times the rate of state education spending in the last twenty years. By 2000 there were nearly a third more black men incarcerated than in universities or colleges. To pay for their prisons, states have increasingly shifted tuition costs to students. Tuition increased from 13 to 25 percent of poor families' income, while Pell Grants covered much less tuition than in the 1980s. Reported in "Study Compares Number of Blacks in Prisons, Higher Education," *Black Issues in Higher Education,* September 26, 2002, 14.

7. Albert Murray, *The Omni-Americans: Black Experience and American Culture* (New York: Da Capo Press, 1970), 44.

8. Franz Fanon, *Black Skin, White Masks* (New York: Grove Press, 1991).

9. Earl Shorris, *Riches for the Poor: The Clemente Course in the Humanities* (New York: W. W. Norton, 2000), 79.

10. Henry Louis Gates Jr., ed., *The Classic Slave Narratives* (New York: Penguin, 1987), 37.

11. David Plotz, personal e-mail, April 17, 2002.

12. Woodson, *Mis-Education,* 133.

13. Murray, *Omni-Americans,* 36.

14. Ralph Ellison, "Shadow and Act," in *The Collected Essays of Ralph Ellison,* ed. John F. Callahan (New York: Modern Library, 1995), 57, 75.

15. Daryl Michael Scott, *Contempt and Pity: Social Policy and the Image of the Damaged Black Psyche 1880–1996* (Chapel Hill: University of North Carolina Press, 1997), 17, xviii.

16. Matthew Brooks, "NAACP, Ashcroft . . . and America," *National Review* Online, January 2, 2001.

17. Woodson, *Mis-Education,* xiv.

18. Gregory Rodriguez, "150 Years Later, Latinos Finally Hit the Mainstream," *New York Times,* April 15, 2001, D4.

19. Cloe Cabreva, "Cashing In on Culture," *Tampa Tribune,* September 23, 2001, Baylife Section, 1.

20. John Derbyshire, "In Defense of Racial Profiling: Where Is Our Common Sense?" *National Review,* February 19, 2001, 40. The quote was not used in reference to either of the quoted phenomena, but is very much in keeping with the way in which it was used.

21. LeRoi Jones [Amiri Baraka], *Blues People: Negro Music in White America* (New York: William Morrow, 1963), 8.

22. But see Note 15 in the Prologue for a discussion of how white supremacy impoverishes whites.

23. DuBois, *Souls of Black Folk,* 52.

24. Franklin Foer, "Reorientation: Asian America Discovers Identity Politics," *New Republic,* July 2, 2001, 15–17.

25. Herbert Stein, "White Male Rage Sweeps America," *Wall Street Journal,* February 9, 1995, A14.

26. Phillip S. Foner, ed. *Frederick Douglass: Selected Speeches and Writings* (Chicago: Lawrence Hill Books, 1999), 618.

27. DuBois, *Souls of Black Folk,* 46.

28. Jeff Jacoby, "No Reparations for Slavery," *Boston Globe,* February 5, 2001, A15.

29. See Part 2.

30. Ann Gerhart, "Frankly, Scarlett, Lawyers Give a . . . Copyright Winds Are Blowing Mightily Over New 'Gone' Novel," *Washington Post,* April 12, 2001, C1.

31. Ron Tarver, "African-American Cowboys," NationalGeographic.com; and Karin Lipson, "An Intriguing Picture of Blacks in Civilization," *Newsday,* February 4, 2003, B2. See also: William Loren Katz, *The Black West* (New York: Touchstone, 1987) and Phillip Durham and Everett L. Jones, *The Negro Cowboys* (Lincoln: University of Nebraska Press, 1965).

32. John Jeremiah Crown, "Horseman, Pass By: Glory, Grief and the Race for the Triple Crown," *Harper's,* October 2002, 51.

33. Murray, *Omni-Americans,* 18–19. See also Note 11 in the Prologue for a discussion of the extent to which the vast majority of fugitives acted with no assistance at all. Slaves, not white "conductors," freed themselves.

34. James Baldwin, *The Fire Next Time,* in *Collected Essays,* ed. Toni Morrison (New York: Library of America, 1998), 344.

35. Associated Press, "N.C. Lawmaker Apologizes for Email," August 22, 2001.

36. Woodson, *Mis-Education,* xiii.

37. DuBois, *Souls of Black Folk,* 275.

38. Suzi Parker and Jake Tapper, "McCain's Ancestors Owned Slaves," Salon.com, February 15, 2000.

39. William Yardley, "Paper's Staffers Protest Editorial Take on Slavery;" *St. Petersburg Times,* January 25, 2000, 1B.

40. John Derbyshire, "Racial Profiling," *National Review,* February 19, 2001, 40.

41. Jon Dougherty, "South Seeks Payback for Civil-War 'Injustices,' " Worldnetdaily.com, April 12, 2001.

42. DuBois, *Souls of Black Folk,* 180.

43. Cheryl Harris, "Whiteness as Property," 106 Harv. L. Rev.

1709–1791, 1724–1737 (1993). See also Michael Patrick Mac-Donald, *All Soul's Day: A Family Story from Southie* (New York: Ballantine, 2000). MacDonald, who grew up one of ten children in the all-white public housing projects of South Boston, confirms that poor whites exhibit all the same "pathologies" of poor blacks but nonetheless see themselves as distinct from and superior to them. As they fight, shoplift, do drugs, and procreate irresponsibly, they count among their meager possessions a vehement antiblack contempt.

44. Tim Wise, "School Shootings and White Denial," AlterNet. org, March 6, 2001.

45. Mike Males, "Tim Wise Didn't Go Far Enough," AlterNet.org, March 27, 2001.

46. Ralph Ellison, "An Extravagance of Laughter," in *Collected Essays,* 631.

47. Murray, *Omni-Americans,* 5.

48. Ibid., 34–35.

49. W.E.B. DuBois, *Souls of Black Folk,* 199.

50. Lowell Ponte, "Clinton Whitewash," FrontPageMagazine.com, February 28, 2001.

51. Jack Greenberg, *Crusaders in the Courts: How a Dedicated Band of Lawyers Fought for the Civil Rights Revolution* (New York: Basic Books, 1994), 465.

52. Charley Taylor, "Black and White and Taboo All Over," Salon. com, February 14, 2000.

53. Dana Canedy, "Boys, 12 and 13, Accused of Killing Father," *New York Times,* November 30, 2001, A18. The two white boys were eventually freed on a technicality that would never have been allowed a black defendant. See also Bill Kaczor, "In Deal, Boys Admit Killing Their Father," Associated Press, November 15, 2002.

54. Lynne Duke, "Red, White and Blue, For Starters: Firefighters (sic) Memorial Stirs Debate," *Washington Post,* January 18, 2002, C1.

55. Hastings Wyman, "The Enduring Burden of my Southern History," *Washington Post,* January 26, 2003, B2.

56. Judy Simmons, "Black and White and Married in Alabama," Africana.com, February 22, 2001.

57. Graves, *Emperor's New Clothes*, 50.

58. Thomas Sowell, *Race and Culture: A World View* (New York: Basic Books, 1994), 214–15.

59. Stephen Glass, "Prophets and Losses," *Harper's,* February 1998, 76.

60. Stephen Glass, "Taxis and the Meaning of Work," *New Republic,* August 5, 1996, 20.

61. DuBois, *Souls of Black Folk,* 274.

62. For instance, Sowell reports that "[b]efore the use of quinine became widespread, the average life expectancy of a European in the interior of sub-Saharan Africa was less than one year. Most European slave traders therefore purchased Africans who had already been captured by others, typically by other Africans." Sowell, *Race and Culture,* 195–96. There is no reason to think whites wouldn't have eliminated the middleman if they could have handled the environment.

63. W.E.B. DuBois, *Black Reconstruction in America, 1860–1880: An Essay Toward a History of the Part Which Black Folk Played in the Attempt to Reconstruct Democracy in America;* quoted in Jones, *Blues People,* x.

64. William Raspberry, "Readers on Reparations," *Washington Post,* June 10, 2002, A21.

65. Andrew Hacker, *Two Nations: Black and White, Separate, Hostile, Unequal* (New York: Ballantine Books, 1992).

66. Brooke Lea Foster, "Golden Children," *Washingtonian,* June 2000, 53.

67. Malcolm X, "After the Bombing," in George Breitman, ed., *Malcolm X Speaks: Selected Speeches and Statements* (New York: Grove Press, 1990), 157.

68. Eric Cohen, "Race and the Republicans," *Weekly Standard,* April 30, 2001, 30.

69. Clinton Collins Jr., "Free the Jackson Five! Affirmative Inaction," Rakemag.com, June 2002.

70. "The Subtle Clues to Racism: A White Sociologist's Nine Criteria for Spotting Veiled Bias," *Los Angeles Times,* January 11, 2001.

71. Craig Lambert, "Stealthy Attitudes," *Harvard Magazine,* July–August 2002, 19.

72. "Debate on Naming School for M. L. King," *Washington Post,* January 5, 1998, A7.

Two
KENTE CLOTH POLITICS

1. Quoted in Charles Johnson and Patricia Smith, *Africans in America: America's Journey through Slavery* (New York: Harcourt Brace & Co., 1998), 27.

2. Chester Himes, *If He Hollers Let Him Go* (New York: Thunder's Mouth Press, 1945), 3.

3. "Six out of every seven persons who crossed the Atlantic to take up life in the Americas in the 300 years before the American Revolution were African slaves." "Penn State Joins Effort to Research Era of Trans-Atlantic Slave Trade," *Black Issues in Higher Education,* January 16, 2003, 12. "From that very first recorded boatload of "twenty Negars" in 1619, most "had already spent some time in the New World, understood the languages of the Atlantic, bore Hispanic and occasionally English names, and were familiar with Christianity and other aspects of European Culture. . . . By the time Europeans began to colonize mainland North America, communities of creoles of African descent similar to those found around the West African feitorias [trading factories] had emerged all along the rim of the Atlantic. In Europe—particularly Portugal and Spain—the number of such Creoles swelled as trade with Africa increased. By the mid-sixteenth century, 10,000 black people resided in Lisbon, where they composed 10 percent of the city's population. Seville had a slave population of 6,000. . . . As the centers of the Iberian slave trade, these cities distributed African slaves throughout Europe." Ira Berlin, *Many Thousands Gone: The First Two Centuries of Slavery in North America* (Cambridge, Mass.: Harvard University Press, 1998), 25–29. "[T]he Venetians increased their imports of black labor such that by 1470, 83 percent of the slaves in Naples were black Africans from South of the Sahara. There were also African slaves in Sicily." Joseph L. Graves Jr., *The Emperor's*

New Clothes: Biological Theories of Race at the Millennium (New Brunswick, N.J.: Rutgers University Press, 2001), 25.

4. W.E.B. DuBois, *The Souls of Black Folk* (1903; rpt. New York: Signet, 1995), 93.

5. The black divorce rate of two-thirds is three times whites' and twice Hispanics'. Orlando Patterson, "Reclaiming Our Family Ties," *Essence,* September 2002, 232.

6. Only 28 percent of black women are married, half the white rate. Ibid.

7. Only 45 percent breastfeed for even a few weeks. Six months after birth only 19 percent were still doing so. Pamela Appea, "Nursing vs. Bottles: Why are African-American Breastfeeding Rates So Low?" Africana.com, December 6, 2000. "In the average Black home, a television is on almost 11 hours a day." "Tuning Out," *Essence,* June 2002, 124.

8. Zora Neale Hurston, *How It Feels to Be Colored Me,* in Alice Walker, ed., *I Love Myself When I Am Laughing . . . and Then Again When I Am Looking Mean and Impressive: A Zora Neale Hurston Reader* (New York: Feminist Press at CUNY, 1989), 152.

9. Harriet A. Jacobs, *Incidents in the Life of a Slave Girl* (Cambridge, Mass.: Harvard University Press, 2000), 365.

10. Himes, *If He Hollers,* 135.

11. "Malcolm X Memorabilia Stolen," Entertainment Urban Report (new.blackvoices.com/entertainment/opinion/eur), December 17, 1999.

12. Malcolm X, "Message to the Grass Roots," speech delivered November 10, 1963, in George Breitman, ed., *Malcolm X Speaks: Selected Speeches and Statements* (New York: Grove Press, 1990), 3.

13. Sanyika Shakur [Scott, Monster Kody], *Monster: The Autobiography of an L.A. Gang Member* (New York: Penguin Books, 1993).

14. Chester Himes, *The Quality of Hurt: The Autobiography of Chester Himes* (New York: Doubleday, 1972), 285.

15. Nikki Giovanni, "feet," in *O Magazine,* August 2002, 169; reprinted from *Quilting the Black-eyed Pea: Poems & Not Quite Poems* (New York: William Morrow, 2002).

16. DuBois, *Souls of Black Folk,* 233.

17. Iyanla Vanzant, *Acts of Faith: Daily Meditations for People of Color* (New York: Simon & Schuster, 1993), entry for February 4.

18. Ibid., entry for February 8.

19. "College Cancels 'Happy Slaves' Class," *Black Issues in Higher Education*, December 10, 1998, 12.

20. K. Anthony Appiah and Amy Gutman, *Color Conscious: The Political Morality of Race* (Princeton, N.J.: Princeton University Press, 1996), 70.

21. Jefferson apologists rarely point out that his slaves were sold, regardless of family ties, to pay his debts after he died. He freed only Sally's children.

22. Ronald Roach, "World Class Educator: Grant Richard Parker," *Black Issues in Higher Education*, January 2, 2003, 24.

23. "First Black Fraternity Chartered at University of Wyoming," *Black Issues in Higher Education*, January 2, 2003, 12.

24. In *How It Feels to Be Colored Me,* Hurston noted, "I am the only Negro in the United States whose grandfather on the mother's side was not an Indian chief" (152).

25. "Measuring the Progress of the Colored Race," 22 May 1886, Douglass Papers, vol. 5, 240.

26. On Elijah Muhammad's orders, Malcolm X, whose mother could pass for white, used to say that he despised every drop of white blood in his veins and that his grandmother had been raped by his white grandfather. After his awakening, the "red-boned" Malcolm admitted that that had been a "political statement." Jan R. Carew, *Ghosts in Our Blood: With Malcolm X in Africa, England, and the Caribbean* (Chicago: Lawrence Hill Books, 1994), 23.

27. Carter G. Woodson, *The Mis-Education of the Negro* (1933; rpt. Trenton, N.J.: Africa World Press, 1998), 190.

28. On the black sitcom *Moesha* starring Brandy Norwood, she once insulted someone by claiming they'd gotten their hair from the Korean flea market. Norwood wore braided extensions then and has a weave now. She has publicly battled with eating disorders and a hatred of her looks.

29. Kevin Baker, "The Magic Reagan," *Harper's*, May 2002, 77.

30. Ann M. Simmons, "South Africa Whites Say Deck Stacked Against Them," *Los Angeles Times,* June 19, 2002, A1.

31. David Plotz personal e-mail, May 26, 2002.

32. "Have you ever noticed that the paths of hurricanes always begin in Africa or near its shores and they take the same path that the slaves took when brought here? And where do they always end up hitting the United States the hardest? The Carolinas and Virginia, which happen to be the place where the plantations and ports were plentiful at the time. Now, do you suppose that all of those souls that were lost at sea in those passages are the same restless ones that gather together to make one strong force and still revenge their lives every hurricane season?" Anonymous, mass forwarded e-mail, October 5, 1999.

33. See Thomas Sowell, *Race and Culture: A World View* (New York: Basic Books, 1994), 246, and Dr. Lisa Yun, "Africans and Asians Breaking Down Barriers," *Black Issues Book Review,* May–June 2000, 58–59.

34. Edward C. Smith, "United States Marks 75th Year of Black History Celebration," NationalGeographic.com, February 1, 2001. A common black conspiracy theory is that "they" made Black History Month February because it's the shortest.

35. W.E.B. DuBois, *The Souls of Black Folk* (1903; rpt. New York: Signet, 1995), 139.

36. Chester Himes, *If He Hollers,*" 88.

37. Monica Davey, "Second Act for Controversial Mayor," *New York Times,* May 16, 2003, A18.

38. Cheo Taylor Tyehimba, "Where There's Will...," *Savoy,* August 2002, 66.

39. Keith B. Richburg, *Out of America: A Black Man Confronts Africa* (New York: Basic Books, 1997).

40. Ibid., 233–35.

41. Hurston, *How It Feels to Be Colored Me,* 152.

42. "While the descendants of slaves carried an indelible stigma for generations in some countries, the male offspring of the Ottoman sultan's harem became his heirs, including his successors as sultan in the Ottoman Empire. In Southeast Asia, Chinese immigrants—

overwhelmingly male—often took local slave women as concubines, in some cases selling them again in later years when the men returned to China, taking their children with them. In other cases, where the original intention to return to China faded away over the years, the concubines might become the wives of those men who remained. Among European men sojourning in Southeast Asia, it was more common to set the women free when the men returned to Europe alone. . . . Among the Circassian [Caucasus Mountain] women who were prized as concubines in the harems of the Ottoman Empire, their treatment was sufficiently mild to cause mothers to deliberately train their daughters for this role and to sell them into bondage in the harems of wealthy Ottoman men, from which they often emerged later with advantageous marriages having been arranged for them by their owners." Sowell, *Race and Culture,* 190–92.

43. Ibid., 230, 236–37, 238.
44. Graves, *Emperor's New Clothes,* 28–29.
45. Sowell, *Race and Culture,* 61, 63–64.
46. Occam's razor is the scientific and philosophic rule that the simplest of competing theories is to be preferred to the more complex or that explanations of unknown phenomena are to be sought first in terms of known quantities. *Merriam Webster Collegiate Dictionary,* Tenth Edition.
47. Richburg, *Out of America,* 237.
48. Woodson, *Mis-Education,* 191.
49. Yaguine Koita and Fodé Tourakana, "A Prayer For Africa," *Harper's,* November 1999, 22.
50. Tom Jones, *Take a Lesson,* excerpted in *Savoy,* May 2001.
51. "Over the centuries, somewhere in the neighborhood of 11 million people were shipped across the Atlantic from Africa as slaves, and another 14 million African slaves were taken across the Sahara Desert or shipped through the Persian Gulf and other waterways to the nations of North Africa and the Middle East." Sowell, *Race and Culture,* 188.
52. "Ignoring the Odds, Alan Keyes Insists His Is the Voice of Moral Victory," *Chatttanooga Times,* September 12, 1999.
53. Jones, *Take a Lesson.*

54. James Baldwin, "Stranger in the Village," in *Collected Essays,* ed. Toni Morrison (New York: Library of America, 1998), 119.

55. DuBois, *Souls of Black Folk,* 131.

56. James Baldwin, "Everybody's Protest Novel," in *Collected Essays,* 18.

57. "Brigham Young University Elects First Black Student Body President," *Black Issues in Higher Education,* March 14, 2002, 21.

58. Associated Press, "Convert Hopes to Become First Black Woman Rabbi in U.S.," May 25, 2002.

59. *Ebony*'s stated definition of *leadership:* "1. Does the individual transcend his or her position and command widespread national influence? 2. Does the individual affect in a decisive and positive way the lives, thinking and actions of large segments of the African-American population, either by his or her position in a key group or by his or her personal reach and influence?" Here is yet another way in which black apologists resemble white apologists: the manipulation of apparently objective rules to achieve dishonest or immoral outcomes. *Ebony,* May 2002, 68.

60. Dr. Carlyle V. Thompson, circulated on the Black Radical Congress listserv, December 17, 1999.

61. "R&B singer in the Hotseat," Entertainment Urban Report (new.blackvoices.com/entertainment/opinion/eur), August 29, 2001.

62. Murray, *Omni-Americans,* 72.

63. Ibid., 111.

64. Adamma Ince, "No Masses No Movement: Black Boomers Shout Reparations in the Court—But Go Silent in the 'Hood," *Village Voice,* May 22, 2002; Bill Maxwell, "We Have No Leaders to Save Our Black Men," *St. Petersburg Times,* July 29, 2001, 1D; William Jones Jr., "Black Leaders Owe Hip Hop an Apology," daveyd.com, August 12, 2002; Lee Hubbard, "Who Shall Lead the Black Race?" *Miami Times,* July 10, 2001, 4A.

65. Jeff Chang, "Generation H," *Village Voice Literary Supplement,* Spring 2002, 81.

66. Bakari Kitwana, *The Hip-Hop Generation: Young Blacks and the Crisis in African-American Culture* (New York: Basic Books, 2002).

67. Colin Channer, "The Problem with Women? Men," *Essence*, May 2002, 114.

68. Joan Morgan, "Their Sweet Success Brings Home Bitter Truth," *Essence*, March 1997, 77.

69. Patterson, "Family Ties," 232.

70. Oliver Williams, "Breaking the Cycle," *Essence*, November 2002, 252.

71. Ibid.

72. According to the National Center for Health Statistics, homicide is the leading cause of death for African American girls aged fifteen to nineteen. (It is the second leading cause for other races.) Vanessa Bush, "A Thin Line Between Love and Hate," *Essence*, November 2002, 194.

73. Murray, *Omni-Americans*, 63.

74. Sowell, *Race and Culture*, 201, 208–209.

75. DuBois, *Souls of Black Folk*, 68.

76. Dan Rather, CBS News Special Report (transcript), July 23, 1999.

77. Carole Stewart McDonnell, "Oreo Blues," in *Life Notes: Personal Writings by Contemporary Black Women*, ed. Patricia Bell-Scott (New York: W. W. Norton, 1994), 127, 141.

78. Six in ten black children are raised by single mothers. Patterson, "Family Ties," 232.

79. Sampson Davis, George Jenkins, and Rameck Hunt with Lisa Frazier Page, *The Pact: Three Young Men Make a Promise and Fulfill a Dream* (New York: Riverhead Books, 2000), 7.

80. DuBois, *Souls of Black Folk*, 41, 45–46.

81. Bomani Jones, "Tiger and Me," Africana.com, May 30, 2002.

82. Charles Dervarics, "Bush Invokes Rare Press to Fill Slot," *Black Issues in Higher Education*, April 25, 2002, 8.

83. Eric Cohen, "Race and the Republicans," *Weekly Standard*, April 30, 2001, 32.

84. Davis et al., *Pact*, 144–45.

85. Tyehimba, "Where There's Will . . . ," 61, and Thamie Dubois, "Taken to the Mat," *Savoy*, August 2002, 74.

86. Ron Susskind, *A Hope in the Unseen: An American Odyssey from the Inner City to the Ivy League* (New York: Broadway

Books, 1998), provides many examples of inner city students' ambivalent jealousy and admiration of high achievers.

87. A study of forty thousand minority high school students conducted by the Minority Student Achievement Network (www.msa network.org) found that African American and Hispanic students are more likely than white or Asian students to report that their friends think it is "very important" to "study hard and get good grades." Overall, the study showed that minority students have as much desire to succeed in schools as whites and Asians. Unfortunately, the study also confirmed that these students know they master the material less well, have less access to resources, and are more likely to live with only one parent or neither parent, and that those parents are less well educated than whites' and Asians'. "Survey Challenges Notions About African American, Hispanic Achievement," *Black Issues in Higher Education,* December 19, 2002, 18.

88. DuBois, *Souls of Black Folk,* 51.

89. E. Franklin Frazier, *Black Bourgeoisie* (New York: Free Press, 1957), 57.

90. "Despite obstacles put in the way of their acquiring the culture of the society around them, blacks nevertheless acquired literacy at a remarkable rate. Most free blacks in the United States were literate as of 1850 and, half a century after emancipation, so were three quarters of the entire black population, most of whom had been either illiterate former slaves or their descendants." Sowell, *Race and Culture,* 221.

91. Murray, *Omni-Americans,* 3.

92. Ibid., 22.

93. Yolanda Adams, "I Don't Want to Be Black Anymore," *Essence,* August 1999, 53.

94. Milfy, New York City, NY Eurextra Thursday Feedback Entertainment Urban Report (new.blackvoices.com/entertainment/ opinion/eur), November 28, 1999.

95. LeRoi Jones [Amiri Baraka], *Blues People: Negro Music in White America* (New York: William Morrow, 193), 134.

96. Ibid., 19.

97. Mina Kumar, "My Hip Hop Id," *New York Times*, August 22, 2001, A14.

98. Jones, *Blues People*, 142, 136.

99. Brent Staples, "A Hemings Family Turns from Black, to White, to Black," *New York Times*, December 17, 2001, A20.

100. Ben Fenton, "Feud from AD 431 Engulfs US Census, *Daily Telegraph*, March 14, 2001, 15.

101. Susan Steindorf, "American Indians on the Rise," *Christian Science Monitor*, December 6, 2001, 11.

102. Julia Goldman, "New Studies Wrestle with 'Who's a Jew,' " *Forward*, December 7, 2001, 14.

103. Ami Eden, "Reform Says No to Ordaining Intermarrieds," *Forward*, February 6, 2002, 1.

104. James Harding, "East of Eden," *New Republic*, November 22, 1999, 18.

105. Brenda de Anda, "Many Crypto Jews Discovering Who They Are and Going Back to Their Roots," National Public Radio, *Morning Edition*, September 20, 1999.

106. Jones, *Blues People*, 20.

107. Quoted in John Jeremiah Crown, "Horseman, Pass By: Glory, Grief and the Race for the Triple Crown," *Harper's*, October 2002, 51.

108. Neely Tucker, "Family Sues in Police Slaying," *Washington Post*, April 6, 2002, B2.

109. Jones, *Blues People*, 59.

110. Claude Brown, *Manchild in the Promised Land* (New York: Touchstone, 1965, 1993), 7–8.

111. Tananarive Due and Patricia Stephens Due, *Freedom in the Family: A Mother-Daughter Memoir of the Fight for Civil Rights* (New York: Ballantine Books, 2003), 156.

112. B. B. King, *King of the Blues* [boxed set], MCA Records, 1992.

113. Dick Gregory, *Nigger* (New York: Pocket Books, 1964), 144.

114. Due and Due, *Freedom in the Family*, 90.

115. John M. McGuire, "20 Years Later, Few Will Let Rocky Sidemann Forget About His Hostage Ordeal in Iran," *St. Louis Post-Dispatch*, November 4, 1999, A1.

116. "[V]ery large numbers (perhaps as many as two-thirds) of

African-Americans have some European forebears; up to two-fifths may have American Indian 'blood'; and at least 5 percent of white Americans are thought to have African roots. It is estimated that 20 to 30 percent of the genes of the average African-American come from European and American Indian ancestors." Appiah and Gutman, *Color Conscious,* 70.

117. When Harriet Jacobs fled her master's house in desperation, she fled to a friendly white neighbor's home. Her master hot on her heels, Jacobs begged the neighboring white slaveowner for sanctuary. She complied but had to slap her own slave's face and threaten her with a beating to keep her from informing. Slavery was complicated.

118. Sowell, *Race and Culture,* 206–207.

Three
GONE NATIVE

1. Ronald Roach, "Learning from the Past," *Black Issues in Higher Education,* February 28, 2002, 28–30.

2. Inga Saffron, "The Visible Man," *Philadelphia Inquirer*, May 29, 2002, E1.

3. W.E.B. DuBois, *The Souls of Black Folk* (1903; rpt. New York: Signet, 1995), 137, 208–209.

4. Ibid., 92.

5. Tananarive Due and Patricia Stephens Due, *Freedom in the Family: A Mother-Daughter Memoir of the Fight for Civil Rights* (New York: Ballantine Books, 2003), 144.

6. Carter G. Woodson, *The Mis-Education of the Negro* (1933; rpt. Trenton, N.J.: Africa World Press, 1998), 197.

7. Ibid., 118–19.

8. DuBois, *Souls of Black Folk,* 91.

9. Ralph Ellison, "That Same Pain," in *The Collected Essays of Ralph Ellison,* ed. John F. Callahan (New York: Modern Library, 1995), 80.

10. Chester Himes, *If He Hollers Let Him Go* (New York: Thunder's Mouth Press, 1945), 152.

ACKNOWLEDGMENTS

This book grew out of my frustration with both the pace of racial progress in America and the role that black people themselves are playing in that progress. Reading newspapers and magazines, or even trying to have a discussion with ostensibly well-informed, well-intentioned people of all races, drove me to madness at the drivel I was expected to take seriously. On the one hand, I was being told that black people's problems were either self-inflicted or innate, given that racism had been eradicated by the civil rights movement (also given that slavery and Jim Crow hadn't been "that" bad, and that blacks had been "just as guilty when you consider" blah blah, and "what about my poor Lebanese, Armenian, Vietnamese buck-toothed, left-handed great-grandmother on my father's side who came here with nothing"). On the other hand, I was told that racism was as potent as it had ever been, Dr. King's dream notwithstanding, and that the answers to black people's problems continued to lie in the never-ending battle to reform the hearts and minds of white people (and, of course, in the never-ending battle to keep the Uncle Toms from diverging from the party line, ideological purity being the *only* currency of the calcified black left). That battle for the perfection of the white soul, the battle to make whites go on apologizing so that weak-minded blacks could get over their cultural embarrassment, took precedence over a focus on practical solutions. So what if Tamika can't read as long as we can go on getting the op-ed page vapors about drunken white college boys behaving badly in Halloween blackface or about any white person anywhere at any time in history using a word with the syllable *nig-* in it?

There is a third alternative. Surely we can acknowledge that overt racism has indeed been officially vanquished by the movement even as we recognize that practical racism remains lodged in many people's hearts, however subconscious, clandestine, and cloaked in seemingly color-blind rhetoric. We can also acknowledge that although some black political tactics, customs, and worldviews are not constructive, in no way are blacks' shortcomings biological or even cultural except as a rational, if regrettable, response to external stimuli (such as police brutality, structural inequality, and substandard education).

I wrote this book to give voice to what I believe is a growing cohort, especially among young blacks, who find few on the national stage who seem more concerned with America's possibilities than with its limitations. It is incredibly frustrating to be spoken for by those for whom one has little respect and with whom one vehemently disagrees; this, I believe, is the case for a great many of the post-movement generation whose "leaders" are assembly-lined for them from the same froth-mouthed, do-nothing, stage-hogging bolt of pseudoactivist remnants who wouldn't couldn't find their way to the 'hood if their lives depended on it. Having inherited the freedom that the movement generation worked so hard to bequeath to them, they feel it only natural to talk back when their intelligence is insulted. Unfortunately, too many members of the movement generation, and their ideological successors, refuse to release their stranglehold on the microphones and spotlights of black progress, even though their ideas have long since stopped being relevant. I have some access to those venues, and I feel duty bound to use them.

Blacks have long described themselves as speaking truth to power, when what they really mean is *white* power. Now it's time for blacks to speak truth to black power, the source of racist and preconceived notions far more pertinent in many blacks' lives than would ever be forthcoming from Republican National Committee headquarters. Young blacks know that racism still exists and still affects their lives. They also know that racism can usually be overcome, sidestepped, planned for, and contained, all without them ever wasting their time on the state of Schuyler's little suburban soul. I hope, with *The End of Blackness,* to help serve notice on that passé state of mind that focuses on white racism instead of black solutions. The future of black progress lies in the black community, in the black heart, and in the black mind that is unafraid to look itself in the mirror and is thereby able, finally, to love and respect itself. No white intransigence has the least chance against a community united in belief in itself and in its future, even if Ku Klux Klan members numbered in the millions (and we all know they do not). The only step required to finish, and thereby end, the civil rights movement is for blacks to free one another from a strangling groupthink. All that's left is to *act free,* as free of black expectation as of white.

Given the astringency of the case I make, I must once again thank my publisher, Pantheon, and my extremely naughty editor, Erroll McDonald, for not only paying me to write this book but also for pushing me to the honesty and leadership required to say what must be said. This is neither the first nor, with luck, the last time I will have to write with his borrowed bravery. He never lets me punk out (brutal mockery being his main prod), and neither does my agent, Sarah Chalfant, at the Wylie Agency (diplomatic chiding being hers). I work independently of any institution, so it's crucial for me to have people to disappoint— intellectually, Erroll and Sarah are those people, though I do plan to work more efficiently in the future so I can widen my works-in-progress readership. Those two can't catch everything. (Jabari Asim, Hasan Hakim, Wil Haygood, Duncan Kennedy, Randy Kennedy, Glenn Loury, Gerald Reynolds, and Gregory Rodriguez got an awful lot of ideas bounced off them though.)

As well and perhaps most importantly, I owe a great deal to the intellectual and political fervor emanating from the hip-hop generation's burgeoning cohort of artists, intellectuals, activists, and entrepreneurs, people like Corey Booker, Chuck D., Davey D, Meri Danquah, Harold Ford, Rob George, Bakari Kitwana, Victor LaValle, Mat Johnson, Mark Anthony Neal, ZZ Packer, Chris Rock, Greg Tate, Chris Tucker, Martha Southgate, Bill Stephney, and Russell Simmons, as well as the wonderful but largely unknown local leaders who toil pragmatically in the shadows while their grandparents hog the stage and the resources. First they shocked me with their irreverence and youthful refusal to be beholden to the past. Now they embolden me and construct frequent intellectual and moral reality checks for me to gauge my ideas against. I have gone from being appalled by them, their music, their comportment, their dress, their frightening open-mindedness, and their nontraditional patterns of thought, to understanding that it's my job to help pave the way for them, even when I disagree. They are not the future. They are the present, and it's my job as a near-elder to help them access the resources they need to consolidate their ascent to their long-overdue leadership of this community. This book is one way of doing that.

Morally, my mother, Johnnie Florence Gooch Dickerson, is my touchstone, and it was she who taught me that silence gives consent. When I was an adolescent, her Mississippi twang grated in my conscience when I tried to stand silent while a bully picked on the defenseless. Now it is her voice that pokes into my brain when I want to bite my tongue and squirm through yet another pointless anti-intellectual, antiwhite rant in silence. The woman haunts me, and she's still alive. I can only pray to achieve the same effect with *my* children. In any event, I had to withdraw my consent to continue being spoken for by the immoral, the mediocre, and the tyrannical. I've sat in silence through my last rant against police brutality while black victims of black abusers go without comfort. I've dodged my last TV producer or op-ed editor seeking comment on the latest kente-clothed "leader" caught shtupping a secretary or preaching to the poor when he should be teaching the poor. I withdraw my consent for allowing the morally bankrupt, intellectually spent, racist rabble to tell the world, let alone the country, what black people think. There is solidarity, and there is capitulation; if they (whom I call the Black Politburo) want a battle for the soul of the black community, they've got one.

Other than that, I'll let *The End of Blackness* speak for itself. There's no point writing a book this merciless, then trying to sugarcoat it. Let me just say this, though. The next time some "new Afrikan" steps up to me at one of my readings—all puffed up with camera-ready umbrage at my incredible "self-hatred"—and questions my Negritude for my interracial marriage or my insufficient (to them) engagement with the black community, they better come loaded for bear. I aim to personally make use of the term "Uncle Tom" as a signifier of political blackmail, moral bankruptcy, and sloppy thinking as clear as "card-carrying liberal" or "credit to their race." Having taken the time to educate myself as to my *true* intellectual and moral heritage, I know that I am not only justified but *required* to speak truth to black power, especially knee-jerk black power. I feel dangerous as hell, and I'm strapped. I've got Martin, Carter, W.E.B., and Franklin in my back pocket, and I'm spoiling for a fight. If you think Derrida, Foucault, or Marx can stand up to those homies, bring it on because I have pulled my last punch with the "blacker than thou" brigade.

The End of Blackness is my gauntlet thrown down to the black powers that be. Pick it up if you dare, but you'd better come correct.

Albany, New York
July 2003

BIBLIOGRAPHY

Allen, James, ed. *Without Sanctuary: Lynching Photography in America.* Santa Fe, N.M.: Twin Palms, 2000.

Appiah, K. Anthony, and Amy Gutman. *Color Conscious: The Political Morality of Race.* Princeton, N.J.: Princeton University Press, 1996.

Baldwin, James. *Collected Essays,* edited by Toni Morrison. New York: Library of America, 1998.

Berlin, Ira. *Many Thousands Gone: The First Two Centuries of Slavery in North America.* Cambridge, Mass.: Harvard University Press, 1998.

Blakely, Robert L., and Judith M. Harrington, eds. *Bones in the Basement: Postmortem Racism in Nineteenth-Century Medical Training.* Washington, D.C.: Smithsonian Institution Press, 1997.

Brown, Claude. *Manchild in the Promised Land.* (New York: Touchstone, 1965, 1993).

Butler, Octavia. *Kindred.* Boston: Beacon Press, 1979.

Carew, Jan R. *Ghosts in Our Blood: With Malcolm X in Africa, England, and the Caribbean.* Chicago: Lawrence Hill Books, 1994.

Davis, Sampson, George Jenkins, and Rameck Hunt with Lisa Frazier Page. *The Pact: Three Young Men Make a Promise and Fulfill a Dream.* New York: Riverhead Books, 2000.

Donald, David. *The Politics of Reconstruction, 1863–1867.* Cambridge, Mass.: Harvard University Press, 1984.

DuBois, W.E.B. *The Souls of Black Folk.* 1903; rpt. New York: Signet, 1995.

Due, Tananarive, and Patricia Stephens Due. *Freedom in the Family: A Mother-Daughter Memoir of the Fight for Civil Rights*. New York: Ballantine Books, 2003.

Durham, Phillip, and Jones, Everett L. *The Negro Cowboy*. Lincoln: University of Nebraska Press, 1965.

Ellison, Ralph. *The Collected Essays of Ralph Ellison*, edited by John F. Callahan. New York: Modern Library, 1995.

Foner, Phillip S., ed. *Frederick Douglass: Selected Speeches and Writings*. Chicago: Lawrence Hill Books, 1999.

Franklin, John Hope, and Loren Schweninger. *Runaway Slaves: Rebels on the Plantation*. New York: Oxford University Press, 1999.

Frazier, E. Franklin. *Black Bourgeoisie*. New York: Free Press, 1957.

Gates, Henry Louis, Jr., ed. *The Classic Slave Narratives*. New York: Penguin, 1987.

Graves, Joseph L., Jr. *The Emperor's New Clothes: Biological Theories of Race at the Millennium*. New Brunswick, N.J.: Rutgers University Press, 2001.

Greenberg, Jack. *Crusaders in the Courts: How a Dedicated Band of Lawyers Fought for the Civil Rights Revolution*. New York: Basic Books, 1994.

Gregory, Dick. *Nigger*. New York: Pocket Books, 1964.

Hacker, Andrew. *Two Nations: Black and White, Separate, Hostile, Unequal*. New York: Ballantine Books, 1992.

Higginbotham, A. Leon, Jr. *In the Matter of Color: Race and the American Legal Process: The Colonial Period*. New York: Oxford University Press, 1978.

Himes, Chester. *If He Hollers Let Him Go*. New York: Thunder's Mouth Press, 1945.

Hudson, Winson, and Constance Curry. *Mississippi Harmony: Memoirs of a Freedom Fighter*. New York: Palgrave Macmillan, 2002.

Jacobs, Harriet A. *Incidents in the Life of a Slave Girl*. Cambridge, Mass.: Harvard University Press, 2000.

Jacoby, Tamar. *Someone Else's House: America's Unfinished Struggle for Integration*. New York: Free Press, 1998.

Johnson, Charles, and Patricia Smith. *Africans in America: America's Journey through Slavery*. New York: Harcourt Brace & Co., 1998.

Jones, LeRoi [Amiri Baraka]. *Blues People: Negro Music in White America*. New York: William Morrow, 1963.

Katz, William Loren. *The Black West: A Documentary and Pictorial History of the African American Role in the Westward Expansion of the United States*. New York: Touchstone, 1987.

King, Martin Luther, Jr. *A Testament of Hope: The Essential Writings and Speeches of Martin Luther King, Jr.,* edited by James M. Washington. New York: HarperCollins, 1986.

Lee, Yueh-Ting, Lee J. Jussim, and Clark R. McCauley, eds. *Stereotype Accuracy: Toward Appreciating Group Differences*. Washington, D.C.: American Psychological Association, 1995.

Lemann, Nicholas. *The Promised Land: The Great Black Migration and How It Changed America*. New York: Vintage Books, 1992.

Lind, Michael. *The Next American Nation: The New Nationalism and the Fourth American Revolution*. New York: Free Press, 1995.

Loury, Glenn C. *The Anatomy of Racial Inequality*. Cambridge, Mass.: Harvard University Press, 2002.

MacDonald, Michael Patrick. *All Soul's Day: A Family Story from Southie*. New York: Ballantine, 2000.

McFeely, William S. *Frederick Douglass*. New York: W. W. Norton, 1991.

McWhorter, John H. *Losing the Race: Self-Sabotage in Black America*. New York: Free Press, 2000.

Murray, Albert. *The Omni-Americans: Black Experience and American Culture*. New York: Da Capo Press, 1970.

Myrdal, Gunnar. *An American Dilemma: The Negro Problem and Modern Democracy*. 1944; rpt. New York: Harper & Row, 1996.

Poussaint, Alvin F., M.D., and Amy Alexander. *Lay My Burden Down: Unraveling Suicide and the Mental Health Crisis Among African-Americans*. Boston: Beacon Press, 2000.

Richburg, Keith B. *Out of America: A Black Man Confronts Africa*. New York: Basic Books, 1997.

Robinson, Randall. *The Debt: What America Owes to Blacks*. New York: Dutton, 2000.

Roediger, David R., ed. *Black on White: Black Writers on What It Means to Be White*. New York: Schocken Books, 1998.

Scott, Daryl Michael. *Contempt and Pity: Social Policy and the Image of the Damaged Black Psyche 1880–1996*. Chapel Hill: University of North Carolina Press, 1997.

Sanyika Shakur [Scott, Monster Kody]. *Monster: The Autobiography of an L.A. Gang Member*. New York: Penguin Books, 1993.

Shorris, Earl. *Riches for the Poor: The Clemente Course in the Humanities*. New York: W. W. Norton, 2000.

Sowell, Thomas. *Race and Culture: A World View*. New York: Basic Books, 1994.

Susskind, Ron. *A Hope in the Unseen: An American Odyssey from the Inner City to the Ivy League*. New York: Broadway Books, 1998.

Tucker, M. Belinda, and Claudia Mitchell-Kernan, eds. *The Decline in Marriage Among African Americans: Causes, Consequences and Policy Implications*. New York: Russell Sage Foundation, 1995.

Twain, Mark. *Huckleberry Finn*. New York: Harper and Brothers, 1884.

Wilkins, Roger. *Jefferson's Pillow: The Founding Fathers and the Dilemma of Black Patriotism*. Boston: Beacon Press, 2001.

Williams, Juan, and Quinton Dixie. *This Far by Faith: Stories from the African American Religious Experience*. New York: William Morrow, 2003.

Woodson, Carter G. *The Mis-Education of the Negro*. 1933; rpt. Trenton, N.J.: Africa World Press, 1998.

INDEX

PERMISSIONS ACKNOWLEDGMENTS

Grateful acknowledgment is made to the following for permission to reprint previously published material:

AFRICA WORLD BOOKS: Excerpt from *The Mis-Education of the Negro* by Carter G. Woodson. Reprinted by permission of Africa World Books, Trenton, N.J.

ALFRED A. KNOPF: Excerpts from *The Promised Land* by Nicholas Lehmann. Copyright © 1990 by Nicholas Lehmann. Reprinted by permission of Alfred A. Knopf, a division of Random House, Inc.

BALLANTINE BOOKS: Excerpt from *Freedom in the Family* by Tananarive Due and Patricia Stephens Due. Copyright © 2003 by Tananarive Due and Patricia Stephens Due. Reprinted by permission of Ballantine Books, a division of Random House, Inc.

THE FREE PRESS: Excerpts from *Black Bourgeoisie* by H. Franklin Frazier. Copyright © 1957, 1962 by The Free Press. Copyright © renewed 1985, 1990 by Thomas L. Jones. All rights reserved. Reprinted by permission of The Free Press, a Division of Simon & Schuster Adult Publishing Group.

HARPERCOLLINS PUBLISHERS INC.: Excerpts from *Blues People* by Leroi Jones. Copyright © 1963 by Leroi Jones. Excerpts from *Quilting the Black-Eyed Pea* by Nikki Giovanni. Copyright © 2002 by Nikki Giovanni. Reprinted by permisssion of HarperCollins Publishers, Inc.

JOHN WILEY & SONS, INC.: Excerpts from *Take a Lesson* by Caro-